W9-BBM-296

Growing Up!

A parent's guide to childhood

Growing Up!

A parent's guide to childhood

**CAROL COOPER, CLAIRE HALSEY,
SU LAURENT, KAREN SULLIVAN**
FOREWORD BY **DR. TANYA BYRON**
CONSULTANT CLINICAL PSYCHOLOGIST

CONSULTANT EDITOR **DR. KATE CRONAN**

London, New York, Melbourne, Munich, and Delhi

Senior Art Editor Glenda Fisher
Senior Editor Jo Godfrey Wood
Managing Art Editor Marianne Markham
Managing Editor Esther Ripley
Production Editor Jenny Woodcock
Production Controller Alice Holloway
Creative Technical Support Sonia Charbonnier
Category Publisher Peggy Vance

Produced for DK by Dawn Bates and Emma Forge
Production Designer Tom Forge
Photography by Vanessa Davies

Jacket design by Glenda Fisher

First American Edition, 2008
Published in the United States by
DK Publishing, 375 Hudson Street
New York, New York 10014
08 09 10 11   10 9 8 7 6 5 4 3 2 1

YD026—8/2008

Published in Great Britain by Dorling Kindersley Limited.

A catalog record for this book is available from the
Library of Congress.
ISBN: 978-0-7566-3671-5

DK books are available at special discounts when purchased
in bulk for sales promotions, premiums, fund-raising, or
educational use. For details, contact: DK Publishing Special
Markets, 375 Hudson Street, New York, New York 10014 or
SpecialSales@dk.com.

Reproduced by MDP, Bath, UK
Printed and bound in China by Sheck Wah Tong

Discover more at
www.dk.com

Contents

8   Foreword
10 Introduction

3–5 years
14 Getting the basics right

Your 3-year-old
20 Growth and development
26 Your child's health
28 Understanding and skills
32 Emotions and personality
40 Childcare and preschool
43 Family life

Your 4-year-old
50 Growth and development
55 Your child's health
57 Understanding and skills

62 Emotions and personality
68 Your child's life

Your 5-year-old
76 Growth and development
82 Your child's health
85 Understanding and skills
90 Emotions and personality
95 Your child's life

6–8 years
102 Getting the basics right

Your 6-year-old
108 Growth and development
112 Your child's health
116 Understanding and skills
122 Emotions and personality
128 Your child's life

Your 7-year-old

134   Growth and development

138   Your child's health

140   Understanding and skills

145   Emotions and personality

150   Your child's life

Your 8-year-old

156   Growth and development

160   Your child's health

164   Understanding and skills

168   Emotions and personality

173   Your child's life

"As a parent you are bound to sometimes question things and wonder what's normal."

9–11 years

178   Getting the basics right

Your 9-year-old

184   Growth and development

188   Your child's health

190   Understanding and skills

194   Emotions and personality

198   Your child's life

Your 10-year-old

204   Growth and development

207   Your child's health

210   Understanding and skills

213   Emotions and personality

218   Your child's life

Your 11-year-old

224   Growth and development

227   Your child's health

229   Understanding and skills

234   Emotions and personality

238   Your child's life

12–14 years

244   Getting the basics right

Your 12-year-old

250   Growth and development

253   Your child's health

255   Understanding and skills

258   Emotions and personality

262   Your child's life

Your 13-year-old

270   Growth and development

273   Your child's health

275   Understanding and skills

280   Emotions and personality

284   Your child's life

Your 14-year-old

292   Growth and development

295   Your child's health

298   Understanding and skills

302   Emotions and personality

306   Your child's life

310   Useful organizations

312   Index and acknowledgments

Foreword

People often ask me if being the mother of my 10-year-old son and my 13-year-old daughter is easier for me because I am also a consultant clinical psychologist. I've specialized in child and adolescent mental health for almost 20 years, so are my children perfect? Is my household one of tranquillity, where we all float through each developmental stage of childhood on a cloud of easy calm? Well, my answer, predictably, is that this is not the case—I say this as my children are rolling around the floor laughing hysterically at the thought that I could somehow be considered the world's totally perfect parent!

And thank goodness I can say "No." Do I want perfect children? No. Do I possess the secret of a one-size-fits-all solution to managing children? No. Do I believe that parenting should be an easy ride? No. No. No. The truth is that being a practitioner in the field of child behavior hasn't made me a better parent, but being a parent has made me a better practitioner. Since becoming a mother (the two happiest days of my life, two years and seven months apart), I can completely empathize with the excitement, fear, bewilderment, joy, and challenges that I hear about from the families I meet and treat. I recognize the feelings of utter helplessness when the children you love are completely incomprehensible and seemingly unmanageable. I respect the frustrations, tears, and guilt that so many parents bring to me as they try to find better ways to help their children through developmental challenges. As one father once said to me, "Parenting—the most difficult job in the world and the only one you get no training for."

All parents need reliable information and advice when times get tough to help them deal with the myriad concerns about all kinds of things, running the gamut of physical, cognitive, and emotional development—but where can we turn? Where can we find straightforward, understandable, and practical advice that will enable us to feel less anxious about what we see in our children and more empowered and positive about supporting them? *Growing Up!* is, I believe, a necessary resource for parents everywhere. This wonderfully inspiring, practical book tells you all you need to know about your children's ongoing development from age 3 to age 14, answering all your questions and offering professional and practical guidance on a range of issues such as what to do if you think your child is being bullied or you are concerned she is not eating, or if she is "addicted" to her cell phone.

> "I wish *Growing Up!* had been around when I started out as a parent 13 years ago!"

Written by four experts in child development—all hands-on parents themselves—*Growing Up!* combines expertise to bring you the latest research-based advice that reads as friendly, reassuring common sense. Carol Cooper, family doctor and medical journalist, gives valuable insights on health and development; clinical psychologist and parenting expert Claire Halsey explores emotional and social development and family issues; pediatrician Su Laurent guides you through the incredible stages of physical growth; and Karen Sullivan, a child-care specialist and writer, looks at aspects of cognitive and social behavior.

The authors tackle the most simple to the most complex, the perplexing to the downright frustrating, in a manner that is accessible and practical. They cover a range of issues, such as how to make sure a picky three-year-old gets a balanced diet without making mealtimes stressful, to how to tell whether your nine-year-old's stomachache is real or a clever ploy to stay home from school, or even to how to negotiate with a 14-year-old who can't see the problem with staying out until 1 am—in a comprehensive and straightforward way. As I have, you will read this book and wonder, "Why on earth didn't I think of that myself?" As I also have, you will find Carol, Claire, Su, and Karen completely reassuring and down-to-earth in their advice. Their useful guidelines will help you realize that parenting is not just doable, but also really enjoyable—even when times feel tough.

Knowledge helps us feel able to manage difficult situations, but emotion can often get in the way and cloud reason. Therefore we often "know" what we ought to be doing, but sometimes feel powerless. We question ourselves and can feel unconfident, particularly when faced with complicated behaviors that are emotionally challenging, and we can feel overwhelmed by advice that can be contradictory. This book provides us all with information to help us understand, take a step back, and feel better able to support our children in a calm, kind, respectful, and, when necessary, authoritative manner. This enables us to have a real and positive influence over how they are developing and to take effective and appropriate action when we need to help that development along. I know that, as I have, you will enjoy this fabulous and inspiring book.

THE JOY OF PARENTING
As a confident parent, you will truly enjoy your children and see their development as a series of joys, not a series of challenges.

DR. TANYA BYRON
Mother of Lily and Jack
Consultant clinical psychologist specializing in child and adolescent behavior and mental health

Introduction

Parenting is as much about instinct as anything else, but we all need a little help sometimes to confirm that we are getting things right, that our children are developing and learning as they should, that the issues they face can be managed, and that they are happy, healthy, and on the road to a fulfilling adult life.

Many of the issues that face today's parents simply never existed before, and we are, therefore, often attempting to navigate uncharted waters without so much as a compass. Our society is increasingly media-driven and stress-ridden; new technologies abound and children are growing up faster than ever. With the birth of the Internet and the self-help book, the plethora of conflicting information about everything from what we should be feeding our children to how much TV they should be watching and when their sex education should begin is confusing and often dispiriting. And so it is not surprising that most parents long for a comprehensive source of good, practical, and sensible advice, based on sound research, firsthand parenting experience, and, above all, common sense. That is precisely what we set out to do with this book. All of us are parents with specialties in different areas of child health and development, so as well as having practical experience, we are in touch with the issues that affect both children and their parents, and the very best ways to resolve them.

Tackling common concerns

Every parent has different concerns at different stages of their child's life. Worries about potty-training, picky eating, language development, growth, and sleep patterns often dominate the preschool years. When a child starts school, makes friends, and begins to take those first steps toward independence, there are new areas with which to contend. From there, the road to middle adolescence seems a veritable minefield of potential doubts. Is this puberty? Why does my child lie? Are his language and reading skills up to scratch? How can I recognize if my child has an eating disorder, depression, or stress, or is being bullied? Is she always going to

BEING PREPARED *There is no such thing as a perfect parent, but by being prepared for the challenges ahead, you can get it right most of the time.*

be shorter than her friends? When should she get her first bra? How do I deal with the question of alcohol when all his friends are drinking it? How can I help him study? Why is he always on his computer? Should I make him visit his grandparents? And the list goes on and on and on. No matter how confident our parenting skills, there will always be times when we question things, and wonder what is normal and appropriate. And kids have an unerring ability to confound even the most organized, savvy parent. If there is one known quantity in the world of raising children, it is unpredictability. This book is for those moments when everything isn't straightforward and when you have questions about anything that relates to your child's life.

THE TEENAGE YEARS
Adolescents often get bad press, but it is possible to enjoy a positive relationship with children during their teenage years.

How the book works

Every age, from 3 to 14, is covered in its own detailed section, looking at the normal range of development, growth, and skills, and what problems are likely to occur. While we have broken this down year by year, many issues do, of course, apply to more than one age group. We've answered questions from parents, and we've worked hard to deal with every issue involved in raising children. So whether you're pulling your hair out about your three-year-old's defiance; concerned that your five-year-old isn't ready for school; wondering why your nine-year-old is sulky; curious about your 12-year-old's physical development; or frustrated by your 14-year-old's apathy, this book is for you.

Parenting is not always easy, but with a little advance knowledge, you can understand your child's ever-changing body, mind, abilities, needs, and concerns, and nurture, love, and guide him through the years ahead. Combined with your natural instincts, we think we've got the perfect recipe for getting it right.

3–5 years

"The toddler years are over, and your child is beginning her schooling and her path to independence. As a parent, your greatest challenge will be to let 'your baby' go, but there will be many rewards in watching her grow into a little individual."

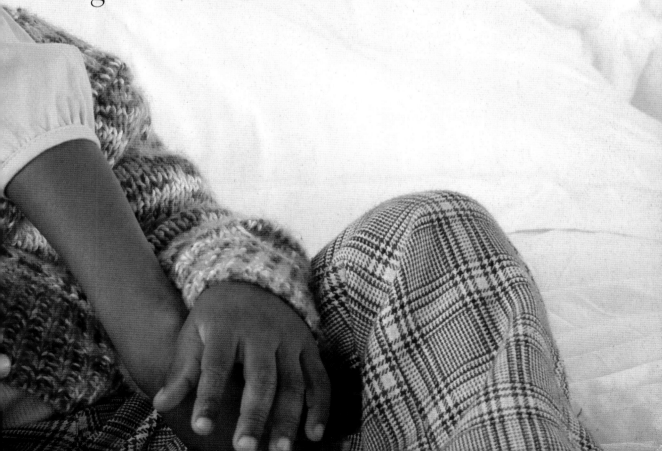

Getting the basics right

This is a crucial period of growth and development, so it is essential to ensure that your child gets enough sleep and plenty of exercise, and eats a healthy diet. If, like many preschoolers, your child is single-minded and often fickle, meeting these basic needs can sometimes be challenging.

The importance of sleep

Despite his high energy levels, and clear exhaustion after a busy day, your preschooler may resist going to bed as a show of independence, and because he doesn't want to miss any of the action. It is, however, crucial that he gets at least 10–12 hours' sleep per 24 hours between the ages of 3 and 5, some of which can be taken as a nap. The best way to ensure healthy sleep patterns is to stick to a nighttime routine. Your child's body clock will adjust, and he will learn that sleep follows his bath and story, for example.

Why sleep is essential:

▶ Research indicates that inadequate sleep lowers immunity: missing even a few hours of sleep per night on a regular basis can affect the way the immune system functions.

▶ A survey in the US found that children who had an inadequate amount of sleep showed impairment of the ability to perform tasks involving memory, learning, logical reasoning, and mathematical calculation. They also found relationships at home and with friends more difficult.

▶ Growth hormones are released during sleep. Research has shown that children who are chronically sleep-deprived—for example, those with severe asthma (see page 163)—can have retarded growth.

EARLY TO BED *Children who get enough sleep are more able to concentrate, accomplish tasks, and handle minor irritations.*

Exercise and leisure

Your preschooler will be naturally active and often on the go from an unseemly hour of the morning. However, spending hours watching TV and doing other sedentary activities, such as playing video games, means many young children don't get enough exercise. It is well documented that regular exercise helps adults to stay healthy, maintain weight, reduce stress, and improve self-esteem, and by being active your child can enjoy these benefits too. Regular exercise will also affect his growth. A recent study reported that children whose activity levels fall far beneath their biological requirements may not achieve optimum development and growth. Furthermore, it found that physical activity naturally stimulates the release of growth hormone into the circulation, and that the healing process (of wounds and in terms of recovering from health conditions) is significantly faster in children who exercise regularly.

Exercise is therefore crucial for your growing child—and in this age group, unstructured, free play outside combined with a few organized activities, such as swimming, soccer, or even dance, will ensure that he gets an adequate amount. Keep sedentary activities, such as watching TV, to a minimum (no more than an hour a day), and encourage your child to run, walk, jump, chase, and climb.

Healthy eating

Your preschooler, like you, should eat a balanced diet (see page 17). This sounds simple in theory, but with the rise of convenience foods, the impact of the media on children's preferences, and, of course, a natural increase in independence that can lead to picky eating habits (see page 25), it may sometimes be a struggle to ensure that your child gets what he needs.

All children require plenty of vitamins and minerals to grow and develop, and to maintain health. The nutrients that are most likely to be deficient in a child's diet are calcium, iron, vitamin C, vitamin A, folic acid, and vitamin B6. It is important, therefore, to include plenty of dairy products, lean meats, dried and fresh fruit, vegetables (in particular, leafy greens and brightly colored vegetables), whole grains, and fish in your child's diet. A balanced diet will almost always provide your child with the recommended daily levels of vitamins and minerals, but you may want to consider giving your child a supplement, particularly if he is a picky eater. Your child should be eating about 5–8 servings of fruit and vegetables a day. That may sound onerous, but a glass of fruit juice, the occasional smoothie, vegetables pureed into sauces or offered as snacks with a dip, and even salad added to sandwiches can all count toward achieving these servings. Many children have a natural distaste for vegetables, but it is

KEEP HER ACTIVE *All children need at least one hour of exercise a day. Set your energetic child free to run and play in the backyard or the park at every opportunity.*

worth persevering. Several studies show that it is often on the tenth or even twelfth offering that a food becomes "familiar" and therefore "worthy" of trying, or even eating.

Drinking water

Water is an essential element of your child's diet, required for the digestive process, healthy elimination, new tissue development, and energy levels. Aim for between 16 and 34 oz (0.5–1 liter) per day. Fruit juices and, indeed, fruit and vegetables, will provide some of this, but whenever possible, choose water over other drinks. It is very easy for children to get hooked on colas and sugary fruit drinks to quench thirst; however, these should be saved for treats only—especially carbonated drinks, which can have a detrimental effect on your child's health (see page 23). Children often mistake thirst for hunger, and a small drink can allay perceived "starvation" close to meals. But don't let your child fill up on drinks— your preschooler's stomach is small, and even a few ounces of juice or water may mean he won't touch his dinner.

FAVORITE FOODS *The aim is for your child to enjoy a range of nutritious foods. If she goes through a phase of eating a limited number at mealtimes, balance her diet with healthy snacks at other times.*

Healthy snacks

Preschoolers need snacks to sustain energy levels and concentration, but look at these as part of your child's overall diet rather than "quick-fills." Keep them small so that he is still hungry at mealtimes.

Snack ideas:

❱ Dried and fresh fruit.

❱ Whole-wheat toast.

❱ Breadsticks and dips, such as hummus.

❱ Low-sugar yogurt.

❱ Raw vegetables.

❱ Nuts, seeds, and rice cakes. Don't give nuts if there is a history of nut allergies in your family.

Balancing your child's diet

	Why it is needed	Daily intake	Food sources	Tips
Protein	Required for growth and development in every part of your child's body. Every cell contains protein, and it is required for cell repair and renewal.	2–3 servings a day of animal and vegetable proteins will provide a healthy balance.	Animal proteins include lean meats, dairy products, fish, and eggs; vegetable proteins include dried beans, whole grains, nuts, seeds, rice, some fruits and vegetables.	Add a handful of seeds or dried beans, or beat an egg into a pasta sauce. Add some lentils or dried beans to soups and stews.
Fat	Necessary for energy and the smooth functioning of your child's body, including providing the calories important for growth and essential nutrients for brain function.	3–4 servings a day.	Healthy fats can be found in vegetable oils, nuts, seeds and oily fish, olive oil, and avocados. Dairy products and red meat should not overwhelm your child's diet, but should be included.	Drizzle olive oil over pasta, use flaxseeds or their oils in salads, offer seeds and nuts as snacks, and give your child fish often. Limit anything containing trans fats.
Carbohydrate	This is energy food and the body's main source of fuel. There are two main kinds, refined and complex (unrefined), and your child's diet should be formed primarily of the latter.	Aim for 4–9 servings a day.	Whole grains, fresh fruit and vegetables, dried beans, and colored rice (brown or red). These are a great source of fiber, and provide crucial nutrients, including B vitamins.	Serve vegetable stir-fries with rice. Offer fresh fruit. Add dried beans to stews. Minimize refined carbs, such as white bread, as these have had the goodness stripped from them.
Fiber	Encourages healthy digestion, helps nutrients be absorbed more efficiently, absorbs toxins, and prevents constipation.	If your child has plenty of the correct foods (see right), he will get the fiber he requires.	Whole grains, fruits and vegetables (with peels when possible), good-quality cereals, rice, and dried beans.	Avoid sugar-coated cereal bars that are high in sugar and often contain refined rather than whole grains.

SERVING GUIDELINES: *A serving is roughly one tablespoon, so your child would need to eat three tablespoons of yogurt to get a "dairy" serving, or three tablespoons of peas for a vegetable portion.*

Your 3-year-old

"She is becoming more independent, but will still want you close by."

SELF-SUFFICIENT It may not always suit your busy schedule, but let her try tasks such as putting her shoes on— it is the only way she will learn.

ADVENTURER As his large muscles develop, activities such as climbing will come more easily to your child. Try to resist being overprotective, even though he may sometimes take a tumble.

YOUR SPECIAL RELATIONSHIP She may be branching out, but you still remain the center of her world.

Growth and development

As she comes out of the toddler years, your child will become stronger and more physically active—opening up a whole new range of activities and opportunities for independent play. You will also notice other more subtle changes, such as the way she grips a pencil.

One of the most obvious ways you will monitor your child's progress is by observing her growth. Genes play their part, but to make sure that your child is growing to her full potential, you will need to give her a combination of good nutrition, lots of sleep, and a warm and caring home environment. If any of these elements is deficient, she may start to fall away from her projected growth pattern, and this will be reflected on her growth chart (see page 22).

Brain development

By the age of three, your child's brain is almost full-grown, but her bones and muscles are still underdeveloped. This is why her head looks much larger in proportion to her body than that of an adult.

However, although her brain doesn't have much more growing to do, it is in a very active phase of development. All the brain cells (known as neurons) your child needs are already there at birth (roughly 100 billion of them!), but during the first decade they grow steadily in length and weight and form trillions of connections with other neurons, which will enable your child to learn and remember. Each neuron can link with as many as 15,000 others. Pathways linking neurons are formed, and if these are used repeatedly they will become permanent. The vast array of networks set up in your child's brain are dependent on her experience of the world. An interactive environment, both at home and elsewhere, that is safe, loving,

STAYING HYDRATED
Because your child is so active, it can be easy for her to become dehydrated. Make sure she drinks plenty, especially water, throughout the day.

"She will be more physically coordinated, stand on one leg, balance, negotiate the stairs, and may even hop."

How your child's bones are formed

Apart from growing in length, bones change in terms of the extent to which they are calcified, the process of calcium being laid down. So, for example, an X-ray of your child's hand and wrist will give a pretty good estimate of her "bone age." Long bones, such as the thigh bone, grow from "centers" at each end, and initially these are made up of cartilage and are not calcified. This means the shaft of the long bone, but not the growing centers, can be seen on an X-ray. In time these centers become calcified and join with the shaft of the bone, eventually forming the shape we are all familiar with.

Healthy bones

A healthy child will usually have a bone age that is roughly the same as her chronological age. An X-ray to assess bone age can be useful to help diagnose why a child is too tall or too short. Your child's bones are likely to be strong and only fracture with a considerable amount of force, such as a fall from a tree. Her growing bones will heal much more quickly than an adult's bones and have the ability to remold into the right shape.

The growth of bones and muscles requires a healthy diet and, in particular, a good daily intake of calcium (see page 84). In children on a dairy-free diet, calcium can be found in soy and green vegetables and is sometimes added to drinks such as orange juice.

"It may sometimes seem as if your child has grown in height between going to bed and getting up."

and supportive has been shown to increase the number of connections between the neurons, allowing children to reach their full potential.

Growing taller

Your child's final adult height will be determined by her genes, half of which have come from each of you, her parents. Most children can be expected, therefore, to achieve a final height of somewhere between the height of their parents, plus or minus 4 in (12 cm). For example, if the father is 6 ft 2 in (195 cm) tall and the mother is 5 ft 6 in (175 cm) tall, a boy's final height should be between 5 ft 10 in and 6 ft 2 in (187 and 195 cm).

From your child's birth, your health-care provider will have been plotting her height and weight on a growth chart. These charts use a system of averages to keep an eye on whether she is growing as expected. If you are worried that your child is growing too slowly, ask your pediatrician or family doctor to measure and plot her height on her growth chart and compare it to previous measurements. If a child is growing too quickly or too slowly, the cause should be investigated.

Keeping your child healthy

To make sure your child grows and develops properly, encourage her to eat healthy and nutritious foods. A well-balanced diet (see page 17) is vital for growth, brain development, immunity, and the development of a healthy cardiovascular system.

There is mounting evidence that nutrition from as early as the fetal stage has a major impact on the risk of developing heart disease and strokes in later life. Childhood obesity is an increasing problem in the Western world, and overfeeding your child, or giving her too much fattening food, may result in the development of lifelong poor eating habits and all the long-term effects on health of obesity. Be aware of how the following will adversely affect your child's health:

A high-fat diet This will cause your child to grow more quickly in both weight and height, but will not make her taller than she would have been on a more balanced diet. It will simply make her reach her final height faster.

Carbonated drinks These are high in sugar, caffeine, and carbon dioxide, and they cause obesity and tooth decay. Some combinations of food additives commonly found in soda have recently been linked to hyperactivity in children (see page 60). Carbonated beverages should be avoided if possible, or reserved for rare "treats."

AN ACTIVE LIFESTYLE
Being constantly on the go is vital for your child's overall health and happiness. By age three, she should be able to run, balance, and jump with ease.

Large muscle development

Your three-year-old's large muscles will be developing well ahead of her small muscles. This means that activities such as climbing and hopping—known as gross motor skills—will come more easily to her.

Children acquire gross motor skills at different ages. Your child may seem very agile and daring and scamper to the top of a jungle gym, way out of your reach, or she may be more cautious and need help and encouragement to achieve each new task. Skills commonly acquired during the fourth year include: riding a push-along car, jumping in place, standing on one foot, and walking along a line or a low wall.

Small muscle development

By using the small muscles in her hand and with effective hand–eye coordination, your three-year-old will start to hold a pencil in a way that will allow her to begin to draw. She may be able to copy a circle and draw an X if she watches you draw it first. Many children will be able to use an adult type of pencil grip, with the thumb on one side and two fingers on the other, giving them good hand control. It is worth showing your child how to do this by drawing and painting with her.

At age three, some children are producing recognizable drawings (although you may have to use a little imagination), while others are either not interested or still drawing basic patterns. Girls' drawings tend to be slightly more recognizable because they develop hand–eye coordination earlier than boys.

Some children can be a little shaky when they concentrate hard. This usually improves with time, but a tremor that doesn't get better should be discussed with your doctor. It is also common for some children to blink a lot when they are concentrating. If this persists, it is worth getting your child's sight checked to rule out any visual problems.

HANDLING SKILLS *Your child will now make use of his fine motor skills to manipulate small objects with precision, improving the quality of his imaginative play and the tasks of everyday life, such as eating.*

Common physical concerns

▶ **My three-year-old refuses to sit on the potty. What can I do?**
Try a gentle approach so that this doesn't become a big issue. Leave the potty in the vicinity, and ask him if he wants to use it, but never force him to sit on it. It can help to play games, such as saying, "Does teddy bear need to pee? Time to put him on the potty." Try to keep it a positive experience.

Your child may prefer to use the toilet because it makes him feel like "a big boy." If so, use a toddler seat and a step to make this easier. Some three-year-olds go through phases of refusing because of constipation (if it hurts him to have a bowel movement, he may associate pain and discomfort with using the potty). Seek advice from your pediatrician.

▶ **My daughter's speech seems very unclear and people often say they can't understand her. How do I know if she has a problem?**
Not all children develop at the same rate, but your three-year-old could have a speech and language problem if she speaks monotonously or too loud; strangers can't understand her much of the time; she omits or swaps consonants (especially at the start or middle of words); she does not ask questions with "where" or "what"; or she does not make sentences of at least three words. Since much speech is learned by imitation, the most common cause is a hearing problem, so the first step is a hearing test that can be arranged through your health-care provider.

▶ **My child will only eat white bread and cereal. How can I get some variety into her diet?**
Some three-year-olds decide to eat only one or two things. Luckily, most "food fads" are over in a few weeks, so making a fuss is pointless and can even be counterproductive. Just serve your child balanced meals, with some of her current favorite food alongside. If she has ketchup on everything, or finishes every meal with cornflakes, there's really no harm in it. Never force your child to eat something she doesn't want—you'll only upset her. However, you can suggest tactfully that she could try a small taste of something. Eating meals with your child is always a good idea because it will encourage her to enjoy a normal diet.

▶ **My son is really chubby and already quite a bit bigger than his friends. What should I do?**
Children develop at different rates, so your child's weight may still not be abnormal even if he's bigger than his friends. See your health-care provider, who can compare your son's measurements against BMI (body mass index) charts for children. If your child seems much heavier than average, you may need a referral to a pediatric dietician.

Unless advised, don't put your child on a "diet"—a preoccupation with food and calories is not healthy. Besides, children need to eat for growth. They also need more fat than adults. However, a three-year-old can safely drink reduced-fat milk instead of whole milk.

Be sure your child has a healthy varied menu and that you are giving child-friendly portions. Offer healthy snacks and do not routinely give junk food for good behavior.

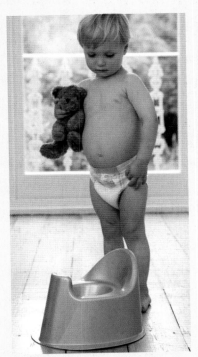

POTTY PROBLEMS *Your child will use the potty eventually. Be patient and persevere, but don't pressure him as this will create more of an issue of it.*

Your child's health

At age three, your child will probably be coming into more contact with other youngsters. You may find she often picks up minor illnesses like colds, coughs, and conjunctivitis, or even bouts of diarrhea or vomiting. In fact, minor infections serve a purpose.

"Over-protecting your child from infections may not serve her well in the long term."

Your child's immune system is developing rapidly and her white cells are learning how to make antibodies to common illnesses. It is only by coming across a variety of cold viruses, for instance, that she can gradually make antibodies and build up resistance to the hundreds of different viruses that can cause the common cold.

Good hygiene

While really strict household hygiene is superfluous, unless perhaps your child has a house dust mite allergy (see page 163), cleanliness in the kitchen and bathroom is vital for preventing food poisoning.

Top tips for protecting your child:

▶ Encourage your child to wash her hands properly after using the toilet, and before eating, to prevent gut bacteria from reaching the mouth.

▶ Wipe your child's nose with a tissue rather than a handkerchief, and throw the tissue away to stop viruses from lingering in the home.

Seeking medical advice

It's best to err on the side of caution if your child is ill and call your pediatrician. Also check with the doctor if your child is sicker than you expect—for instance, if she is lethargic or vomits repeatedly, or her skin feels cold and clammy.

Treating a fever
As well as making your child feel unwell, a high fever increases the risk of dehydration. Between the ages of six months and four years, there's also the possibility of a febrile convulsion (fit or seizure)

from a high temperature. So lower your child's temperature if it is over 102.2°F (39°C). Make sure she has plenty to drink and does not have too much clothing on. A dose of liquid acetaminophen or ibuprofen for children also helps.

⟩ Teach your child not to pick up discarded objects in the street, park, or playground. Dog and cat feces can contain parasitic roundworms called *Toxocara*, which, if ingested, can migrate to the eyes and cause permanent partial loss of vision. Cat feces can also transmit toxoplasmosis, another potentially serious infection. If you have a sandbox, keep it covered when not in use to prevent animals from eliminating in it.

⟩ Use separate chopping boards for cutting up vegetables and raw meat or poultry, and always cook meat thoroughly to kill bacteria.

⟩ Set your refrigerator temperature no higher than 41°F (5°C). To prevent contamination, keep raw items at the bottom and cooked foods at the top. Keep stored food well covered, whether it is raw or cooked.

Immunizations

Vaccination gives lasting protection against more serious infections. From the age of three years and four months, your child will be offered a booster against diphtheria, tetanus, pertussis (whooping cough), and polio. At the same time, an MMR booster is also available to enhance your child's immunity to measles, mumps, and rubella (German measles). Any side-effects from these injections are usually mild. They can include a short-lived fever, sore arm, and a rash about 10 days after the MMR shot. If you want to discuss the immunizations further, speak to your pediatrician.

Dental care

Milk teeth are important for your child's jaw development—for both the bone and the muscle—and so, although tiny, these first teeth have a role in speech and language. Since they stay in until the second set of teeth are ready to come through, they also serve as a position guide for the permanent teeth. Regular brushing with children's toothpaste will keep your child's teeth and gums healthy, and set up good habits for the future.

Top tips for brushing teeth:

⟩ Your child will probably want to hold her own toothbrush now, but you need to supervise very closely and often finish the job for her.

⟩ Make sure she brushes up and down to effectively clean between the teeth. You may need to stand behind her, while she watches in the mirror.

⟩ Encourage her to rinse well, as toothpaste can be an irritant if swallowed.

MILK TEETH *Let him get used to the idea of having his teeth examined by taking him with you to the dentist from babyhood.*

Understanding and skills

Your three-year-old's language will be improving all the time and you will find yourself conversing in a more interesting way. She will begin to get a basic grasp of preschool skills, such as learning numbers, beginning to understand time, and comprehending stories you read to her.

BEING ABLE TO COUNT
Encourage her to count while she is playing and during everyday activities such as food shopping.

Learning to concentrate

Three-year-olds vary in size and personality, but one thing most have in common is a short attention span. By now your child should be able to play well on her own some of the time, but even when she is interested in an activity, she may only stay focused on it for three minutes or so. The ability to concentrate is an essential life skill, with huge implications for school success and for the world of work.

Try encouraging your child to concentrate by sitting with her as she plays, so you can help her stay on task, but don't force her to continue with a toy or game. When a toy no longer amuses her, put it away so that it does not distract her from the next activity. The important thing at this age is that your child should be able to concentrate when something has grabbed her attention.

Numbers and the concept of time

Your child will know many numbers and may be able to count up to five, but this is likely to be an exercise in memory rather than a true understanding of numbers.
To help your child:
▶ Pass her toys one by one as you say, "Here's one for you," "Here are two for you," and so on.
▶ Count as you put toys away together.

▶ Point out numbers in everyday life—for instance, on buses or doors.

▶ Read nursery rhymes that incorporate numbers or counting.

▶ Use dough or modeling clay to make number shapes. The feel of each shape will help your child remember the different numbers.

▶ Play dominoes together—those that have both colors and dots are ideal for children of this age.

Your child's memory will be improving, so she will be able to recall what happened yesterday or even last week. She will have some grasp of time and may know the names of a few days of the week. While it is still probably too soon for her to use a clock, she will understand the

Toys and activities for three-year-olds

When choosing any toy for your child, the simplest ones are usually the best. The more complex the toy, the less your child uses her imagination and the less she gets out of her play.

You may find that your child uses many objects for other than their intended purpose. For example, she might tip a toy wheelbarrow up to make a chair. Making her own fun is part of her creative thinking and her problem-solving, so let her play freely as long as she is not being destructive or getting into danger.

Try these toys and activities:

★ **Simple jigsaw puzzles** help your child concentrate, recognize shapes, and solve problems.

★ **Books** enhance her speech and language. Your child is now old enough to handle books made with paper pages, not board.

★ **Construction toys** enhance creativity, fuel the imagination, and even teach your child the basics of maths and physics.

★ **Playing with dough or clay** entertains your child and encourages her creativity. She also learns some basic concepts, such as the fact that whatever shape you make, the amount of dough remains the same.

★ **Drawing and painting** exercise her creativity and hone her manual skills. By now she may be able to draw people to some degree. Give her the freedom to draw or paint what she wants, even if her efforts are still messy.

★ **Making things**—your child may be able to handle a pair of children's scissors. Help her with cutting, gluing, and other creative activities. She will find it fun and stimulating to use fabrics of

different textures and colors. She will need your help, but let her lead the activity as much as possible.

★ **Make-believe and pretend play** will begin to occupy much of your child's time. Provide simple props, such as a toy tea-set or a dress-up box. If she doesn't have a tent or playhouse, you can make do with a sheet draped over a table or a couple of chairs.

Sometimes she will want you to play too; at other times you should stay in the background. Take your cue from your child. As well as "pretending," she may want to help with simple cooking and setting the table. This will help her feel "big," and boost her learning, too.

★ **Memory games**—Lay out several items on a tray. Ask your child to look at them and then close her eyes. Take an item away and ask her what has been removed.

"On average, three-year-olds learn one new word every two hours; a rate that continues until adolescence."

difference between "before" and "after," "morning," "afternoon," and so on. "Later" and "soon" are also familiar concepts now.

Language skills

This is a rich time for speech and language development. Your three-year-old will listen intently and understand almost everything you say. She is likely to be chatty, to mimic, and to express herself well. She will speak in three-word or perhaps even five-word sentences, often using "and" to construct even longer sentences. Some children will do this earlier.

She will have a grasp of grammar, too, though it will be imperfect. She may for example, say "sheeps" and "eated." She will recognize many letters, especially those used in her name, and may recite sections of the alphabet as well as favorite nursery rhymes. Her vocabulary will expand and she will echo new words and phrases, so avoid saying anything you would rather she didn't repeat. Language and thought are closely linked. Your three-year-old's word power helps her grasp new ideas and plan her activities, so playing with her toys becomes increasingly well thought out. At three, your child will be brimming with curiosity about her surroundings and the wider world. She will want to know everything, and soon her favorite word "Why?" will help her unlock big ideas, such as "Why is the sky blue?" and "Why does Grandpa wear a hat?" Always try to answer your child's questions, even though they can get tedious. If you say you will tell her later, remember to stick to your promise.

Learning from books

Reading books to your child is a pleasurable activity and will encourage her language skills. She will probably be able to turn the pages without tearing the paper, at least most of the time, and she will enjoy doing this as you read. Don't worry if your child wants to look at the same book over and over. She will be discovering something new each time. Even familiar pictures contain details she may not have studied before.

Pause before or during a story and ask your child what happens next. She will love telling you, and it is a useful pre-reading exercise. Just for fun, you could occasionally change a word in a well-known story. For example, instead of "The big hungry caterpillar," say "The big hungry giraffe." This will amuse your child and she is likely to tease you about your mistake.

Pronunciation

Your three-year-old's diction is bound to be
babyish and she may lisp. She may also leave
out consonants such as "k" or "t" at the end
of a word. She may have trouble pronouncing
"sh," "z," and "v" sounds until she is four. But
you will have no trouble understanding her, and
her speech will be clear to most other adults.
When she mispronounces a word or makes a
grammatical mistake, it is more helpful if you
don't correct her explicitly. Just use the correct
version in your reply, and if possible stretch
her learning by adding more detail. So if, for
example, she says: "Dog eated food," reply by
saying, "Yes, the dog ate all her food. She was
hungry, wasn't she?" To stimulate your child's
speech and language:

Speak to her often, making eye contact when
you can. Use an adult voice, but you may still
need to exaggerate the sounds of new words.

Talk about feelings and moods You can speculate on how someone in
a story might feel when, for instance, their teddy bear gets lost. While such
conversations benefit both sexes, they are probably most helpful for boys,
who sometimes grow up lacking the vocabulary and the inclination to talk
about emotions.

Play letter games Magnetic letters may interest your child, as can jigsaw
puzzles and blocks with letters on them. If possible, these should have
lower-case letters, as that is what she will learn when she starts writing.

Sing nursery rhymes to encourage your child to learn rhythms of speech.
The repetition involved also helps your child articulate sounds.

Play with puppets together—either hand-puppets or finger-puppets will
engage your three-year-old's imagination and really stretch her vocabulary
and grammar as she makes up dialogue for new situations.

Follow your child's lead Don't force her to talk or play when she doesn't
want to. There will be times when she is more reflective, or just tired.

LEARNING LETTERS
*You can introduce her
to the alphabet at this
early age by playing
with letter cards, and
encourage her to
think of three words
that begin with "b,"
for example.*

Emotions and personality

By the time your child is three years old, you will be able to read her moods and respond quickly to her needs, and she will understand you quite well, too. She will know that your love for her is unconditional and that, although sometimes you may not like her behavior, you will always love her.

Practicing letting go

While your three-year-old may be playing more independently, she will still want you to stay close. You can help her separate more easily by giving her plenty of practice in getting your attention but then letting it go. You can do this by giving frequent small bursts of attention, as little as a minute or two, and then leaving her to play alone before you return again to show your interest in what she is doing. This way she gets plenty of experience of letting you go and learning that you always come back.

A typical three-year-old will be happy to run off to play, then come back to touch base every once in a while. Your supervision of her is crucial at this age, as she will have little sense of danger and may become very distressed if she can't find you.

Managing separation anxiety

In the baby and toddler years, it is normal for children to become anxious when they are separated from a parent, especially their main caregiver. It takes time for them to understand and trust that the person they love and depend on will always come back to them.

At around three years of age, your child will feel more confident about being separated from you. You will be surprised how quickly she is ready to play once you have left her with her caregiver.

Make separation easier:

▶ Let your child know you will be back for her, give her a quick kiss and hug, and leave calmly. Hovering, or being tearful yourself, will prolong the distress for both you and your child.

▶ If your child has a favorite toy, leave this with her for extra comfort.

A STRONG BOND *Your love forms the basis of your child's sense of security and self-esteem and will provide her with the confidence to explore her world.*

SAYING GOODBYE
While there may still be tears as you leave him at daycare or with a babysitter, remember that they are unlikely to last long after you have departed.

▶ If you are worried because your child was distressed when you left her, call the caregiver a little later to check that she has calmed down.

▶ If your child still struggles to separate from you, have some practice sessions starting with a short time away; 20 minutes at first, then building up each time. This way she will grow in confidence about being apart and that you will come back for her. Remember, child-care professionals are experienced in helping children cope with separation and will be sensitive to your child and know how to handle the situation.

Battles of will

At age three your child will begin to assert herself as an individual, and will often resist doing as she is told. "No" may be her favorite word. Even though this behavior can be challenging, there are plenty of advantages to having a strong-willed child: she is likely to express her needs clearly and develop firm opinions, and is less likely to be bullied both now and in the years to come.

However, to succeed at home and preschool, she needs to know how to do as she is asked. To reduce battles of will:

Keep things in perspective You can lessen clashes by deciding "not to sweat the small stuff." Ask yourself if the issue is big enough to battle over. Does it really matter, for example, that she has odd socks on or that she wants her drink in the red cup, not the blue cup, this morning? If the issue is important, such as putting on a coat in cold weather or brushing her teeth, then it is worth standing your ground; otherwise, resist the temptation to battle over every small thing.

Be clear about what you want Your child will be more likely to cooperate if you give clear instructions that are reasonable and fair. If you want to give her a reason for doing something, keep it simple such as "It's cold out, please put on your coat." She will thrive when you are consistent and when you mean what you say.

"If rules change depending on whether you are tired, run down, or too busy, your child will be confused about what is wanted and find it more difficult to behave well."

Dealing with tantrums

Embarrassing and hard to ignore, tantrums are a common cause of parental stress. They often happen in public, meaning you have to contend with a large audience watching you manage your child's screaming and shouting. Around age 18–24 months, tantrums really get going and continue into early childhood. Everyday activities such as getting dressed, going to the supermarket, or visiting others can become stressful as you try to stay calm while your child acts out her worst tantrum yet.

The good news is that tantrums help your child learn to handle frustration. They allow her to show how angry she is and give you a chance to work with her to manage her emotions, by talking to her about how she feels once the tantrum has passed. When you remain calm in the face of her waves of anger and frustration, you teach your three-year-old that strong feelings need not be scary and can be contained. So try to keep your cool, and stay nearby to make sure your child is safe. Avoid reasoning with your child in the midst of her emotional eruption—she won't be able to take in what you are saying during this time.

Remember:

❯ Managing tantrums by giving in or distracting your child with a treat is very much a short-term solution. In the long term she will learn that tantrums work and you will be in for many more.

❯ If you get angry and harsh when your child has a tantrum, she will learn that her feelings cannot be safely controlled and may become confused by her own emotions.

DIFFICULT BEHAVIOR
Be reassured that tantrums have a purpose—they teach your child that strong feelings can be managed.

Getting the behavior you want

Your praise and interest are very powerful in getting the good behavior you want, and your habit of giving positive attention will probably be well established by the time your child is three years old. By praising her and recognizing her achievements when she does something well, you will build her confidence and self-esteem.

When you notice your child playing nicely or when she is cooperative, take the time to show your approval. A simple hug, pat, or a few words of praise let her know she has done the right thing and make it much more likely she will do the same again. The way you give praise can make a

difference to whether your child gets the positive message. When you say her name, use a warm and loving tone of voice, look her in the eye, and really mean what you say—this way your praise will have a greater effect. **Remember:**

❯ Your three-year-old needs your attention; if she doesn't feel you have noticed her being good, then she will try misbehaving to see if you react.

❯ To keep your child behaving well, make sure she gets much more attention for good behavior than for misbehaving.

Becoming self-sufficient

Your three-year-old is beginning to tackle a challenge that will last a lifetime—to become independent. This stage will last for years as she tries increasingly complex tasks starting with bathing and dressing, and gradually begins to make her own decisions. She will be testing the limits of her coordination and thinking, so you can expect plenty of frustration as she keeps trying each new task, but she will grasp things quickly when you calmly give a little help, without taking over. The desire to become independent will make her motivated to try to do things for herself.

To encourage independence:

❯ Set your three-year-old up for success by practicing the simplest skills first. For example, begin teaching dressing using underpants and pajamas. These have no fastenings, tend to be looser and easier to handle, and often have a picture on the front, making it clearer which way around they go.

❯ Break each skill down into smaller parts—for example, if your child is learning to put on her coat, you may at first hold it open for her so all she needs to do is put her arms in the sleeves. As she grows in confidence, encourage her to pick up the coat and find the armholes herself. Eventually, she will be able to get her coat from the peg, find the armholes, and put it on without any help at all.

GROWING CONFIDENCE
You will build your child's self-esteem and increase her confidence if you speak positively five times for every one time you scold her.

Making friends

Your 3-year-old is ready to make friends and play cooperatively with other children. Through daycare, child care, and family friends, she will be having regular contact with a group of children her own age and may start to gravitate toward children whose company she enjoys. She will build her fledgling friendships by working together with her peers on simple games and activities organized by the adults around her. As she is only just learning to share, she will still need plenty of supervision to avoid disputes over toy ownership and taking turns.

A shy child

Children vary in how quiet or outgoing they are, and it is normal in any group of three-year-olds to find those who are shy and prefer to play alone alongside those with more active and sociable personalities. Shyness is not necessarily a problem; it may simply reflect your child's temperament and preferences. It tends to run in families, so if you are a shy parent you are more likely to have a shy child; this can be hereditary or simply because your child is copying the way you react to the world.

Some parents worry that their child's shyness will get in the way of the development of friendships and shy children may need extra help to mix with others and be confident in new situations.

To help a shy child:
◗ You can help a shy child develop friendships by inviting a playmate over to visit and by planning simple activities that encourage the children to play together. This is less overwhelming than meeting other children at toddler and preschool playgroups.
◗ Shyness can also be reduced when a child's overall confidence is raised. Plenty of praise for achievements involving playing or cooperating with others can be helpful.

A developing sense of humor

Your three-year-old will love simple jokes and slapstick, and begin to start appreciating potty humor. Being able to see the funny side of life grows with children's language skills and their ability to notice when things are absurd. Lightheartedness is a very appealing quality, and your child's ability to joke and laugh will set her up to get along well with others.

Things that will make her laugh:
◗ Young children will laugh when they see things that shouldn't go together, such as cows with fins or cars with legs.
◗ She will be amused by adults in slapstick routines as she enjoys the

BRANCHING OUT
Your child's early friendships, if well formed, can last through elementary school and beyond.

"Your three-year-old will find many things funny and learn a great deal through jokes and silly word play."

BEING SILLY *You will rediscover your own sense of fun through your child.*

concept that grown-ups have accidents, fall down, or get covered in goo. She will find it even funnier if it is you, or someone else close to her, who is being silly, and will laugh readily when you make funny faces, tell simple jokes, surprise her with a whoopee cushion, and make up silly stories and rhymes.

▶ She will like to share jokes with you, and may start to be the "joker" and learn how to tease someone else. For example, she might find it hard to suppress a giggle when you are trying to find her during a game of *Hide and Seek* or watch with glee as you try to find possessions that she has taken away. This aspect of teasing shows your child is able to understand your perspective—she can put herself in your shoes as you look for something, for example your keys, she has hidden.

While it is wonderful to share a joke, bear in mind that this kind of humor is very different from making fun of someone else, which develops later in your child's life and should be discouraged. At this age, though, your child might be confused by what is okay to laugh at.

Keeping your child safe

Your three-year-old is too young to effectively protect herself from harm, either from a stranger or from someone she knows. Your supervision and attention to where she is and who she is with are her best defense. This can be challenging, especially in the park or playground, where you want her to run around, but it is essential to keep her in view at all times.

Safety with dogs
In public places, animals, especially dogs, can be a problem. While you don't want your child to become afraid of dogs, it is advisable to exercise caution around them because they can become overexcited by small children and even move into "attack" mode, and this applies to family pets as well as "strange" dogs. It doesn't help when owners try to reassure by saying how much the dog "loves" children. To get your child used to dealing with dogs, point to the animal and talk about it positively, but explain that it is best not to touch a dog she doesn't know.

A child should never be left alone with a dog, even if it is the family pet.

Common behavioral concerns

▶ **My three-year-old daughter still insists on using her pacifier all the time. Does it matter?**
Using a pacifier at this age can interfere with speech development because your daughter will have fewer opportunities to speak, and it may cause her to replace "t" and "d" sounds with "k" and "g" sounds. Leave the pacifier at home so your child can't have it. When you've achieved outings without a pacifier, you can try restricting it to bedtime only. Explain to your daughter that "big" children don't use pacifiers, or tell her the "binky fairy" has taken it, and try replacing it with another comfort object (see below).

▶ **My little boy drags his teddy bear around with him all the time and throws a tantrum if he leaves it anywhere. Is this normal?**
The use of comfort toys is normal at this age and beyond. Psychologists call them "transitional objects." Your child will stop carrying his comfort toy once he no longer needs the security it gives him. When he decides he's "big," he'll probably discard his toy or use it only at night.

Meanwhile, don't make fun of him or try to wrench his toy away. You may need to patch it up often because he hugs it to pieces. Favorite toys are hard to replace, and their loss can be very distressing for a child, so if possible, buy a spare.

▶ **My daughter cries and clings to me when I try to drop her at daycare. What can I do?**
If your child becomes anxious away from you, there's a reason—she feels she needs your presence. Not all children become independent and self-reliant at the same age, so give your child the security she still depends on. Always say goodbye when you go, and make sure you're always back when you promised. Try to let her leave you, not the other way around. This helps because the decision to move away and play is hers, not yours. Give your child your time whenever you can. Try to address triggers for her anxiety—for instance, a new baby in the family may now be the focus of attention. Remember that some of the clingiest toddlers mature into the most confident young adults.

▶ **My little girl bites when she gets frustrated. How should I handle this behavior?**
At three, your daughter should know that biting is wrong, but she will also know that the drama that ensues is an excellent way to get attention. When your daughter bites, remove her from her victim. Say "No, biting hurts," but don't make an unnecessary fuss. Instead, give time and attention to the child she bit. Whatever you do, don't bite back. It's cruel, and it only teaches your child that, whatever you may say, biting is acceptable.

▶ **My twins have gained a reputation for their bad behavior. Why are they so naughty?**
Twins can be a challenge, as unwanted behavior is common, and often a bid for attention (it works, too). Try to make time for each twin. Talk to them individually, and read to each separately when you can. Let them have their own toys, clothes, and other things, as this helps their social development as individuals.

Twins can benefit from time spent away from each other. See if any friends can invite one of your twins at a time to play. You could also consider some individual sessions at playgroup.

DOUBLE THE TROUBLE *Twins may compete for your attention by behaving badly. Although it's difficult, do your best to give them individual positive attention to avoid this.*

YOUR CHILD'S WELL-BEING *You can get him prepared for preschool, but once he's there, you need to trust that he's well cared for in a safe and stimulating environment.*

Child care and preschool

Finding appropriate child care and choosing a good preschool can be daunting. The most important thing to remember is that you need to tailor your choice to your individual child. If you are in a position to choose, ensure that the environment you select will bring out the best in her.

Choosing child care

At this age, your child requires continuity and routine—a mixture of different caregivers and facilities will be unsettling and confusing. Even if your resources are limited, try to stick to a routine where each day and week represents much the same level of care. For example, you may have a grandparent to help a couple of days a week, and use a local daycare center for other days; or send your three-year-old to preschool in the mornings and have her picked up by a babysitter who brings her back to her home or yours. These are all viable, acceptable options, but try to ensure that each week is roughly the same.

When looking for child care:

▶ Try to find care where there are other children of the same age; socialization skills develop enormously in the preschool years, and contact and play is important at the age of three (see page 42).

▶ Always check references and follow them up, and ask to see any inspection documents.

▶ Don't be afraid to ask questions, and to bring any concerns you have about your child to a prospective caregiver's attention.

▶ Pay a visit. A healthy environment will be obvious to you and, conversely, shortcomings, such as children looking bored, will stand out.

▶ Always look for a good staff-to-child ratio; for a three-year-old, no more than around 5–7 children per caregiver is preferable.

▶ Go for a trial session. Even the best caregivers or daycares may not be right for your child, so test them out for a few hours.

▶ Make sure your child's basic needs will be met—that she will be provided with healthy food and given plenty of opportunity for exercise, and that there are age-appropriate learning activities. If she has an interest in music, for example, ask what is provided at the facility.

》 Find out the procedure for emergencies. You will feel much more confident about leaving your child if you know she is well taken care of, and that you will be alerted to any potential problems.

》 Follow your instincts. If you and your child like the atmosphere of a child care facility, or the personality of a prospective caregiver, and your child responds positively, it is a good starting point.

》 Don't rule out family members as caregivers; although it can cause some tension, studies show that children who are cared for within the family unit fare better emotionally.

Assessing a preschool

You will be looking for much the same qualities in your three-year-old's first preschool experience as you will in her child care. Most early learning education organizations are effectively providing child care as well as learning opportunities, and they should get the balance right by offering plenty of nurturing care alongside a stimulating program of activities.

If you feel that your child isn't ready to be "educated" in an aspirational environment, there is certainly no harm in waiting. Many three-year-olds respond better to programs based around play, interspersed with a few structured activities; research indicates that this is an effective learning environment for young children. At preschool your child should be presented with age-appropriate challenges and learning opportunities, balanced by plenty of unstructured play, exercise, supportive care, and time for rest and relaxation.

A POSITIVE ENVIRONMENT *A good preschool should have a "buzz" and a focused set of ideals. The children should look happy and be occupied.*

Preparing your child

When you find an appropriate preschool for your three-year-old, give her time to adjust to the idea before she starts going there.

Starting elementary school

Not all of the world's children begin academic school careers at the same time. In the US, it's usual for children to start at around age five, but in other countries, age six or above is the norm.

A big transition

When your child makes the transition from home or child care into a more structured educational environment, it can be daunting, and also poignant for you. One of the first things you need to consider is whether or not your child is actually ready to begin school (see page 70). You will need to provide plenty of support and reassurance, and understand that anxiety about leaving you is a normal sign of healthy bonding and emotional development.

Being with other children

A healthy home environment will provide most things a young child needs, but for healthy emotional and cognitive development, being with children of the same age can be invaluable. If your child is home with you, rather than at daycare or school, make sure she has regular contact and opportunities to play with other children.

PLAYMATES *Being with other children regularly in a learning environment will hugely benefit your child's social development and encourage new skills.*

To help your child:

▶ Talk about starting preschool and read books about it.

▶ Explain the routine, from getting ready in the morning and walking or driving to preschool, to what is likely to happen during the day.

▶ Make sure your child meets her first teacher before the big day.

▶ Take her to the preschool and her classroom before the first day so that she has some idea of what to expect.

▶ Make going to preschool a celebration—buy a new backpack and lunchbox and ask her to help you pack a snack or lunch.

▶ Reassure your child by making it clear who will be picking her up and when—and, of course, make sure you arrive to pick her up on time.

▶ Allow her to take along a favorite comfort item if she wishes; this can help make the transition from home to preschool easier.

▶ Expect some distress—it is normal and to be expected.

▶ Don't hover around—it will make it more difficult for both of you.

▶ Remember, many children resist going to preschool and school, but come out beaming. And that is what you are looking for!

Family life

For a harmonious family life, you will need to help your three-year-old develop a positive relationship with any siblings. She will sometimes irritate older siblings by playing with their possessions and may be overzealous with a younger child or new baby.

Brothers and sisters are good for each other. They form strong bonds, and look out for and learn from each other now and through to adulthood. But from very early on in life, even under two years of age, children are already skilled at annoying and tormenting their brothers and sisters as well as being caring toward them. You will have your work cut out for you!

Disagreements between brothers and sisters are a normal part of everyday life as children live and play together and compete for your time and attention. This rivalry acts as your child's first learning opportunity to manage conflict with others. She is practicing a crucial social skill that she will use outside the home whenever tempers flare. At age three, your child will need a lot of supervision to make sure she gets along with her siblings, and encouragement to use words rather than physical force to resolve disagreements. Research tells us that when parents explain to an older child the emotions and reasons behind the behavior of a younger child, then they do get along better. This way, empathy between children is developed.

PEACEFUL PLAYTIME
Your three-year-old will not be completely comfortable about sharing, so you'll need to monitor playtime with siblings to help prevent disagreements.

Handling disagreements

It is easy to fall into the trap of giving more attention when children disagree than when they play well together, or to rush in and assume it is the older child who has started the conflict. It can be tempting to leave children alone when they are playing quietly and only go to them when there is a quarrel. Cooperation is built up when parents go to children often and praise them for playing well together. To avoid unnecessary arguments, ensure that anything precious to an older child is kept out of reach. At the other end of the scale, your three-year-old should not be left alone with infants and needs to be well supervised with younger toddlers.

Sharing your time

Every child in your family needs your love and attention, but this can be a challenge when you are balancing child care, work, household tasks, and a life of your own. Having around 15–20 minutes alone with each child every day will reassure them that, no matter how busy family life can be, they are very important to you.

Personality differences

If you have more than one child, you might be surprised at their differing personalities. Your first child may have been a placid and easy-going infant and the second a whirlwind of activity and prone to tantrums. These

Spending time with you

To give your three-year-old positive attention, you don't always have to sit down and play. She will love to do what you do so that she can be just like Mommy or Daddy. Copying what you do is your child's delight.

Your three-year-old will love to push her toy vacuum around the room after you and splash plastic cups and plates in a bowl as you do the dishes. As well as enjoying herself, she is learning plenty from copying. She will understand your routine and might want to show

how grown up she is by carrying out simple tasks such as pulling up her comforter every morning. Don't, however, treat these tasks as your child's job or responsibility. They are the first step in that direction, but children as young as three aren't ready to have a chore list just yet.

MAKING JOBS EASY *To encourage your child to try tasks for himself, make it easier by lowering things to his height.*

individual differences in temperament are created through genetics but are also shaped by your child's environment. The differences and similarities between your children will help them to develop as individuals within your family, and each one will present you with unique joys and challenges as they grow and develop. If you expect your children to think, react, and act alike, you may be in for a surprise; even children as similar as identical twins have a unique personality.

Resist labeling and pigeonholing your child, because if you decide at an early age that she is "the wild one," for example, you might find that she lives up to this reputation. Furthermore, depending on your own personality, you may decide, for instance, that extroverted behavior is more positive than introverted behavior when, in fact, there is no right or wrong. The key is to think of and treat your child as an individual.

Introducing a new baby

Having a new baby in the family, while a great joy, is usually a real upheaval, not only for you as new parents, but for older children too. Your child's world will change because she will need to learn to share your attention and be patient while the new baby is cared for first.

Your three-year-old will cope better if you involve her in your pregnancy. For example, ask her to help choose a name, let her feel your baby move, and involve her in getting the new baby's bedroom ready. When the new baby is born, your three-year-old will feel included if she too receives gifts or gets a present "from the baby." Having a doll to care for will allow her to copy you as you bathe and tend to the baby. This gives you a chance to be close even when you are caring for the latest addition. To help your child get used to the new baby's arrival:

Maintain a routine To avoid disruption, do your best to keep to the same routines and outings as before the baby was born—children feel more settled when things stay the same.

Accept some regression Expect your three-year-old to regress to some extent and try out some old baby behaviors, such as asking for a bottle. Be sympathetic to these behavioral changes, as they are her way of letting you know she has needs, too, and wants to be included. You will find that these behaviors will pass once life settles down into a routine again.

DIFFERENT INTERESTS
Treat each child as an individual. Some will enjoy quiet, practical activities while others will be more carefree. Neither is wrong.

Make time if possible Your three-year-old will know she still holds a special place in your heart when she has some loving one-to-one time with you, so try to make time for this every day.

Sharing a room

When space is scarce, it can work well to have children share a bedroom. There may be problems, but room-sharing can build close bonds between brothers and sisters if noise and territory disputes are managed well.

Top tips for room sharing:

❯ Room sharing works well when each child has their own well-defined space. Personalize each child's bed area with their own storage, color scheme, posters, and toys, but expect them to share floor space for playing.

❯ Make it a joint responsibility for them to keep their room neat. Your three-year-old will be able to help you put her toys away.

❯ If your three-year-old is sharing with an older brother or sister, lay down some rules for the older child, such as being quiet when the other is sleeping, and storing their belongings in their part of the room.

❯ Avoid problems of accidental breakage by making sure older children's prized possessions are kept out of reach of the youngster.

You may worry that different bedtimes or night waking will mean children keep each other awake. However, most children, once they are fully asleep, will snooze through even the loudest disturbance. It helps if your home is not too quiet, as your children will be used to tuning out some of this background noise, making it easier for them to sleep through commotion during the night.

Family time

Children thrive if they are part of a family that makes time to "play" together. Spending time together as a family, when you are doing something fun or relaxing and your attention is on each other, will give both you and your children an opportunity to communicate, share an interest, and have fun together.

According to a recent survey, families have less time together than they would like, with almost half of parents spending an hour or less with their children every day. Parents say that work and technology, such as watching

QUALITY TIME *It isn't always easy to set aside time for play, but a period focused entirely on your child and his interests is a powerful way to show him that you care.*

"When family members spend time together, they create a shared identity alongside a store of happy memories, which help children gain a sense of who they are and where they belong."

TV and playing electronic games, often get in the way of family time. It takes plenty of motivation to set aside family time amid the demands of day-to-day chores, child care, and work, yet 72 percent of parents do want to spend more time being active as a family. Spending time together does make you feel better: a recent survey found that 86 percent of parents said family time left them feeling happier and closer.

Take a look at your own family and assess how you spend your leisure time. The things you do together don't have to be complex or expensive. It is those simple, everyday activities that create good times. Whether it is having a meal together, splashing around washing the car, or helping each other clean out the hamster cage, children get quality and quantity of family time when it is a part of the daily routine. Whether you are a single-parent family, have little time together because of shift work, or divide up care of the children because you are separated or divorced, these moments of family time are important.

Keeping your cool

Parenting can be stressful and will undoubtedly stretch your patience at times.

To keep your cool:

★ Count slowly to 20, then ask yourself, "Am I calm?" If the answer is "No," keep counting.

★ Take two deep breaths, let your shoulders drop, shake out tension from your hands, and notice your body relaxing.

★ Look at a photograph of your three-year-old as a little baby and bring back that rush of love you had for her as an infant.

★ Call a friend and talk about how you are feeling. This can help you to get things in perspective and perhaps find a solution.

★ Make sure your child is safe and then step away—for example, walk to your mailbox and back.

★ Have a reality check and ask yourself, "Is this issue worth losing my cool over?" If you can't cope, seek professional help (see pages 310–311).

Your 4-year-old

"Watch him grow and change as he ventures into the wider world."

SCHOOL TIME He may be starting preschool this year—a big milestone for the whole family.

FOCUSING ON KEY SKILLS A structured environment gives him the chance to focus on a range of important learning activities.

PLAYTIME Having fun and playing imaginatively at home help to stimulate your child's development.

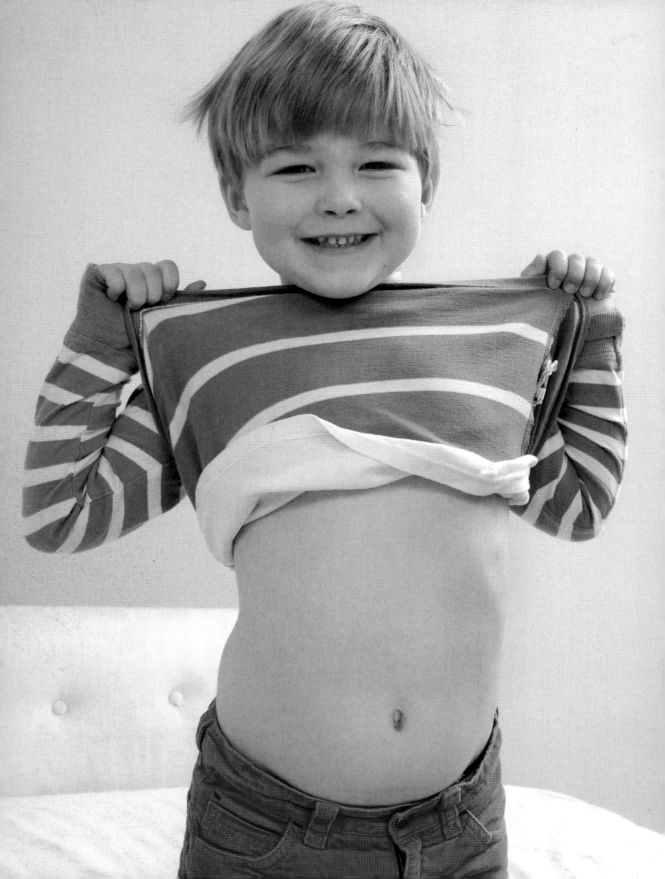

Growth and development

You will notice your child's body looking less toddlerlike, and any early baby fat will begin to disappear. Your child's lungs will grow in capacity and he will have increasing stamina. Soon you will find you don't have to "let him win" every race—and you may even find it hard to keep up with him!

Physical changes

From now until his teenage growth spurt, your child will be growing slowly but steadily at a minimum rate of 1½ in (4 cm) a year overall. This can appear to happen in fits and starts, so you may start to worry that he has been wearing the same-sized clothes for a year, then find that he has outgrown some pants you just bought.

His feet will grow slowly but also in an unpredictable way, so he may outgrow one pair of shoes rapidly and remain in the next pair until he wears them out. In general, your child's feet and hands will grow in proportion to his overall height. If you are measuring your child against a door frame and note that he has grown less than ¾ in (2 cm) in six months, seek advice from your health-care provider. If you are worried that your child is too chubby, work out his BMI (body mass index) and check on the chart on page 52 whether he falls into the overweight or obese category. You will notice that the BMI increases with age. This is because as your child grows, he becomes relatively heavier due to increasing muscle mass.

Just as your child's body is changing, so is his brain. To maximize his brain development, he requires stimulation, warmth, security, good nutrition (see page 17), and plenty of sleep. Your child's brain is laying down neural pathways (see page 21), which become permanent and allow him to remember many sequences.

New skills

By now your four-year-old will probably be able to jump, skip, hop, throw a ball overhand, kick a ball, and climb confidently. He will be able to dress

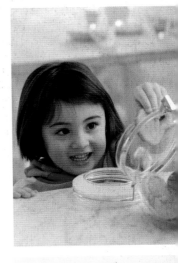

SWEET TREATS *The occasional cookie won't make your child overweight, but make sure unhealthy snacking doesn't become a habit.*

> "Simple physical activities, such as kicking and throwing a ball, will greatly enhance your four-year-old's physical and coordination skills."

himself, but may still need some help from you. Coordination improves with practice. A child who is having difficulty climbing or kicking a ball may lack confidence and simply need a little encouragement.

At this age, your child may make a good attempt at using scissors and be able to draw something that resembles a person. He may hold a pencil in a more mature way, although many children still have an awkward grip. With encouragement, he may try writing his name. Some four-year-olds (not many) are able to tie shoelaces. If your child is using his fist to hold his crayon, he should be encouraged to use a more mature pencil grip. His

Body Mass Index (BMI)

BMI is calculated by dividing weight in kilograms by height in meters squared.*

Age	Boys: at risk of overweight	Boys: overweight	Girls: at risk of overweight	Girls: overweight
4	16.9–17.8	above 17.8	16.8–18.0	above 18.0
5	16.8–17.9	above 17.9	16.8–18.2	above 18.2
6	17.0–18.4	above 18.4	17–18.8	above 18.8
7	17.4–19.2	above 19.2	17.6–19.6	above 19.6
8	17.9–20.0	above 20.0	18.3–20.6	above 20.6
9	18.6–21.0	above 21.0	19.2–21.8	above 21.8
10	19.3–22.2	above 22.2	20.0–22.9	above 22.9
11	20.2–23.3	above 23.3	20.8–24.2	above 24.2
12	21.0–24.2	above 24.2	21.7–25.3	above 25.3
13	21.7–25.2	above 25.2	22.6–26.3	above 26.3
14	22.6–26.0	above 26.0	23.3–27.3	above 27.3

* See http://apps.nccd.cdc.gov/dnpabmi/Calculator.aspx for a BMI calculator.

Omega-3 fatty acids

There is a growing view that deficiencies of omega-3 fatty acids, found in fish oil, can play a part in the development of childhood disorders including learning difficulties, behavioral problems, and depression.

The results of trials so far have been conflicting, with some showing encouraging improvement in areas such as learning and behavior, while others have shown no differences after treatment. One trial showed an improvement in reading, spelling, and behavior in children with dyspraxia (see below). There was no improvement in their motor skills (see page 24).

Only one trial has looked at the effect of giving fish oils combined with many vitamins and minerals to healthy children. The results showed an improvement in memory and in verbal learning, but not in any other areas of learning or IQ.

More research is needed, but in the meantime, you should aim to include a source of omega-3 fatty acids—for instance, from oily fish such as salmon and mackerel—in your child's diet at least twice a week.

teacher can recommend a triangular-shaped rubber "grip," which is slipped over the lower part of the pencil and makes it easier for some children to arrange their fingers and thumb around the pencil. The range of abilities among four-year-olds is huge, and it is vital not to start worrying if your child is still scribbling while his friends appear to be producing minor masterpieces.

Dyspraxia

About 5 percent of otherwise healthy school-age children have difficulty with tasks such as using a knife and fork, tying shoelaces, and catching balls. For some, this is just a question of time, but for others it may be the result of a developmental condition called dyspraxia, which affects movement and coordination because the brain is unable to sequence in the correct way. Symptoms include swinging and tapping feet when seated, being unable to sit still, and being clumsy. There may also be language difficulties.

As a parent, the two most important ways you can help your child are by encouraging him to keep trying the tasks he is struggling with, without expressing impatience, and by building his self-esteem by focusing on things he does well. Most children with dyspraxia do not need to see a doctor, but a few, particularly those with other problems such as learning difficulties, may benefit from a medical assessment and occupational therapy.

NEW SKILLS *Cutting out effectively is an important skill to practice, as it makes so many craft activities possible.*

Common physical concerns

▶ **My four-year-old often soils her underpants. What should I do?**
The medical term for soiling is "encopresis." About three percent of children suffer from this condition, which can be caused by a traumatic event during potty training, such as pain during a bowel movement or a fear of toilet flushing. Other risk factors include eating a high-fat or high-sugar diet, inadequate exercise, and recurrent stress.

Children with ADHD (see page 60) and other attention disorders are also more likely to suffer. It may also be that your child doesn't want to stop whatever activity she's doing to spend time on the toilet. Once you have addressed dietary issues, set up a star chart for when she uses the toilet. Avoid becoming angry, which will compound any fears, and praise and encourage her when she gets it right.

If your child suffers from constipation or regular loose bowel movements, see your doctor, who can look for underlying causes.

▶ **Should I be concerned that my four-year-old son wets the bed?**
No, don't worry. Until the age of four or five, bedwetting is common. Potty training may not have sunk into your child's subconscious, so he doesn't wake when he needs to urinate. Bedwetting is also genetic. Some 75 percent of bedwetters had a parent who wet the bed as a child. There is also some research indicating that many bedwetters

have a deficiency of a hormonelike substance that directs the kidneys to concentrate the urine, so that less is produced at night and a child's small bladder can hold it. In bedwetters, inadequate amounts of this chemical are secreted at night, so more urine is produced than the bladder can hold.

The medical term for bedwetting at night is "nocturnal enuresis," and there may be some concern if this is happening after bladder control is normally established. Your doctor may recommend a moisture alarm for your child's bed, and, in extreme cases, medication. In the meantime, make sure your child drinks plenty during the day so that he learns to recognize and act on the feeling of his bladder being full. Also consider waking him to put him on the toilet before you go to bed, and work on "retention control," which means encouraging your son to wait a little longer each time before going to the bathroom during the day; this can expand the capacity of his bladder. Above all, be calm and avoid judging or showing anger. After age three or four, most children are embarrassed by bedwetting.

▶ **My four-year-old twins play doctors and nurses, and examine each other's private parts. Is this normal?**
It is indeed. As children learn about their bodies, and those of the opposite sex, they are naturally

curious and have no concept of what is and isn't "appropriate." It is natural and healthy for children to explore their bodies, and many children in this age group masturbate. Avoid embarrassing your twins, or making them feel ashamed about their actions; body image is established early on, and you don't want them to associate shame with bodies. Turn a blind eye unless the games are causing anyone distress.

▶ **My four-year old daughter flatly refuses to use a car seat. Do I have to use one?**
Yes. Because vehicle safety belts don't fit the physical and developmental needs of young children, appropriate child safety seats or booster seats are necessary, and must be used as long as legally required. Check with your state or province—seat belt laws vary depending on where you live. According to the American Academy of Pediatrics, a child should use a booster seat until the adult seat belt fits correctly. This usually occurs when the child reaches about 4' 9" (1.45 m) in height, between ages 8 and 12.

Choose a seat that meets current safety standards. If your child is resistant to using a car seat, try a booster seat, which is less confining, and safe as long as the adult belt fits appropriately. Let her decorate it with stickers to make it "cool" or unique, if this helps!

Your child's health

As your child becomes more active and spends time playing outdoors and interacting with other children, good hygiene becomes even more important to help protect him from infection. If he will be starting preschool this year, now is the time to have his eyesight checked, if you haven't already.

Encouraging physical activity

Regular exercise is a great habit for life, and now is a formative time to get active for your child's future. What he does now sets the pattern for his whole life, so it can impact his later risk of obesity, heart disease, osteoporosis, diabetes, and even some cancers.

Many four-year-olds develop a passion for TV, so try to encourage more active pursuits. You could participate in activities together. For instance, you might develop a liking for swimming or playing soccer in the park, which will coincide nicely with your child's improving coordination at this age (see page 52). It is good to have a daily outing, even in bad weather—not only to get some fresh air and exercise, but also to have a change of scenery. Wearing warm clothes and waterproof footwear means your child can get out and about every day, even if it is only to jump in puddles in the park.

Preventing illnesses

There is no point being obsessive about hygiene (see page 26), but simple measures will help to reduce infections such as food poisoning, and prevent colds. Your child's immune system still doesn't equip him to fight every infection, though you may notice that he now has fewer illnesses.

Colds are still very common, however, with the average child having 6–10 each year. Since each cold can last up to three weeks, expect your child's nose to be runny much of the time, and be ready with tissues as much as you can. Four-year-olds can't usually blow their own nose, so when he has a cold you may need to help with this, or at least to teach him not to use his sleeve.

ON THE MOVE *Buying your four-year-old his first bike will encourage him to get out and about and be active. Exercising now will affect his future health.*

WEARING GLASSES
Children's glasses now come in a wide range of styles, and many have arms that curl around the ears— very important in boisterous activity.

Since your four-year-old will be starting school before long, this is a good time to teach him to wash his hands properly himself and get him in the habit of doing it without being reminded. He should be taught to do this after using the toilet and before eating meals, especially when he has been playing outside. At this age, he will need supervision, as he is likely to rush and not wash his hands thoroughly. In the bathtub, your child can wash himself to some extent, though you will still need to wash his hair.

Your child's eyesight

During the first seven years of your child's life, the part of the brain that processes vision is still developing, so it is important to pick up visual problems as early as possible. Research studies suggest that one six-year-old in 20 has an uncorrected eye problem, so don't wait for symptoms such as straining to see the TV or squinting at books before taking your child to the optometrist for a check. If a child cannot see properly with one eye or has a squint, his brain learns to cut out the image from the weak eye so that eventually there is serious vision loss in that eye. Most children's visual problems can be corrected by wearing glasses or by patching the good eye to encourage use of the weaker one.

It is a good idea to take your child for an eye test before he starts preschool, as this can preempt problems in class. Even if you think your four-year-old's eyesight is good, it is worth having his vision checked by an optometrist. Ideally, this should be an annual appointment from this year onward. Most four-year-olds are happy to cooperate with eye testing, but it is advisable to find an optometrist who is used to dealing with young children and can put them at ease.

If your child needs glasses:

❯ Try to get two pairs in case he loses or breaks a pair.

❯ Find out when during the day he should be wearing them and make sure he does so (alert his teacher to this).

❯ Ask what he should do when he is playing sports.

❯ Establish when your child should be seen again for a sight test.

❯ Inquire whether he is likely to need glasses long-term. A child's eyes continue to develop until about the age of seven, so your child may outgrow the need for glasses.

Understanding and skills

Your child now understands much more than he did before. Because he can retain information in his mind for longer, he is better able to follow instructions and complete simple tasks. This is an important life skill, which will stand him in good stead for when he starts school.

Learning new concepts

Your four-year-old can probably count up to 20, perhaps with help, and will have a good understanding of what numbers mean. He will have a better grasp of time now and may show an interest in clocks, but he is unlikely to be reliable at telling the time properly for another year or more. Even so, talking to your child about how long an hour is, for instance, can help his understanding of time and numbers, especially when he has to wait a certain amount of time for something he wants.

Your child may be able to name and match several colors accurately, and sort objects, such as different animal shapes. He will also pair related objects easily, such as a cup and saucer, and a sock and shoe. He will enjoy rearranging his toys, assorted pebbles or shells, and other items into groups, and then perhaps mixing them up again. All this deepens his understanding of sets and groups, which underpins much of mathematics. Shape discrimination is also important when it comes to learning to read, since it enables your child to distinguish between letters. You can help his recognition of shapes by playing games in which your child is required to match up images, and by providing slightly more complex jigsaw puzzles.

Emotional understanding

At four, children can show a range of emotions. Your child may cry if you read a sad story. He may also try to comfort you when he thinks you are sad. You can help to develop his compassionate side by talking about situations that you see. For instance, if you see someone waiting for a bus in the rain, you and he could speculate on how that person might feel if they miss the bus.

QUANTITIES *From an early age, filling and emptying containers with sand or water will teach your child concepts such as more/ less, bigger/smaller, and heavier/lighter.*

"At first, your child's attempts at writing are really an extension of drawing. In other words, they are just scribbles."

Your child's own need for privacy is increasing, and this is important to his sense of self. There may be secrets he shares with a friend or with a favorite teddy bear. You could consider providing a space of his own, even if this is just a corner of a shared bedroom.

Early writing

By now your child will have learned two vital things: how to hold a pencil or crayon, and the fact that written symbols can convey messages. The first word your child is likely to try writing is his name.

To help him with letters and words:

▶ Show him how to write lower case letters. Don't worry if his earliest efforts bear little resemblance to the right letters.

▶ Label a coat hook or door, and items such as a chair, with his name.

Speech and language development

At four, your child will speak clearly. He will know what he wants to say, and most of the time know how to say it. His words will be in the right order. In addition to "and," he will use "when," "if," and "but," enabling him to tell long stories. Expect him to talk a lot, sometimes very fast.

At times he may become insistent or argumentative and sound rude, though he is probably just animated. Some of his consonants will still be

Helping him to remember and concentrate

Your four-year-old's memory will be improving all the time, and he will be more able to focus on tasks for a longer period of time.

To help your child:

★ Talk to him about events that happened yesterday, the day before, or even last week.

★ Recite nursery rhymes and songs together. Try leaving out some of the words or lines.

★ Play the memory game: one of you starts with "I went to the beach on my vacation, and in my suitcase I took..." Each player in turn recites the list of items so far and adds one more.

★ Show your child different coins or stamps, then get him to find the same kind among others in a drawer or box. A variation on this is looking through a catalog to find pictures of objects that are already in the house.

★ Play a game known as Concentration or Pairs, which involves arranging all the cards face down, then taking turns flipping over two cards at a time, until a player finds a matching pair. There are many varieties of this game, some with very easy cards designed for young children.

a bit unclear. At four he can manage to pronounce "sh," "z," and "v"
sounds, but he won't master "ch," "j," or "l" until he is five. He is unlikely
to pronounce "th" or "r" properly until the age of six or seven. Consonants
are more challenging for your child when they occur in clusters, as in the
words "strike," "tempting," or "library." Occasionally adults will fail to
understand what your child is saying, and he may find this frustrating.

"Why" questions continue throughout this year, and increase in their
depth. Now he might want the answers to more difficult questions, such
as why his pet guinea pig died. To help his speech and language:

Avoid using baby talk Your four-year-old needs to learn to say words
properly, especially if he is at school now. However, using one or two baby
words (like "blanky" for "blanket") won't be a problem.

Continue to use eye contact and emphasize new or difficult words.

Don't correct him all the time Just use the correct version in your reply,
rather than overtly correcting his pronunciation or grammar.

Answer your child's questions If you don't know the answer, then look
it up. It is good for your child to learn that answers can be found from
books or the Internet, or by asking others who have more expertise.

Ask questions Sometimes open-ended questions are good, but often your
four-year old will just need to be given simple choices, such as "Would you
like milk or apple juice?"

LEARNING THROUGH PLAY *He will understand new concepts and develop language through play. By joining in sometimes, you can answer his questions and help him learn.*

Expand your child's language and thinking by having "what if" conversations. You could ask what might happen if, for instance, there were a blizzard and it snowed all night.

Pre-reading skills

Learning to read is a continuous and gradual process that starts early on, when your child first makes connections between the words he hears you read and the marks and symbols on a printed page. Once your child begins to read for himself, he improves gradually over many years.

There are two main methods of learning to read:

▌ Phonics—your child learns the sound of each letter (or groups of letters) and puts them together.

▌ Look-and-say—your child looks at a whole word (or even a whole sentence) and learns to recognize it as an entity.

A formal method isn't needed at age four. Just continue reading to your child and looking at books together, at his pace. He will engage with

Common learning concerns

▶ **My four-year-old daughter shows no interest in letters, numbers, or anything else that she needs to prepare her for school. What should I do?**
If your child is particularly weak in certain areas, talk to your health-care provider, who can arrange tests. However, do bear in mind that many children are late bloomers, and develop cognitively in a short space of time, when they are older. For example, a few children don't say much until almost three, and then at age four speak in full sentences and go on to read early. Many disorders can be detected in the preschool years, and with early intervention, they pose fewer problems later on.

▶ **My son has difficulty concentrating. Could he have ADHD and what should I do?**
Attention Deficit Hyperactivity Disorder covers a range of symptoms including poor concentration, restlessness, impulsive behavior, and poor social skills. More boys than girls have ADHD. It's a neuro-developmental disorder with a strong genetic element, although there's no single definitive test and the exact cause is unknown.

Your child may have ADHD if he never needs much sleep, fidgets constantly, flits from one activity to another, finds it hard to listen to a story, and is very active and boisterous. Sensitive but firm handling will help but cannot cure ADHD. You should get a specialist assessment early on. For many children, ADHD is a lifelong condition that makes it difficult to do well at school, but with the right help your child should be able to fulfill his potential.

Speech and language problems

Children develop language skills at different times. Boys and twins are most likely to be late developers in this area. A delay in learning speech or reading doesn't always mean there is a problem; children often catch up. However, some children really do have a disorder that needs attention. Your four-year-old is more likely to have a genuine problem if:

★ He often looks blank or does not understand you.

★ He switches consonants around, or omits them.

★ He stutters or stammers.

★ He speaks little compared with other children his age.

The first step is to talk to your health-care provider without delay, or get the opinion of a speech and language therapist. Ask your pediatrician or family doctor for a referral to a suitable specialist.

a story even more if you talk about it. You could pose questions such as "Goldilocks was very hungry, wasn't she?" Your child may recognize a word or two, or maybe just a few letters. Some children pretend to read, which is good preparation for reading because your child is practicing the rhythms used in reading aloud.

To help his pre-reading skills:

▶ Underline words with your finger as you read.

▶ Try playing together with magnetic letters.

▶ Play "I Spy" when you are out and about, or even just at home.

▶ Write down six or seven names and ask your child to pick out his name from among them (use lower case, except for the initial letter).

Visiting the library

Your four-year-old can get a lot out of the library, so go often. As well as being stimulating for your child, it is quite a peaceful activity for you. Your local library will have a children's section and may have storytimes for youngsters, too. These are usually given by library staff or volunteers, but occasionally authors also do readings. There may be changing themes and displays, helping your child come across books and ideas you and he had not considered before. At the library, your child will also see other children enjoying reading. If he has his own card for borrowing, it will encourage him to value and take care of books if you explain that they have to be taken back for another child to use.

"At this age, your child's experience of books should be fun—neither a lesson nor a chore."

Emotions and personality

You remain the center of your four-year-old's world, but he will be beginning to build other important relationships outside the home. These form his wider circle of attachments, but it is his strong bond with you that allows him to develop successful relationships with others.

LOVE AND SECURITY
When your child is secure in your love, he will feel confident that others will care about him, too. This is an important part of his emotional development.

Your four-year-old will now separate from you with little or no fuss the majority of the time, and be eager to get to the playground each day to see his friends and start the school day. This phase of developing relationships outside of the family, and stress-free separation, may leave you feeling less important, but don't worry: your attention, praise, and unconditional love continue to be the biggest influences on your child.

Making friends

With one or two friends he looks forward to seeing, your child will be playing more cooperatively. He will tend to build friendships in the obvious way—being closest to children he sees most often and those who like the same activities, whether that is rough-and-tumble play or arts and crafts. Having friends when you are four is important, as it affects how you play. When your four-year-old plays with a friend, rather than someone he doesn't know well, the activity will be more complex and he will communicate more ideas to keep it going. About two-thirds of children of age four will choose friends of the same sex. To strengthen your child's friendships, make arrangements for playtime at home as well as school.

Your four-year-old is developing the skills needed to be a good friend: being good at listening, being aware of the feelings of others, and being able to share. These abilities will make your child more popular.

To help your child learn these skills:

❯ Teach listening by giving your child a simple message to pass on to someone else in your household.

❯ Raise an awareness of emotions by talking about and naming everyday feelings such as "annoyed," "happy," "jealous," and "proud."

◗ Practice sharing by praising your child when he is generous with his toys and encourage taking turns by playing games such as Candy Land.

Types of play

Imagination guides your four-year-old's play as he starts to act out different roles and scenarios—for example, taking the part of "Daddy" or "the teacher." Research shows that girls tend to act out domestic scenes, while boys most frequently play out characters from books, television, or movies. This imaginative play is fun and helps your child understand the roles and relationships of those around him. As well as mimicking what you do, you will notice your four-year-old copying things he has heard you say; his accurate parroting of your favorite phrases may sometimes shock you. You can promote imaginative play by providing props such as dress-up clothes and play kitchens or stores, and by taking your child to places where he will see people in different roles, such as a farm or a hospital.

PLAYING NICELY
Your child's play will start to become more cooperative, especially with those children he knows well.

Your four-year-old will be getting more involved in organized physical play. His developing coordination and ability (see page 51) to throw and kick mean he will enjoy playing sports at a basic level. These activities are good for his health, his ability to take turns, and his coordination. Practice is essential for all these skills, so opportunities for physical play at home will back up the learning from games and sports organized at school. This activity will, of course, keep you in shape, too.

Imaginary playmates

Your child may develop an imaginary friend at this or an earlier age. Boys' imaginary friends tend to be very competent and may be used as an example to work toward. Girls tend to create imaginary friends who are less able and

"Imaginary playmates coincide with a child's developing imagination and occur at a time when fantasy and reality may be blurred."

need help, and then use them to boost their own confidence and practice caring skills. Studies suggest that more girls than boys and more first-born children have an imaginary friend.

There is no need to worry about your child having an imaginary friend as long as he continues to play with "real life" friends and his everyday activities are not hampered. The imaginary playmate could be helping your child get through a difficult time; perhaps a friend or family member has moved away, or changes at home have made your child feel insecure. The comfort an imaginary friend provides may be just what your child requires for a short time; the majority of children let their imaginary friend go as their need for this companionship reduces.

If your four-year-old has few friends and relies too heavily on his imaginary playmate, he may need your help to meet some new children. For example, try inviting other children over to play, or spend more time with relatives and friends who have children the same age.

Learning to share

Your child is still learning about sharing, and although by age four he will realize that not everything belongs to him, he won't be entirely happy about it. He may be impulsive, and his desire to play with a toy or go on the slide, for example, may make him impatient and unwilling to wait for his turn. He is starting to understand about give-and-take, and that he will benefit if he learns to share. You can help reduce the stress of sharing when other children come to visit by getting your child put away his most

House rules

Your four-year-old is beginning to understand what is expected of him, so a few clear, simple household ground rules that everybody knows and understands can make family life run more smoothly. They can also help your child behave properly in environments outside the home. Rules bring a sense of security: your four-year-old needs to know what to expect and where he stands. Simple rules mean you can be consistent as parents and, when they apply to everyone, enable you and older children to set a good example. Make rules positive: they should state what you want family members to do, rather than what you don't want them to do. **Some useful rules are:**
★ "We use a quiet voice."
★ "We clean up after ourselves."
★ "We are gentle when we touch."

precious toys and bring out only those he is comfortable sharing with someone else.

Remember:

▹ Sharing is a developing skill, so your child will share perfectly well sometimes and be unable to do so at other times.

▹ Saying you can play with it "in five minutes" won't mean much to your child. His understanding of time is still developing, so help him wait his turn by counting out loud or watching the second hand on a clock.

Getting the behavior you want

Your four-year-old will have the beginning of a sense of right and wrong based on the behavior you value and the behavior you punish. He will be quite concrete in his thinking—for example, he will consider it worse to break a big toy than a smaller one, even if the smaller one is more precious or expensive.

At age four, he will be able to understand that behavior that hurts others, such as hitting another child, is less acceptable than, for example, breaking household rules by not putting away toys or hanging up his coat. He will be motivated to behave well to get your praise and avoid disapproval, so this is an ideal age to start teaching your values. Encourage him to own up if something has gone wrong, and show how pleased you are when he is caring and thinks of others. Your reactions show him the behavior and standards that you value and will help him live up to them.

Your child may become confused about what is correct and incorrect behavior if, as parents, you undermine each other's decisions. For example, your child may be in the habit of asking one of you for a treat, then, if he is told "No," going to the other for a different answer.

To avoid giving conflicting advice:

▹ Always check back with your partner to see if a decision has already been given. If this can't be done easily, delay giving your answer until you have had a chance to talk it through together. This way your child sees you as a parenting team who back each other up.

HIS POSSESSIONS
Sharing is bound to be harder when he is playing with his own toys. Be sympathetic to this, but teach him about being giving.

"A child of four will laugh around three hundred times a day, while an adult laughs on average just seventeen times."

▶ If you do disagree—and this is bound to happen sometimes—do it away from your child, and then let him know your joint decision.
▶ Remember that consistency is everything when trying to manage your four-year-old's behavior, and being given one clear message or boundary will be much less confusing for him.

Sense of humor

The development of your child's sense of humor is linked to his rapidly developing language skills. These include the ability to tell a very simple story and an increased understanding of words and rhyming. Four-year-olds can form little rhymes and word plays and be highly amused by them. They will alter words to make them rhyme, and this causes much hilarity.

Your four-year-old is also more aware of manners and therefore of what is taboo, so mentions of burping, bottoms, or poop will make him giggle. He may find it immensely funny to say a "naughty" word, not least because it usually gets some sort of reaction. If he is doing this in public, simply distract him with something else rather than making a big deal of it.

Being bossy

Many four-year-olds are noisy and assertive. They are still working out how to get what they want, and many try the tactic of simply ordering others around or being demanding to get their way. This can appear rude and often ends in sulking or tantrums if their orders are not obeyed. How you react to this behavior will shape your child's future social skills.

Developing empathy

Your four-year-old is beginning to understand his emotions and those of others. He may notice when someone looks upset and offer to console them. This can happen five or six times an hour when he is with other children, and the amount of comfort given does not differ between young boys and girls. Being able to notice and understand other people's emotional state is an essential social skill. Encourage empathy by being responsive to your child's emotional states, by talking about and naming feelings, and by explaining to your child how his actions affect others. This will work better than scolding your child when he is not caring toward others.

Remember:

▶ If you give in to orders, then your child will learn that bossy behavior is effective and use it more often.

▶ If you react by prompting your child to ask politely, you are helping him to develop a skill that is useful at home and elsewhere. Many parents make it a rule that children must use the magic word "please" before requests will be granted and must say "thank you" afterward.

▶ Always set a good example yourself by using "please" and "thank you" when you make requests of your four-year-old and others.

Common behavioral concerns

▶ How can I cope with my daughter's regular tantrums?
By age four, your daughter should have a vocabulary that allows her to express herself emotionally, so ignore her tantrums, and make it clear that you will listen to her complaints or concerns if she speaks calmly and explains, "I'm mad," or "I'm scared," for example, and why. Make sure she has some choices in her life—for instance, allow her to choose what to wear around the house—so she feels she has some control over her life.

▶ I've noticed my little boy tells lies. Should I be worried?
Your son is still trying to distinguish between fantasy and reality at this age, so he will believe that if he says he was good, then he was, and will deny wrongdoing even when caught in the act. He is motivated not to get into trouble and may lie about simple things, such as whether he broke a toy, to avoid being scolded. Remember, he is not lying in a manipulative way—he just wants the problem to go away. Rewarding honesty is a good tactic. Avoid accusations or anger and stay calm when your child is untruthful. Set a good example—your son will be confused if he hears you lie, even if it's a little white lie.

▶ My son wakes in the night screaming. Is this a night terror?
Yes. Night terrors are marked by a sudden awakening and intense fear. Your child may scream and appear extremely distressed. You may think he is awake, but he probably isn't. The terror may continue for several minutes. Night terrors usually occur in the first third of the night—suddenly, from a deep sleep. Some night terrors might be caused by frightening stories or TV programs. Other children suffer from deeper-seated anxieties that will need to be brought to the surface and looked at. Night terrors rarely indicate a serious problem. Children don't remember the bad dreams when they have experienced a night terror.

Take steps to address any anxiety that your child might be experiencing, and if the terrors occur frequently, consult your doctor. Remain calm during an episode, providing a reassuring and safe presence for your child. Some experts recommend waking your child about 15 minutes before the terror usually occurs to preempt it. Comfort your child, and stay with him for a few minutes while he goes back to sleep. This normally breaks the cycle, and if the terrors do recur, they should be much less dramatic.

REAL-LIFE QUESTIONS

Your child's life

You all face an exciting, but daunting, milestone as your child starts preschool, but there are many ways you can prepare him. When your child is at home, you can begin to hope for slightly more responsible behavior, such as being helpful and being more calm and well-mannered at mealtimes.

Starting school

Whether or not your child has attended a playgroup or daycare prior to his first day at school, you can expect some reluctance or concern as he comes in contact with unfamiliar environments and people.

To help your child:

) Remember that your child's temperament will dictate his response to a new challenge or environment. Some four-year-olds are robust and outgoing; others cling to parents and do not respond well to change or separation; in fact, both types of children can exist in the same family.

) Discuss the changes that will be taking place. Before the new school year begins, talk with your child about the changes in his daily routine, and give him an opportunity to ask questions. Be reassuring and upbeat, and focus on the positives, such as making new friends, and doing lots of exciting activities, like painting and playing in the sandbox.

) Start his school-year bedtime and morning routine a few days early. This may prevent him from being confused, groggy, or cranky on the first day of school. Arrange a play date with another child from his class, preferably one-on-one, so that he knows someone and will be more comfortable.

) Always say goodbye, and let him know you will see him at the end of the day. Your child will have an easier time with separation if he is confident that you will return to pick him up.

) Take him to the school to get used to the layout—show him his classroom, the restrooms, and his cubby, and introduce him to the teacher.

) Let him know it is normal to feel nervous or worried about being away from you, and suggest that he takes a familiar toy or a family picture to school for comfort.

"Give your child an opportunity to express any fears, which can then be discussed and resolved."

"It is important to handle your own emotions about your child starting school."

▶ Remember that your own feelings will affect your child's attitude to preschool. If you are upset or feeling fearful or guilty, you can be sure your child will pick up on that. Be as positive as you can be, and while it is fine to say that you will miss him, focus on the fact that he is going to have much more fun at school than you will at home or work.

Teaching basic skills

Your child will develop at his own pace, but your involvement and encouragement will help him prepare for some of the circumstances and activities he will face at school.

Before starting school, your child should be able to:

▶ Listen to instructions and concentrate when required.

▶ Sit still when required.

▶ Use the toilet independently, including flushing, and be able to wash his hands thoroughly.

▶ Hold a pencil or crayon.

▶ Answer and ask a question.

▶ Understand sharing.

▶ Solve problems when angry or frustrated, without being aggressive.

▶ Do simple tasks by himself, such as put items in his bag.

▶ Put puzzles together.

▶ Cut roughly with children's scissors.

▶ Run, jump, and climb.

▶ Put on a coat and shoes that have Velcro fasteners.

▶ Say his first and last name and his age.

▶ Sing some songs and rhymes.

▶ Recite a familiar story.

   If your child is not managing most of these skills, you can work on them gently and regularly to get them right.

Encourage independence Use everyday activities as an opportunity for learning, such as putting on shoes together before you go out.

Teach him about his personal details, such as his full name and age.

Make sure he has playmates Playing with other children helps to form bonds and teaches him sharing and negotiation skills.

Teach him to sit quietly and concentrate—practice this while you are on the bus, in the doctor's office, or even when your child is sitting at the kitchen table doing a quiet activity, such as cutting out.

Do craft activities together, such as cutting and pasting and drawing, so that he is confident in using small implements.

Teaching tolerance

For the first time, your four-year-old may be in contact with children of different races, religions, and family structures from your own. It is, therefore, extremely important to teach him tolerance—to explain that differences are good, and to be celebrated. Talk about why people have different skin colors, why they wear different clothes, and why they speak differently. Talk about people's backgrounds and cultures, and how variety can make life much more exciting. If you eat international foods, use this as an opportunity to talk about differences.

From the earliest possible age, it is important to make it clear to your child that people are people, no matter what they look like or how they speak. Teaching respect is fundamental to this, so actively look for opportunities to discuss differences (even the different colors of cats or dogs) and similarities, to make your point clear. If you get a whiff of prejudice, step in early to counter it. Try not to let any prejudice slip into your own speech or approach to others.

HOME LEARNING
Encourage your child to do simple activities at home, such as drawing with a pen or crayon. This will help prepare her for similar activities she will do at school.

Packed lunches

First packed lunches, whether they are required daily or for special outings, should be fun and child-friendly. Four-year-olds are easily distracted, and if they have to peel fruit, open yogurt cartons, or handle a big sandwich, they are likely to give up before they have even begun. Don't be tempted to fill a lunchbox with unhealthy snacks, either—your child's mood and performance will be negatively affected by foods that contain lots of sugar.

For a healthy packed lunch, offer a selection of items such as small squares of sandwiches, peeled orange segments, tiny pieces of fruit dipped in lemon juice to prevent browning (skewered on a kebab stick with the ends cut off), drinkable yogurt, boxes of raisins or other dried fruit, rice cakes, or miniature tubs of hummus, and a bottle of water.

"Shared activities give your child a sense of belonging that is important as he branches out to form friendships away from home."

Family life

When you have fun together as a family, you will create good times and memories that will help build your four-year-old's identity as part of the family. As well as going to the playground and park together, take up shared interests such as swimming and outdoor activities.

Of course there is indoor family playtime, too: your four-year-old is ready for simple board games, such as Chutes and Ladders, and will enjoy games of suspense, such as those that have a pop-up element. Remember that your child's attention span for these games will be short—up to 10 minutes—so don't be disappointed if he wants to move on to the next activity before the game is over.

The importance of eating together

Family life is full of everyday rituals that help us "touch base" and communicate with each other. One of the best ways for people to catch up is by sharing a meal, though fewer than half of American and Canadian families eat dinner together at home four or more times a week.

The benefits of eating together:

▶ Your child is more likely to eat healthily and have a balanced diet.

▶ Family bonds are made stronger through sharing the events of the day, and your four-year-old will learn good table manners and pick up vocabulary from both listening to and joining in with mealtime chatter.

▶ At shared mealtimes, your child can receive plenty of praise for his dexterity with cutlery and his good behavior.

Getting used to a babysitter

Your child may now come home to a babysitter after school rather than to you. You can help ease the process by ensuring that your sitter is familiar with your child and all of his routines, and has spent time with him before he starts school or daycare, or you return to work. Make sure his normal routine is in place, and that your child is happy and confident about expressing his needs. Don't be surprised if he resists or complains; most children prefer the company of parents to others. If you are sure about your choice, be firm. A good babysitter will have the skills to keep your child happy and occupied in your absence, and you should be confident in this.

Helping around the house

Your four-year-old is ready to get into some good household habits, such as cleaning up after himself and helping you with simple tasks.

It is not unreasonable to expect him to put his toys in a box or closet. He will still need your help if there is a lot to put away, but will love to have you work alongside him. Help him to develop neat habits by having easy-to-handle, child-level storage.

He can manage some small jobs too, such as taking his cup and plate into the kitchen at the end of meals, or helping you feed a pet. He is not ready to have a list of chores to do on his own, but will enjoy being helpful most of the time, so just follow his lead.

SIMPLE RESPONSIBILITIES *Giving your child easy tasks at this age paves the way for later helpfulness.*

Your four-year-old will get the most out of mealtimes when there is a set time for dinner that is part of his routine. Distractions such as the TV or handheld games can get in the way of talking, so it is advisable to turn them off for the duration of the meal. Mealtimes may sometimes be a battleground rather than a pleasure as your child asserts his opinion about what he will eat and how long he is prepared to sit still. He will stay seated for longer, and be less messy, when you stay at the table with him and remain calm. Avoid pressuring or pleading with him to eat.

Up until now, your four-year-old has been more concerned with learning to use his cutlery, but as this is mastered, you can start to teach him the finer points of good table manners. Four-year-olds learn most quickly when the older children and adults set a good example. Watching you handle a knife and fork, pass food to others at the table, and eat slowly will guide your child. He will be motivated to do well when you notice he is eating without spilling and praise him for being helpful. Of course, there will be times when he makes you all giggle uncontrollably as a burp escapes or food is accidentally sent flying. While you will laugh naturally when these things are a surprise, prevent them from becoming routine by gently letting your child know that you don't want this behavior repeated every day.

"Keep strong emotions away from mealtimes, as they may make your child anxious, which can in turn reduce appetite."

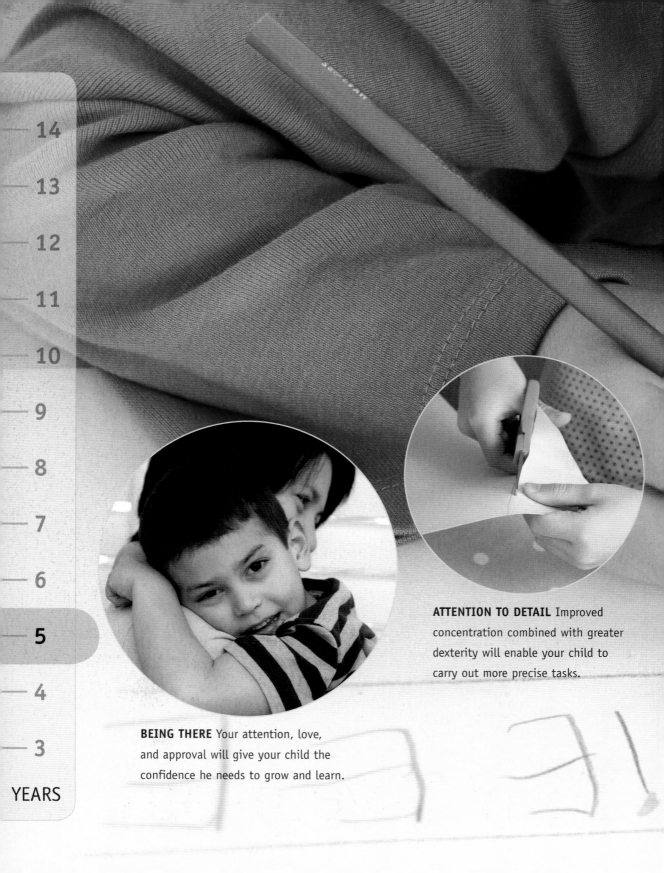

14

13

12

11

10

9

8

7

6

5

4

3

YEARS

ATTENTION TO DETAIL Improved
concentration combined with greater
dexterity will enable your child to
carry out more precise tasks.

BEING THERE Your attention, love,
and approval will give your child the
confidence he needs to grow and learn.

NEW INTERESTS He may begin to show a preference for particular activities that he enjoys.

"She will become more capable and independent as she rapidly learns new skills."

Your 5-year-old

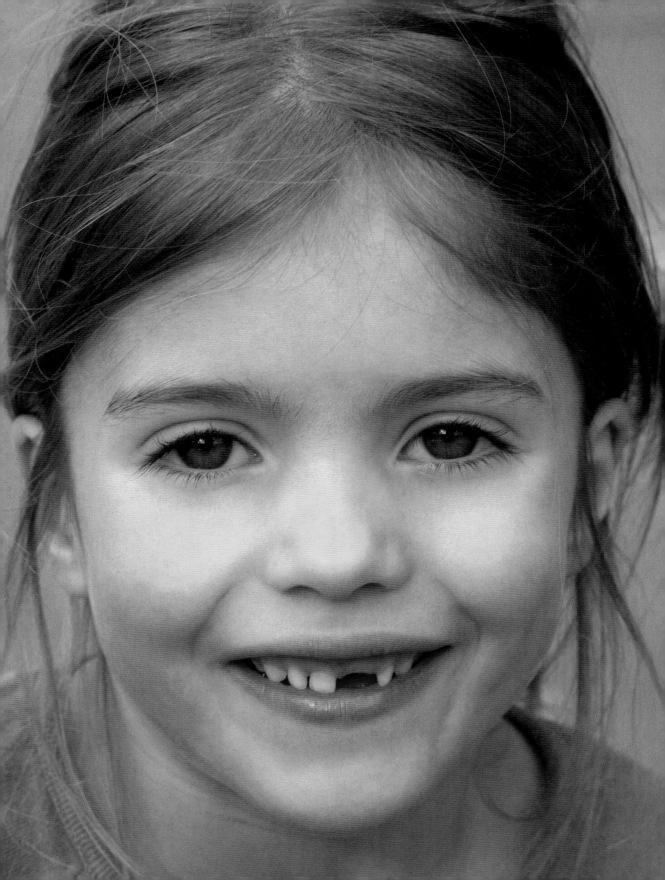

Growth and development

A milestone will be reached as your five-year-old's first teeth begin to fall out. Her height and weight will continue to increase slowly and steadily. You may notice that her face slims down as fat is replaced by muscle, and many children will look this way from now until puberty.

Losing teeth

Usually milk teeth (see page 27) only start to fall out when secondary teeth are coming through. A loose tooth will be exciting for your child because it is a sign of growing up, and she will know that the tooth fairy might visit. It may, however, also make her anxious because a loose tooth can be painful and cause the gum to bleed. The process can linger on, with the tooth hanging by a strand for days. Any parent who has watched their child suffer with the first tooth will be quick to pull out subsequent teeth when they become very loose. If a tooth is hanging by a thread and you don't want it to fall out while your child is asleep, wrap a tissue around it and pull quickly. Hardly any force should be needed. Make sure you don't lose it, as this may distress your child. Always have a good excuse ready in case the tooth fairy "forgets" to come—for example, say, "The weather was bad so she couldn't make it, but I'm sure she'll try again tonight!"

Secondary teeth

While primary teeth are usually pearly white and even, quite often secondary teeth have darker enamel that may look disappointingly yellow in comparison. This is normal. It is also normal for secondary teeth to come through crooked. Sometimes a new tooth will appear before the primary tooth has fallen out, and in many children there is quite a long gap between the loss of a primary tooth and the appearance of the secondary one. The good news is that teeth usually straighten out by themselves. However crooked your child's new teeth seem, there is a good chance she won't need years of orthodontic treatment. Take care of your child's new teeth—she should brush them twice a day, and you should supervise this.

GROWING STRONGER
Muscle strength will increase, and this will enable your child to develop his motor skills, such as running and climbing, at a rapid pace.

"If your child is a picky eater, you must think carefully about sources of iron and vitamins."

Iron deficiency

Iron deficiency anemia has been shown to cause problems such as poor behavior, slow growth, tiredness, and recurrent infections. Children who get most of their calories from milk and starchy foods and eat no meat or green vegetables are prone to iron deficiency. If your child looks pale and seems excessively tired, she may be anemic and you should see your doctor. Anemia is diagnosed by a blood test, but can also be indicated by the color of the nails and the pink area just inside the lower eyelids, which will look pale. Iron pills or liquid will be recommended. This must be given at the prescribed dosage because an excess amount can cause iron poisoning.

If you suspect that your child doesn't eat a balanced diet (see page 17), it is advisable to give a daily dose of a vitamin mixture suitable for children that contains iron. Vitamin C is particularly important, as it helps the body absorb iron. Good sources of iron are red meat, green vegetables, and breakfast cereals fortified with iron. Vitamin C is found in many fruits and vegetables, particularly citrus fruits and tomatoes, and in some fruit juices.

Calorie needs for healthy growth

Calories are a measure of the energy value of food. In order to grow in height and weight, a child needs slightly more calories going into her body than are being used up in exercise, whereas adults need to avoid gaining weight by creating a perfect balance in terms of what they eat

Calorie intake

As your child grows, her calorie needs increase, but it is rarely helpful to worry about exactly how many calories she eats. If your child is healthy and gets plenty of exercise, she will eat as much as she needs, but it is your responsibility to ensure she eats well and is active. This chart shows the recommended calories per day for boys and girls at different ages.

Age	Boys	Girls
1–3 years	1,230	1,165
4–6 years	1,715	1,545
7–10 years	1,970	1,740
11–14 years	2,220	1,845
15–18 years	2,755	2,110
Adult	2,550	1,940

versus how many calories they use. Obesity in children is a simple
matter of consuming too many calories and not burning enough. Try to
encourage your child to eat a balanced combination of starch, fruits and
vegetables, and fat, and keep junk food, which contains "empty calories,"
to a minimum.

Large muscle development

By age five, your child will probably be able to ride a bike with training
wheels and use a scooter, and her increased muscle power, together with
her ever-improving coordination, means she will be able to manage skills
such as standing on one leg and skipping over a jump rope.

Now is a good time to consider taking your child for lessons in
activities such as swimming, ice skating, or dance. However, this is an age
when competitive parenting can be a fine art, and it is easy to find yourself
feeling anxious that your child is only doing two after-school activities per
week when her friends are doing four or more.

Remember:

▶ When choosing activities, go at your child's pace and don't forget that,
at age five, a whole day at school is exhausting enough for your child.
One or possibly two after-school or weekend activities per week is plenty.

▶ Any hobbies should be fun, so only do them if your child is eager and
appears to be getting something out of taking part in an activity (with the
possible exception of swimming, see overleaf).

Small muscle development

At this stage, the small muscles are continuing to develop, and hand–eye
coordination is so good that your five-year-old may enjoy spending long
periods drawing, coloring, and doing simple puzzles. Although for most
children their "handedness" has been clear from the age of 18 months
or so, now is the time when they will stick to one hand for writing (see
overleaf). Many children still find it hard to tie laces, so Velcro fastenings
on shoes are highly recommended.

Once again, the range of abilities at this age is huge: if your child can't
do a simple puzzle, she may simply have no interest, or she may just need
to practice. Children really benefit from the time adults or older children

BALL SKILLS *With
better hand–eye
coordination now, he
may be able to catch
and throw a large ball.
Some may even be able
to catch a tennis ball.*

"Being left-handed is normal, so there is no reason for your child to feel different or for her to be forced to use her right hand."

spend playing with them. If your child is struggling to learn something new, she may need to be shown many times and given lots of praise for her achievements. If your child is having problems in any area of development, you should be informed by your child's teacher.

Helping your left-handed child

The discovery that you have a left-handed child can come as a surprise if you are an entirely right-handed family. Unless you are a left-hander, you will not realize how much the world is set up for right-handers. Scissors, for example, are usually made for right-handers, but there are versions for left-handers. Holding a pen is probably the greatest challenge. All may be fine when your left-handed child writes in pencil, but switching to ink can lead to a smudgy mess.

Most children will find their own writing style with their hand held either above or below the words as they write them. Apparently, there are more left-handed than right-handed geniuses, which is always worth remembering if you are trying to reassure your child.

Learning to swim

Many children needlessly drown each year, so, for reasons of safety, learning to swim is an essential skill. Swimming is also wonderful exercise, as it uses many muscle groups without placing stress on any of them. It is a skill that is much easier to learn at an early age. It will teach your child coordination and build strength.

Sign up for lessons at your local pool and keep going for as many months or years as necessary, until your child is a confident swimmer.

Choose classes that have no more than six per class in a warm pool. Swimming is a lesson that is worth persevering with even if you meet a lot of resistance.

If you can't find, or don't want to pay for, lessons, try to teach your child basic swimming skills yourself.

CONFIDENT SWIMMER *The earlier you take your child swimming, the more natural and at ease he will be in the water.*

Common physical concerns

▶ **My five-year-old has started to wet himself in the daytime. What's the best thing to do?**
Your child could have a urinary tract infection, so take him to your doctor for a test. Or there may be something preventing your child from using the toilet. Perhaps at school he's not allowed to go when he needs to, or the bathrooms are dirty; a recent upset or trauma, such as a house move, parental separation or conflict, a new baby in the family, or bullying at school, can also be factors.

Your knowledge of your own child and his situation should enable you to form some idea of what might be worrying him, and how to address the problem. If not, do talk to your health-care provider. Talk to your child's teacher, too, of course, to find out if he is having any problems in the classroom or on the playground. Above all, be gentle and sympathetic with your child. Wetting is rarely, if ever, the child's fault.

▶ **My daughter often says she has a tummyache. How will I know if she is really ill?**
Your child may say she has a stomachache if she doesn't want to go to school, for example, but it's not safe to ignore. If she is vomiting, has a fever, or looks unwell, seek advice from your doctor, at least until it's established that your child doesn't have a serious medical problem.

Recurrent stomachaches can be difficult to deal with, but once physical problems are excluded, any emotional aspects usually become clearer. Your daughter may offer insight, and tell you that her tummy hurts when, for instance, she has to read aloud in class. Take her concerns seriously and help reassure her to overcome her fears.

▶ **I'm concerned that my son may be too pudgy, but I don't want him to be skinny, either.**
There's little doubt that overweight kids usually become overweight adults. But, as you're probably

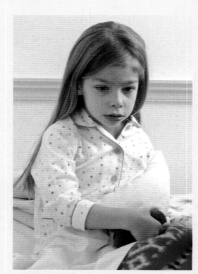

TUMMY ACHE *When a young child is anxious about something, it is quite common for her to say that her tummy hurts, but always take her complaints seriously.*

aware, anorexia and other eating disorders are also a risk, most often in children age seven and beyond. The best policy is to offer your child a healthy range of foods. If you think he's getting chubby, serve smaller dessert portions, and consider offering low-fat options (reduced-fat milk is suitable at age five). But don't obsess about nutrition; your son needs to learn a healthy attitude toward eating.

Your doctor can offer further advice on your child's size and growth, and work out his BMI (see page 52). Don't cut out whole food groups or put your child on a diet without advice from a pediatric dietician. Your doctor can refer your child if this is necessary.

▶ **How can I teach my five-year-old daughter road safety?**
Your child should already have a growing appreciation of the dangers of cars and be naturally wary of them. Encourage her to stay on the sidewalk, and to stop, look, and listen when crossing. Always do the same yourself by using crosswalks, and never jaywalk or cross against the lights.

At this age, you should still hold your child's hand when crossing, at least on busy streets. Road safety develops over a matter of years. Many children are not truly reliable in heavy traffic until they are about 10 years old, so don't expect too much too soon.

Your child's health

At five, your child will probably glow with health and vitality, at least most of the time. She will still catch many infections, of course, especially once she starts school and spends long periods of time with other children. As a parent, you will develop a good instinct for when all is not well with your child.

"Growing pains do appear to exist, but the exact cause, and why some children get them more than others, isn't known."

Growing pains

Between the ages of five and ten, so-called "growing pains" are common. Your child might complain of intermittent leg or arm pains, often during the night. It can help to rub the ache and reassure your child. Although some pediatricians believe physical growth is painless, it is possible that fast-growing bone ends (see page 22) could give rise to pain.

Not all pains are growing pains: being stressed, minor injuries, infections, and even juvenile arthritis can also cause limb pain. A few children develop joint pains because they are double-jointed (a condition known as hypermobility). Very rarely, night pain in only one place can be a symptom of a bone tumor. If your child's symptoms are persistent, see your pediatrician or family doctor and ask for a referral to a specialist.

Feeling thirsty

As your child races around, she is likely to get dehydrated and will need to consume lots of fluid. Thirst is a normal mechanism, but extreme thirst is sometimes a sign of diabetes, a condition that has become more common in children. Symptoms can develop over a few weeks, or even days. As well as drinking a lot, a child with diabetes is often unwell and listless; may have abdominal pain; may have lost weight; and usually passes lots of urine.

If your child looks well, and drinks a lot but does not urinate very often, then she is probably not diabetic. She is just filling up on the fluids she needs. However, if you are concerned, don't hesitate to check with your health-care provider, who can test your child's urine and/or blood to check her glucose (sugar) levels.

Hearing loss

Some five-year-olds have undiagnosed hearing problems, as a result of repeated ear infections, or for no obvious reason. Hearing loss can be hard to detect, because hearing can fluctuate from day to day. But it is vital to spot it, as this is a crucial time for your child's learning. It is also important to diagnose hearing problems so your child can socialize with others, and keep herself safe. Be aware of possible symptoms, such as watching TV with the volume high, appearing inattentive or dreamy, struggling to learn at school, and talking too loudly or mispronouncing words. If you suspect there is a problem, ask your pediatrician to refer your child for a hearing test.

Diagnosing an illness

It can be a challenge to know when to keep your child home from school—sometimes a child who appears unwell in the morning can rally quickly. Symptoms like fever or vomiting are common at this age, and can change from hour to hour. If your child appears to be ill, ask yourself:

Is she feverish? Or was she feverish during last night? If so, she should not be sent to school.

Is she drinking and eating less? A child who has been ill may not have regained her appetite, but she will be at least drinking fluids and picking at some food. If she wasn't well enough to have any breakfast, she is probably not fit for school.

Does she have diarrhea or vomiting? If she vomited in the night, or had diarrhea this morning, she should stay at home, because the virus causing the upset can be contagious. She could also be at risk of dehydration.

Does she have conjunctivitis? Infections of the eyelids and lining of the eyes can be very contagious. Even though your child feels well, some schools will not want her to attend until it is treated. You may not need to keep her off school for the whole five days of treatment, though, as the condition becomes rapidly less contagious once eyedrops are used.

IS HE ILL? *You will know your child well and should be able to gauge when he is genuinely ill. Always follow your instincts and never be afraid to seek medical advice.*

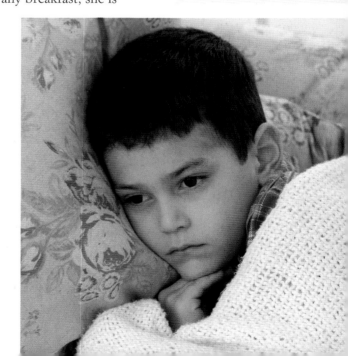

The importance of calcium

Calcium is one of the most important and abundant minerals in the body. Around 99 percent of it is found in bones and teeth. It is vital for building strong bones, and even for preventing osteoporosis in midlife and beyond. When it comes to building strong bones, exercise is also important.

Calcium is also needed for heart health, muscle strength, and even blood clotting. Note that cooking in aluminum pans can reduce calcium absorption. At five, your child needs 800 mg per day of calcium. Give her:

★ Milk and dairy products, including yogurt.
★ Nuts, grains, and chickpeas.
★ Green leafy vegetables, such as broccoli and kale.
★ Dried fruit, such as figs and prunes.
★ Tofu and soy.
★ Meat, poultry, and eggs.
★ Sardines, mackerel, and other fish where the small bones are eaten.
★ Cereals fortified with calcium—the milk they're served with will, of course, also include calcium.

Carbonated drinks
It is worth reducing your child's intake of carbonated drinks, preferably to zero. These contain phosphates, which almost certainly increase calcium loss from bones.

NUTRITIOUS MILK *Give your child milk to drink regularly, in addition to any she has on cereal, for calcium intake.*

Does she have an undiagnosed rash? Rashes are common, and occasionally they are signs of serious conditions. Other rashes, such as chicken pox, can pose a risk to other people. So keep your child home from school if she has a widespread rash and take her to your doctor for a diagnosis. A small red or scaly patch is unlikely to be anything serious, especially if your child seems well.

Impetigo (see page 115) or shingles are both infections that can pose a risk to others, but are less contagious if the area of the rash is small and it is concealed by clothing. In this case, it is not unreasonable to send your child to school that morning and take her to your doctor later in the day for a proper diagnosis.

Is she very clingy? You will have to use your instincts as well as look out for any other symptoms. If your child is clingy and you decide to send her to school, be sure that the teacher can contact you easily if your child's condition deteriorates during the day.

Understanding and skills

Your five-year-old is likely to be unrecognizable from her four-year-old self. Things will suddenly start to "click," and she will probably be able to confidently match her colors, copy letters, and point out words. Although she will be learning at school, there is plenty you can teach her at home.

Your five-year-old will be a fountain of information and be confident about her ability to impart it. Her experiences define her world and teach her more than any book. So allow her space to explore. Take her out and let her stop to discover and learn. Give her plenty of toys and games, such as building blocks, beading kits, and dolls with clothes to dress. All these allow her to produce an imaginary world in which she is in charge.

Drawing and imagination

Ask your child to explain what she has drawn, and show interest in details, to help her to find the words to describe what she has done. Offer plenty of tools that she can use to create her masterpieces, and encourage her to

CREATING PICTURES *Her drawing will be more detailed—for example, her house will have a chimney and a door, and her "people" will have heads and limbs.*

"There's plenty of evidence to suggest that children use drawings and creative endeavors to express themselves."

put her feelings into her artwork. Don't forget that the average five-year-old might have a good vocabulary, and some emotional intelligence, but she will also be aware of other people's feelings and the impact of her worries. For example, if you are stressed, your child will intuitively know that it isn't a good time to talk, and she might hold in her concerns. So not only is drawing a fantastic outlet for the imagination, it can also provide an outlet for her emotions.

Fun and games

There is now greater scope to play games with your five-year-old, not least because she is able to understand and respect rules.

Board games These can encourage lateral thinking, teamwork, tactics, and concentration, which aid cognitive development.

Memory games Your child can probably recite her full name, address, and telephone number, so encourage the learning process by playing memory games (see page 58).

Role play Emulation is a key feature of this age group, so set good examples and purchase some mini-sized cooking pots, tools, or gardening implements. Show her life skills and encourage her to try them out. She will love to copy you and also enjoy role play. Try listening to an audio book with your child. When it is finished, adapt a few hand-me-downs into "costumes" for your five-year-old to help her create the same world.

Your individual child

Depending on schooling, the stimulation she has at home or school, and even genetics and personality, your child may fall short of some developmental milestones. Some children (particularly girls) take huge cognitive leaps at age five, and because their fine motor control (see page 24) is better, appear more advanced than boys of the same age. Boys may lag behind girls, partly because their physical development doesn't match, but also because boys tend not to be naturally interested in the minutiae of school activities.

Your five-year-old girl may be able to recite the names of all the characters in her favorite TV program, but give her a book to read, and she may lose interest. Don't despair! Most of the skills required for reading and writing, and, indeed, socialization, are cemented when a child reaches six or seven, so there is plenty of time. If, however, you are concerned about your child's development, consult your health-care provider.

Physical games Always look for ways to keep your child physically active—for example, by making sure she has equipment such as a ball and racket or a jump rope.

Speech and language

Your five-year-old's speech will be developing rapidly, and you may be surprised by her capabilities, and, undoubtedly, her growing powers of negotiation. She will now have had her first experiences outside the home, in play-date, daycare, or school settings, and you may find that her interests are changing, and that she has a natural curiosity about the world—fed by the different experiences and people she now encounters.

Your five-year-old may:

▶ Have a vocabulary of up to 15,000 words, and speak clearly.

▶ Be able to hold a conversation, describe events and experiences, ask the meaning of words, and even remember and tell a joke.

▶ Use the word "because" more as she begins to develop her powers of reasoning, and her negotiation or arguing skills.

▶ Confidently memorize personal details (see left) and be able to remember and repeat stories that have been read to her.

Your five-year-old will love stories, and understand that they have a beginning, middle, and end. Encouraging this process ignites creativity and will help develop your child's comprehension. For example, stop a story

PHYSICAL FUN *She will begin to initiate her own activities when playing with friends.*

Learning to tell the time

Most five-year-olds have some idea of the passage of time, but won't understand the workings of a clock. **To help your child:**

★ Make a chart with the numbers 1–12 in a column and a picture of a clock next to each entry, showing where the hands will be. Your child will probably understand hours and half-hours; you can move on to explaining quarter-hours and smaller divisions at a later stage.

★ Encourage telling time by showing your child a clock, and indicating when you expect her to take a certain action. With analog clocks, show her where the clock hands will be when you will call her to take her bath, for example. For a digital clock, follow the target time with the three or four readings after that. For instance, if 7:35 is bathtime, explain that 7:36, 7:37, 7:38, and 7:39 mean she is late!

★ Talk her through her day: for example, tell her, "At 7 o'clock, we get up, at 8 o'clock we eat our breakfast, at 9 o'clock we leave for school."

LEARNING FROM BOOKS
The more she reads, the more she'll learn and understand, and the greater her grasp of language and words will be.

before the end and ask "What do you think will happen?" Anything that sparks imagination and instills an understanding of storytelling will encourage healthy cognitive development. Ask your child to tell her own stories. Praise her profusely, ignoring discrepancies. Some children master reading at this age, and take great delight in "teaching" what they have learned. Studies show that the act of explaining reinforces knowledge, much more than any other form of education, so encourage your child to let you know what she is doing, and describe how it works and why.

Her attention span will be increasing, so you can spend a little longer poring over books. The more time you spend talking and explaining, the more her curiosity and her use of words will expand. Dramatic play is a feature of this age group, so give her every opportunity to express herself in this way, giving her words and even short "scripts" from which to work. Make jokes, and play word games—talk about letters and how they sound. Games are the best way to encourage interest and to cement knowledge in five-year-olds.

Regular communication is essential for the development of speech and language, and if your child is not talking and listening, she is not learning. Although it may seem difficult and time-consuming at times, the more you converse with your child at this age, the better. Even if it seems like mindless chatter on both sides, it is helping her learn.

Word recognition

Some experts recommend a combination of phonics (sounding out letters) and flash cards to promote word recognition. The most important thing is not to pressure your child.

To help your child:

▶ Pin up words around the house (the word "refrigerator" on the refrigerator or "door" on the door, for example).

▶ Play with the flash cards and show supreme enthusiasm when your child recognizes a word or even gets it nearly right. Try to make sentences by lining the cards up across your living area.

▶ Point out letters and words when you are reading to your child—and when you are out and about, on signs and at the store, for example.

▶ Ask her to circle familiar words (in pencil!) in a favorite book, and go through them together.

Speaking and describing

Use every opportunity to allow your child to describe both the way she feels and what she perceives. For example, talk about the colors of buses, cars, and trains, the displays you see in a store, the way a piece of sandpaper feels, and the way a flower smells. Encourage your child to find words to describe what she sees, feels, hears, and thinks, and to draw comparisons—for example, this rose smells like honey; that angry moment felt like a volcano; the little boy made the girl feel very happy when he said he would play a game with her.

The more your child learns to identify the world around her, and her experiences, at this young age, the more she will understand how to express her feelings, thereby expanding her use of language—as well as encouraging her emotional intelligence.

Is your child ready to read?

Your child is ready to read when she can master the following:

★ Is interested in sounds, letters, and words.

★ Can hold a book the right way and turn the pages properly.

★ Knows letters and the sounds they represent.

★ Recognizes stories and anticipates what happens next.

★ Can repeat sentences of at least eight consecutive words.

★ Knows some nursery rhymes, songs, or stories by heart.

★ Can recognize her own name— and perhaps other words—in print.

★ Can explain the meaning of words told in a story.

Electronic reading devices
You may be interested in some of the computer or handheld products now available to help with the process of learning to read. In reality, these can do no harm as long as your child is interested, and she doesn't spend hours alone using them. Don't force her to use one. She will learn when she is ready, and be enthusiastic as long as it's fun. The moment you begin to put pressure on her to learn, her interest is likely to wane.

Emotions and personality

You may have noticed a change in your child since she started preschool and find that different aspects of her personality are starting to emerge. This may bring with it a change in behavior as she begins to assert herself. She will be more in touch with her emotions and need your help to handle them.

"Sometimes what starts out as rough-and-tumble play can turn into aggressive behavior, perhaps causing one child to get hurt."

Your five-year-old is on a steep learning curve when it comes to her own and other people's emotions. She is now able to identify many emotions and make the link between an event and the associated feeling. For example, if you tell her a story about someone receiving a treat, she will be able to predict that the person will feel happy or excited. You can assist your child to learn about feelings by labeling her emotions and linking them to the physical sensations that go with them. For example, if you think your child is excited, you might say, "Is your tummy tickly? Maybe you're excited." This way, your five-year-old will learn to recognize her emotions and the physical sensations associated with them.

Aggressive behavior

You can expect your five-year-old to show a certain amount of aggressive behavior. This is normal and can happen because she is still learning the difference between being assertive, by asking clearly for what she wants, and being aggressive, by taking what she wants regardless of the feelings of others. She will also find frustration hard to handle and may react physically by hitting or being destructive.

If your five-year-old is being very aggressive:

▎ Supervise her play more closely. Get more involved in her games so you can guide her to share and control her frustration.

▎ Alongside this watchful eye, give lots of praise when your child plays cooperatively or handles disappointment well, saying, for example, "You're doing so well with that puzzle" or "Thanks for playing so nicely together."

▎ If things do escalate to aggression, step in quickly to defuse the situation. You can do this by calmly separating the children if they are hurting each other. Then, once tempers have cooled, ask each child to tell you what happened and explain to them how they could have reacted differently. For example, help them to use words, rather than hurtful actions, to express themselves. Or, if they can't solve the problem, teach them to find an adult and ask for help.

Handling fears

Although your child will still have a vivid imagination, she is increasingly able to tell the difference between fantasy and reality. Her fears, therefore, have become rather more concrete. Common fears for five-year-olds are of animals, such as dogs and snakes, and natural phenomena, such as thunderstorms and fire. Your five-year-old will also be taking in more about what is happening in the world through news reporting, and may worry about floods, illnesses, and epidemics. While five is a common age to develop fears, for most children these are mild and do not affect their everyday life for very long. It is very rare for a young child to experience levels of anxiety that require treatment. Girls tend to show more fears and anxieties than boys, although why this happens is little understood.

Respond calmly to your child's fears and comfort her. Her fears can sometimes be irritating if, for example, she is reluctant to visit the park because she is scared of dogs. Take a gradual and gentle approach. It may take a while as you encourage your child to approach the thing she fears, but, for example, introducing your child to a dog before she feels confident to do so may make her fear worse. Remember, though, that some fears are legitimate: for example, some dogs really are dangerous, and a useful rule to teach is that she should not go near or touch a dog that she doesn't know (see page 38).

BEING FEARFUL *What scares your child may not seem frightening to you, but respect that it is difficult for him. Don't tell him he's "being silly."*

Pester power

By now your five-year-old may have perfected her ability to pester. Pestering can be a very effective tactic to get what she wants and will

"Whether she is pestering for treats, a later bedtime, or having friends over, you will be surprised how persistent your five-year-old can be."

often be used impulsively when she requires something immediately. While many parents resolve to be firm, they often give in just to make their lives easier. When pestering works, children learn just how long and how loudly they must go on until they get what they want.

The good news is that it's possible to tackle pestering and get it under control. When your child's request is reasonable, you can avoid pestering by agreeing right away; this way, she won't have to nag you and will learn that you consider what she asks for. For example, it is nice to have an occasional small reward like an ice cream cone at the park on a hot day, or be bought a sticker book at the end of a shopping trip when she has behaved well. However, if you feel your five-year-old's request is not reasonable, then use all your willpower and don't give in, no matter how much your child demands. You could try out being a "broken record," repeating your decision in a monotone voice each time she pesters.

At first, sticking to your decision will be met with increased demands as your child tries to figure out if you are really serious. You could give a brief reason for your decision, but don't get into a debate on the point. If you can keep calm and not give in, then your child will learn at this age that pestering isn't the best way to get what she wants.

How she plays

At age five, your child will be motivated to play structured games and revel in the excitement of trying to be first. She will want to win and may become very upset if she is not first or best at the game. This can make games quite stressful as you begin to dread your child's reaction to losing.
To help your child:

▶ It is wise to have your child win most, but not all, of the games. She does need experience of winning graciously without gloating, as well as losing without sulking or having a tantrum.

▶ Talk with your five-year-old about playing as well as she can, but explain that it is important that other people get a chance to feel excited and win.

▶ Your child may take a while to get used to not winning every game, but keep playing. It is not easy at her age to cope with losing.

Children vary greatly in how sociable or solitary they are, but at age five, most spend little time alone, and even when their play is solitary they are usually in the shared part of the home rather than alone in their room. Children of five thrive on company and attention, so playing with others is beneficial. Your child may want some quiet time alone after hectic activity or as she winds down before bed. She will probably enjoy looking at books or sorting through her toys as a quiet way to spend time.

Handling boasting

Your five-year-old will now be able to give you a fairly accurate assessment of her own capabilities, especially telling you what she is good at. At this age, she will be motivated to share her achievements with you because your approval is highly sought after. She will not see this as boasting, but simply as a statement of fact. Encourage her to recognize her achievements, but help her be sensitive to others. For example, if she has received a school award, she should know not to keep repeating the fact in front of a friend who hasn't received one.

COMPETITIVE PLAY *Your child will be driven to win when she plays games. Help her manage emotions whether she wins or loses, and explain that it's only a game!*

Seeking approval

Your child does not just want your attention—she wants your social approval, which includes being praised, liked, and trusted. A common cry at this age is "Watch this!" or "Look at me!" The timing of these requests may be difficult, as your child will want you to notice her immediately. Try to avoid delaying tactics such as saying, "I'm busy, wait a minute." Often, the minute turns into much longer, and the opportunity passes. If possible, stop what you are doing when your child asks you to watch her and give your undivided attention.

Knowing how much your five-year-old loves your approval can also guide you in getting good behavior. She will be much more interested in behaving well if you have been clear that there will be a reward for being good, rather than threatening a punishment for poor behavior. The most effective rewards involve extra time with you, such as offering more stories

PRECIOUS MOMENTS
Try to stop what you are doing to watch her if she asks, and respond if she wants a cuddle. This attention will help her emotional development.

at bedtime. Sometimes your five-year-old may seem to go overboard to get you to notice her. She will prefer to get your positive reaction for good behavior, but second-best is your attention for misbehavior. She would rather be reprimanded than ignored.

If you find you are constantly scolding your five-year-old, it is time to switch tactics and pay lots of attention when she is being helpful, playing nicely, and using a quiet voice. This will give her the positive attention she needs, remind her of how you want her to act, and reduce her motivation to misbehave.

Your energetic child

Your five-year-old will need some physical activity every day. When she doesn't get this opportunity, you will find that she becomes restless and irritable, and that she releases her energy indoors—for example, by climbing on furniture. The solution to getting enough physical activity is to create outdoor opportunities for play every day and to find acceptable indoor ideas. Playing musical chairs, dancing to music, and acting out nursery rhymes are all great ways to get moving inside the house, and your child will love it if you join in, too.

For a small number of children, their energy levels will be challenging no matter how much running around they have done outside. If you feel your five-year-old is consistently overactive, no matter how much you have tried to keep her occupied and tire her out, then visit your doctor or other health professional for advice.

Laughter and jokes

You may find yourself living with a practical joker. Your child may, for example, try to surprise you by pretending there is a monster sneaking up on you, or switch plates at dinner to see if you notice. She will continue to find potty humor amusing and may dissolve into fits of giggles if someone burps or passes wind. Your child will be able to understand simple spoken jokes and will try to learn and repeat them. She will also be motivated to read books with a funny storyline, and this can be a great way to encourage a reluctant reader.

While laughter should be encouraged, explain to your child that there is a time and a place for joking and that she must not be too silly when she is at school.

Your child's life

By now your child will be used to preschool or kindergarten. You will need to ensure that her routine and any child-care arrangements are problem-free, and that she has established good relationships with her teachers and classmates. At home, sibling relationships may become more challenging.

After-school care

Depending on your work routine, your child may need someone to care for her at the end of the school day. The challenge is to choose the setting that best meets the needs of your child and yourself. Even if the care is just for a couple of hours a day, or to cover school vacations, it is still important to make a careful assessment (see page 40).

When choosing an after-school babysitter:

▶ Arrange to meet her and observe how she interacts with your child.

▶ Ask the babysitter for references and get her to describe her experience of caring for other children this age. Make contact with other parents she worked for and ask about the care she provided.

▶ Make sure she knows basic first aid and is confident about what to do in an emergency. Provide her with your contact details.

▶ Make sure your babysitter knows how closely you want your child to be supervised. Also talk over how she should handle any difficult behavior. Make sure her ideas on child management are similar to your own.

▶ If you use a child care agency to find a babysitter for your child, ask what checks they carry out on their employees to make sure they are suitable to work with children.

> "A settled routine is important. It will help your child if she knows who will be caring for her and that you will definitely be home at the same time each day."

Doing "homework"

At five years of age, your child may start to get some basic "homework" or be given a reading book to bring home. At this age, any assignments should be very low-key, brief, and fun, not time-consuming or pressured. You can get involved by listening to your five-year-old read, reading to her, or helping her with simple projects.

Classroom behavior

Your five-year-old's teacher will expect your child to be well-mannered, sit in her seat when she is working, listen to instructions, and do as she is asked. This may seem like an ideal and, while your child won't, of course, behave perfectly all the time, you can help her by encouraging and practicing at home the skills she needs for school.

To help your child:

» When your five-year-old follows simple instructions, such as hanging up her coat, praise her. She will be thrilled and be more likely to cooperate and do these tasks for herself at school.

» Teach her good manners by demonstrating them yourself as much as possible—children learn to be polite from watching adults.

» Sitting and concentrating can be encouraged by giving your child plenty of tabletop activities when she is at home, such as modeling with clay and drawing; this kind of activity will help her get used to sitting still for at least 5–10 minutes.

» Listening skills can be encouraged by reading together. After you finish a story, ask your child if she can remember what happened to the characters

Early bullying

At five years of age, bullying is most likely to be physical, such as pushing and shoving, and taking other people's belongings—for example, your child may have her pencil case taken. It is also more likely to be a single child, rather than a gang, doing the bullying.

Bullying can happen in any setting, at school, in the home by a brother or sister, or at after-school clubs. If you have noticed your five-year-old isn't enjoying school as much as before, if tummy-aches or headaches bother her on school days, or if she seems to have lost confidence, then bullying could be the cause. If you are concerned, make your child's teachers aware so that you can work together to stop the bullying from happening.

SPOTTING THE SIGNS *At this young age, a child who is being bullied may not be able to express what his happening. Look for signs, such as becoming withdrawn.*

Being organized

At age five, your child is ready to take on some small responsibilities, such as choosing her clothes, getting dressed in the morning, and putting dirty laundry in a basket. She will not, however, get this right every day and will do better with a little assistance from you. You can help by making it easier to be organized; for example, make sure storage, drawers, and closets are easy to open and at the right height. Create storage that is simple to understand by sticking pictures on the outside of the boxes showing what should be in each one. Pictorial reminders work well for five-year-olds.

and some of the details of the plot; she will soon get in the habit of listening to the story carefully so that she can explain it to you afterward.

▶ Talking and listening to each other during mealtimes is another way to build up useful skills for school.

Teaching respect

By the age of five, your child will have an understanding about personal possessions, and will know that items such as toys and books always belong to someone. She may be fiercely possessive of her own favorite belongings, yet assume that everyone else should share. You can build on her understanding by teaching your five-year-old to ask before taking someone else's possession. Five-year-olds can get the impression that just asking is enough, without waiting to hear the "Yes" or "No" response. Explain to her that if someone says "No," then she may not take the item. If your child does take something without agreement, make sure she gives it back, otherwise she will learn that asking does not matter.

Your child will be clumsy or careless at times and may damage or break someone else's belongings. Make it your family policy that everyone has to own up when there is a breakage and make amends if possible. Respecting others and using good manners is learned most effectively when your five-year-old watches how you talk about and treat other people. If you speak respectfully about others, and treat them equally, whether they hold opposing views, have a different religious background, or are from a different culture than yours, then your child will grow up with an attitude of respect for everyone she meets.

MODEL PUPIL *At school your child will be expected to focus on tasks, such as listening to a story, so have storytime sessions at home.*

DAILY CONFLICT *To some extent, you need to allow siblings to resolve battles for themselves. Do, however, monitor their disagreements and make sure that neither child is bullying.*

Sibling rivalry

It is no wonder that your five-year-old child gets into conflict with her brothers and sisters; your children are, after all, in competition for the most precious thing in their world: your love and attention. When they are not in school, siblings are in close proximity for a lot of the day, perhaps even sharing a bedroom, and will certainly battle it out over sharing toys and watching TV programs. Be reassured that this sort of conflict is normal.

Most disputes between siblings are part of growing up and will give your five-year-old a way to practice dealing with conflict, which will help her manage disagreements outside of home. Each argument is an opportunity to learn, so before you step in, always give your child a chance to solve the problem herself. You may be pleasantly surprised at how creative her solutions will be.

If you must intervene:

▸ Keep the children together when you address the difficulty.

▸ Speak in a calm voice, as your children will pick up on your mood and adopt this tone. Don't shout, or they may shout back.

▸ Ask each child to describe the problem, and then prompt each to say how it could be solved. Offer ideas only if you need to. If the problem is sharing, for example, then you are hoping your five- year-old will suggest ideas, such as "Can I have the dance mat now, then we can trade games?"

▸ Use the "stop" technique if, for example, you are driving and the children are squabbling. Pull over as soon as it's safe to do so, and say nothing. The simple act of stopping will help them realize what they are doing and calm the situation.

When there are a lot of squabbles, closely supervise your children's play and give them positive attention for cooperating and getting along. Do make sure that each child is lavished with as much love and attention as the other and, as far as possible, be fair and try to avoid favoritism.

Of course, you can make sibling rivalry worse by comparing children to each other. Your five-year-old is still developing her sense of self, and making comparisons such as, "If only you behaved as well as your brother," or "When your sister was your age she didn't always run to me for attention," can be harmful to your child's self-esteem and create resentment between siblings. These comparisons are best avoided by you and by other adults in your child's life, such as grandparents.

Extended family relationships

It takes more than a mom or dad to raise a child, and your five-year-old will be full of curiosity about who is in her extended family and how everyone fits together and relates to each other. Your child will be exploring the world outside of home, developing her identity as part of the wider family and local community. This means she will be curious and receptive to knowledge about her relatives and family history.

Grandparents play a special part in helping children understand how the family fits together. You may get along well with your five-year-old's grandparents or struggle to agree with them, but whatever your relationship, don't let that get in the way of their relationship with your child. The same is true of other family members—even if you aren't that close to them, it doesn't mean they shouldn't be part of your child's life.

"Your child's extended family is very important. Getting to know and learning about relatives helps your child to establish her sense of identity and belonging."

In modern society, people often live miles away from their closest relatives. When possible, bring the generations together through simple family celebrations; a special meal, an outing, or family reunion can be moving and an enjoyable experience for your child. If relatives do live far away, making a phone call, or sending an email, card, or even a video of family life can bring you all closer. If you have plenty of photos of relatives around your home, these can be used to prompt stories and bring to life these absent, but important, family members.

6–8 years

"As friends become more important and influential, your child will become more sociable and outgoing."

HEALTHY LIVING *When it comes to exercise and diet, the key is to guide your child. At this age, forcing him to do something will be met with resistance.*

Getting the basics right

With growing independence, your child may begin to have clear ideas that don't match your own about what to eat, when to go to bed, and what activities she enjoys. It can be challenging to keep her on the right track, but it is important to instill good habits that promote a healthy lifestyle.

As other children become a significant part of your child's life, she is likely to develop different and new habits, likes, and dislikes. If her friends' habits aren't especially "healthy," you may end up with a battle on your hands. For example, she may want to eat junk food or sit and watch TV after school if that is what her friends are allowed to do.

Good nutrition

Your child will continue to grow and develop quickly, and what she eats is paramount to her health and well-being. She may have friends who have their own money to buy soda and snacks, and who are allowed to choose what they take to school for lunch. Do your best not to be pressured by this, and continue to make providing a healthy diet your aim.

There are two crucial nutrients your child needs at this stage of her development: calcium and iron. Calcium lays down the foundation for bones and teeth, and this is key at a stage when both are being developed. Calcium also affects many other bodily functions, and even plays a role in mood and sleep. For calcium intake, give your child foods such as dairy products, plenty of leafy greens, canned salmon, and soy. If she doesn't like them, try hiding leafy greens by pureeing them in soup, adding them to pasta sauces and casseroles, and layering them in lasagna dishes.

Iron is required for energy and the transportation and manufacture of red blood cells, which carry oxygen, but it also affects cell growth—and, through that, your child's growth. It is found in all animal meats, such as beef, pork, and chicken, although red meats are a more powerful source. Iron is also found in dried fruits, beans, soy products, some whole grains, dark, leafy vegetables, and even oatmeal.

To encourage healthy eating:

❱ Continue to offer the same foods that you did for the preschool years (see page 17), and when you meet resistance, or are faced with demands for junk or processed foods, start teaching your child about nutrition. Kids love facts, and if you tell her that by eating healthily, she has more chance of becoming the next great tennis player or Olympic athlete, or the smartest student in her class, she will take heed.

❱ Take your child with you when you go grocery shopping, and talk about what is fresh, what is healthy, and what is not.

❱ Engage her in planning balanced meals that contain three vegetables, one source of protein, and a couple of carbohydrates. Choosing recipes from a book and helping to buy the ingredients, or getting them out of the cupboard, can often inspire some enthusiasm for new foods.

❱ Involve her in food preparation, and ask her to help create salads, chop ingredients, and choose herbs and spices that might work well. Ask her questions such as how a zucchini could be cooked, for example, or beets prepared. Would the lentils be good with cheese and rice, or with salsa? The more your child learns to think about and understand good food, and gets involved in preparing it, the more likely she is to eat it.

❱ If your child is a pick eater, try inviting a child who you know is a more adventurous eater. She may be more influenced by that than by your asking her to taste something.

❱ Stick to your guns about junk food. The odd treat outside the house will never do any harm, but junk food should always be seen as an aberration rather than everyday fare.

❱ Introduce your child to different cuisines, cooking methods, and ingredients. Be enthusiastic both when you taste things and when she does.

❱ If your child doesn't eat what is on her plate, don't make a fuss, as this is likely to make

THE RIGHT CHOICE
If the food you serve from an early age is healthy and balanced, your child will accept this as the norm and relish eating it.

mealtimes stressful. Most importantly, don't offer to cook her something different or you could soon find yourself making three different meals at a time for different family members, making your child an even fussier eater and creating even more work for you.

"Bedtime battles may ensue, but a good bedtime routine is as important to your child's health and development now as it was in the preschool years."

Healthy sleep

Being at school may make your child tired and grumpy—not only because she has had to concentrate all day, and probably be on her best behavior, but also because she is growing and developing, and together these factors create a drain on energy levels. In this age group, children need at least 10 hours of sleep. Naps are a rarity, and tend to disrupt nighttime sleep patterns, but if your child is tired at midday on weekends, let her rest.

What is most important is that your child's body dictates the amount of sleep it needs. Stick to a regular bedtime and a routine, and be firm if she resists. If she insists that her friends are allowed to stay up until 10 pm, point out that by going to bed at 8 pm, she gets a bedtime story and some quiet time with you. Hopefully, she will be asleep before she can argue.

Exercise and leisure

Many children develop an obsession or fascination for technology, and it can be difficult to get them away from their "favorite" shows, or the end of a game. While there is no harm in the odd PlayStation or TV session, if it takes up more than an hour a day at this stage, it can be problematic. TV and video games have been linked with poor sleep habits and lack of concentration, not to mention family disruption.

It is important to establish priorities. Children of this age must get at least an hour of exercise every single day, preferably outdoors, and preferably unstructured. Add to this some structured activity, perhaps two or three times a week, and you have a healthy child on your hands. When any homework has been done, the requisite exercise achieved, and

WATCHING TV *There is no harm in letting him watch his favorite programs, as long as he also gets exercise and stimulation from other activities.*

a healthy dinner consumed, then certainly allow your child to relax by watching TV or playing video games, but limit it to that one hour, and set the timer so you both know where you stand.

Starting school

Your child will need your support whatever age she first goes to school—be it when she is three or six. Young children are great copiers and very aspirational, so show them their older siblings heading off to school, or a neighbor's child. Talk well in advance about how much fun it must be, and how much more interesting it is than being at home or with a babysitter. Reiterate that you or someone your child knows well will pick her up at a certain time. Focus on the good things—a new lunch box or backpack, a "grown-up" outfit or school uniform, or a class she will enjoy, such as crafts. Do your best not to let your concerns show.

Traveling to school

By the time your child is eight years old, you may find that she wants a little more independence, and she may start to ask to walk to school alone, especially if her older friends are allowed to do so. However, she is too young to walk by herself.

★ Some schools have a "walking bus" initiative, in which parents take turns accompanying a group of children walking to school. This means children get some exercise rather than sitting in the car, and have a chance to chat, too.

★ She can, of course, ride the school bus at this age, but you should keep a close eye on her while she waits for the bus.

Your child may be ready to walk to school alone by the time she is around age 11, a time when many children start secondary school. Before any independence is allowed, you must be confident that your child knows the rules of the road, is sensible enough to stick to a designated route, and knows what to do in case a problem arises.

If she is not ready—perhaps she is easily distracted, hasn't taken on board the rules of the road, lacks basic navigational sense, or seems frightened in unfamiliar situations—don't allow her to travel to school alone. Only you will know your child's capabilities.

LETTING HER GO *Independence is good for your child. Trust that she will listen and abide by any rules you set, in return for more freedom.*

Your 6-year-old

"He'll know what's expected of him and how to behave—when he wants to!"

NEW SKILLS You will notice a huge improvement in his hand–eye coordination, making him more accurate and capable in his play.

MAKING CHOICES Your child may begin to have firm opinions about everyday things, such as what she wants to wear and what she wants to eat.

BEING GIVING Your child now enjoys the company of other children and is more willing to share.

Growth and development

During this year, the way in which your child grows and develops will give him more opportunity for independent play, especially sports. He will also be more capable of doing detailed tasks, such as crafts. His permanent teeth will probably be coming through—a sign that he is growing up!

Growth rate

From now until puberty (this begins at varying ages), your child should continue to follow a steady rate of growth in terms of height and weight. What really matters is height, and if at this age your child is falling away from his height curve (see page 22), you should talk to your doctor. This can be due to a hormone problem or, rarely, a sign of chronic illness.

Growth often seems to go in spurts, but overall the rate of growth should be approximately 1½–2½ in (4–6 cm) per year. Weight can be more variable—for example, an illness will often result in temporary weight loss, while a sedentary period where a lot of food is consumed, such as holiday periods, can lead to temporary weight gain.

Large muscle development

Your child will be building on his physical skills and may start to play more complicated team games, such as soccer and baseball. Ball skills will improve, and he may be able to catch small balls. All this comes with practice, and there is a wide range of abilities in six-year-olds.

It is not surprising that athletic parents frequently have athletic children. While there is probably a genetic element to this, children's sporting ability is closely related to the amount of practice and motivation they have. If you realize you are a couch potato and would like your child to grow up with a healthy love of exercise, it is up to you to make the effort and, for example, play soccer with him or take him swimming. Motivate your child by exuding enthusiasm for sports, even if you would rather watch it on TV than play it. Some schools may not start team sports as early as six, so if your child loves soccer, for example, it is worth looking

"Team activities are a good way of making friends, building self-esteem, and learning about cooperation."

for a local kids' team. Team sports are a wonderful way of getting exercise and practicing fine motor skills (see page 24) and coordination. They can also help to boost confidence—children who are struggling to adjust to school may shine on the soccer field and, even if they don't, it is never too early to learn about how to be a good loser!

If you are worried that your child has poor coordination, is clumsy, or is struggling to do activities that seem to come easily to his friends, talk to your health-care provider.

Small muscle development

Your six-year-old is likely to be adept at using scissors (make sure you get left-handed scissors if you have a left-handed child) and small tools. He will draw confidently, using the correct pencil grip, and be able to write both letters and numbers. It is normal for some of these to be written backwards until your child becomes more familiar with them. This improvement in fine motor control means that your child will be able to cut with a butter knife and become more independent in his eating.

COLORING SKILLS
Being more focused and being able to manipulate a pen accurately will allow your child to draw and color neatly.

Learning to ride a bike

Age six is a good time to teach your child to ride a bicycle. Make sure he starts with a bike that is the right size for his height. You can use training wheels, or try the following method.

To teach your child:

★ Start by removing the pedals. Sit him on the saddle and allow him to get his balance.

★ Place the bike on a gentle slope and encourage him to lift his feet up and let the bike roll forward, with the knowledge that he can put a foot down if he loses his balance.

★ Put the pedals back on when he is confident that he can stop without falling over, and encourage him to start pedaling, while you hold the back of the saddle.

★ Before you know it, you will have a confident cyclist, without the need to listen to months of squeaking training wheels.

Safety first

When cycling, your child should wear a helmet and some brightly colored outer clothing. In poor lighting, it needs to be reflective, too. Keep an eye on the condition of the helmet and its fit, as your child's head will grow. Wear a helmet yourself when out cycling, to set a good example.

Teach your child rules for road and park safety. Make him aware that children on bikes are less easy for others to see. Provide a bicycle bell or horn and teach him when to use it. This is especially useful when he is at the wobbling stage.

Permanent teeth

As your child's primary teeth fall out (see page 77), secondary or permanent teeth will appear, but the age at which this process starts and ends can vary enormously. A few six-year-olds will already have some of their permanent teeth, whereas some eight-year-olds won't even have lost any primary teeth. By the age of 14, most children will have 28 permanent teeth (eight more than primary teeth). A further four teeth, the wisdom teeth, usually appear later, in the late teens or early 20s.

The addition of fluoride to toothpaste—and, in many municipalities, to drinking water—has produced a significant improvement in dental health, but there are still alarming numbers of children who have to have several of their primary teeth pulled out under anaesthetic due to poor diet and poor dental care.

It is important to have your child brush his teeth with supervision twice a day. At this young age, children, although often willing, are not able to effectively brush all parts of their teeth on their own, and taking good care of teeth now will greatly reduce the risk of cavities. Food and drinks containing sugar are the main cause of tooth decay.

Your child's health

At this age, your child should be energized and active, but poor lifestyle choices, such as eating too much—or eating the wrong food—can have a very negative impact on health and development. Good nutrition continues to be important, especially now that your child has more outside influences.

Watching your child's weight

Once your child starts full-time education, both you and he will begin to compare him to his peers. Bear in mind that six-year-olds vary a lot in size and shape, and while many are lean, others may seem a little overweight. This is often harmless unless it is excessive, but if it appears to coincide with a marked decrease in physical activity or increase in snacking, try to encourage your child to become more active, and offer healthier foods. Since the early 1980s, the number of overweight children in the developed world has risen. In the US, approximately one child in three is overweight or at risk of being so, and around 15 percent of children are obese.

Clues that your child may be overweight:
▶ Shortness of breath on exertion.
▶ Waddling when he walks.

Development checks

Once your child reaches age six, he is unlikely to have regular development checks unless there is a particular concern.

You are bound to wonder whether he is developing at the correct rate, but try not to get too obsessed about his progress as long as he is healthy and happy.

As a rough guide, you can expect your six-year-old to:
★ Have a lively and inquiring mind.
★ Be able to communicate thoughts and feelings.
★ Be able to concentrate.
★ Be sociable.
★ See and hear as well as you can.
★ Read a bit and write a little.
★ Be physically active.
★ Be well coordinated.
★ Sleep more or less regular hours.
★ Have a good appetite, at least for foods that he likes.
★ Be dry by day and at night (barring occasional "accidents").

If you have any worries, seek advice from your doctor.

A GOOD START *Eating breakfast will benefit your child physically and mentally. It is important to learn this good lifetime habit at an early age.*

▶ Painful knees.

▶ Snacking all the time.

▶ Already the heaviest in the class for no good reason.

The best way of assessing whether your child is overweight is to measure and weigh him accurately and calculate his BMI (body mass index) (see page 52). Ethnicity should be considered in the assessment, too, as different growth curves may apply.

If your child is seriously overweight, you will need advice from a pediatric dietician. If he is only modestly overweight, it may be enough to encourage healthier habits and see the doctor periodically for weighing and measuring. As a parent, it can be easy to ignore weight problems in your child, especially if you or your partner also carry excess weight. Not acting to reduce your child's weight will adversely affect him; on his way to becoming an overweight adult, he could suffer physically, socially, and emotionally, especially if he becomes a victim of bullying.

The importance of breakfast

As well as fuel for growth, a good breakfast provides carbohydrates for sustained energy and alertness, both of which are vital to learning. Teachers often say that they can tell which children have skipped breakfast because they are less alert in class, less able to concentrate, and don't participate as much. Breakfast also plays a part in maintaining a healthy body weight, because it stabilizes metabolism and helps prevent snacking.

Remember:

▶ A small breakfast is better than none.

▶ If you go without breakfast yourself, then your child will see little point in eating it.

Try tempting your child with the following:

▶ Scrambled eggs or pancakes, when you have time.

▶ Oatmeal with a little sugar or cinnamon sprinkled on top.

▶ A different cereal from usual; there are many aimed at children, fortified with added vitamins.

▶ A different toast topping from usual, such as homemade jam or preserves, cheese, ham, or other cold meats.

▶ Fresh fruit in a fruit salad or smoothie. Let your child help prepare it.

Your child's skin

Here are some common skin conditions that can occur in young children.

Dry skin and chapped lips

This is common in winter, so your child may need a thin layer of lotion on his face and an inconspicuous lip balm during the colder months.

Sunburn

Sunlight contains ultraviolet radiation that can damage the skin permanently. Even on winter days, your child's skin needs protection if he is outside a lot, although the areas needing sunscreen are smaller in cold weather. UVA ages the skin, while UVB burns. Your child needs protection from both, so look for the ratings on sunscreen products.

Eczema

This common skin condition often runs in families. Scratching makes things worse and the skin may become cracked. This can lead to infection by bacteria, which can cause inflammation and weeping.

Unfortunately, a tendency to develop eczema is in the genes. The good news is that eczema improves with age.

To help prevent a flare-up:

★ Dress your child in cotton, rather than wool or synthetic fabrics.
★ Use nonbiological laundry detergents.
★ Use soap substitutes.
★ Use special eczema products in your child's bath and encourage him to pat himself dry, rather than rubbing with a towel.
★ Don't be afraid to use steroid creams on red itchy patches for a few days to clear them up quickly.
★ See your doctor if your child's skin is red, crusty (may be yellow), and weepy, as it may be infected.

To treat the rash once it appears:

★ Apply emollients (moisturizers) to your child's dry skin at least twice a day.

Cold sores

A cold sore is an infection of the lip (or sometimes the nostril) that is due to herpes simplex virus. It is

SKIN PROTECTION *Your child's skin is delicate and easily harmed by UV rays. Always be rigorous in your use of sunscreens, especially when you are in a hot climate. Also protect your child's head with a hat.*

very contagious and tends to recur. Cold sores can be triggered by cold weather, injury, picking the lips, infection, or even strong sunlight.

The initial symptom is usually tingling, followed some hours later by a large blister or cluster of blisters. If you act early, then you may be able to stop the attack with acyclovir cream, which has an antiviral action, or even just with an ice cube applied to the tingling area. Try to stop your child from picking or even touching his cold sore. Ensure that he uses his own towels and cutlery. Keep him home from school until the sore has completely crusted over.

Get medical advice if:

★ There is a large crop of sores, or sores in more than one place.
★ There is a sore very near the eye.
★ Your child is unwell—for instance, if he is refusing to eat or drink (there may be sores inside his mouth and throat).

Impetigo

This bacterial skin infection, which causes a red, yellow, and crusty rash, is common in school-age children and can be spread by dirty hands and nails. Hygiene is important, as it helps limit these common infections, as well as gut infections and threadworms. Try to prevent your child from picking the rash—although this isn't always easy—and apply creams as instructed by your doctor.

Understanding and skills

Your six-year-old is likely to have a good attention span, especially for the things he likes. You may notice him becoming more pensive because, while he is still highly imaginative and creative, he is becoming more cerebral and may need quiet thinking time occasionally.

Numbers and math

USING LOGIC *His understanding of how things work enables him to play with more complex toys. He will enjoy tackling these with friends.*

Although he will still make mistakes, your six-year-old will have a better understanding of numbers and may be able to count to 100. You can help by encouraging him to think of tens and units. For instance, show him that two stacks of 10 blocks plus seven more equals 27. Use coins to help him distinguish between shapes and sizes, and learn about value. He will be amazed to discover that smaller coins aren't necessarily worth less than larger ones.

Your child may even be ready for simple sums, though often six-year-olds find it hard to grasp basic mathematical concepts such as addition

and subtraction. You can help by putting together and taking away from groups of small objects such as buttons and building blocks. Don't criticize when he gets a sum wrong; just show him how to do it again.

Telling time relies heavily on math, especially if you use an analog timepiece. Your child might like to have a simple clock in his bedroom, so he can relate the time of day to his various activities.

Being creative

Your six-year-old will enjoy creative activities, such as drawing, coloring, and painting. His pictures will be more figurative now, but don't worry if his efforts are less detailed than those of other children. You could try letting him have different media to work with—for instance, chalk or clay—to encourage experimentation and creativity. Clay or modeling dough is especially good for creativity because your child will use both hands to mold it. This is thought to be good for brain development because it keeps both sides of the brain working equally. It also teaches some of the basic rules of physics such as conservation of mass; whatever shape you make, you still have the same amount of dough you started with.

Individual interests and skills

At age six, children vary a great deal in their interests and what they are good at. For instance, some children devour books, while others are fascinated by different cars (perhaps even being able to tell them apart by the sound of their engines). Gauge and encourage your child's interests, and try not to compare him with other children too much.

Logic and problem-solving

Your six-year-old will learn a lot from you as well as from school. You can encourage his logical reasoning by talking through some things he may so far have taken for granted.

Try having conversations about the following:

◗ How clothes are made (from pieces of cloth and balls of wool).

◗ How plumbing works (the toilet is flushed when the tank empties into the bowl).

◗ How money is earned and spent.

TELLING TIME
Once she has a better grasp of numbers, she is better equipped to understand the concept of time and how to tell it.

Teaching cause and effect

Your six-year-old will have a good grasp of cause and effect. For example, he will understand that when you step on the dog's paw, it hurts the dog. There are so many examples in daily life that you won't have to look far for them.

Just use everyday experiences as opportunities to enrich your child's knowledge. For example, increase scientific understanding by explaining why it feels cooler after sunset and why the sidewalk is slippery when it is raining.

By learning about cause and effect, your child will understand how his behavior affects others. With this knowledge, he will, hopefully, think twice before behaving badly. He will also understand that discipline follows bad behavior.

BEING CLUMSY *There will be everyday upsets such as spilled milk and broken toys, but he will now know the difference between doing something accidentally and on purpose.*

❯ What to do if the weather is cold or the heating doesn't work.
❯ How people on the top floor of a building get out if there is a fire.
❯ How to get all the groceries into the car or onto the bus.
❯ How a pile of pebbles or shells fit into a jar. (The most efficient way is to put the large pebbles in first so that the smaller ones fill the gaps!)

Some of the problems can be more creative in nature—for example, ask him how he would make a garage out of a large box. Your everyday world will provide many more problems to ponder. In this way your child will discover and hone skills that will help him solve a far greater range of problems in life.

Intention and opinion

By the time your child is six, he will probably have dropped plenty of things, but he is old enough to know that he shouldn't do it on purpose. He will also be aware of different views and opinions, something he will encounter more and more of at school. For example, he might know that his friend Charlie likes chocolate ice cream, while Leila prefers strawberry. Encourage him to think of other people's views by asking what he thinks others might be thinking or feeling.

Speech and language

In your child's seventh year, his speaking and listening vocabulary will double, and he may show a major interest in reading. A longer attention span (usually about 15 minutes) and natural curiosity mean he will be asking questions and querying the meaning of words. This coincides with an increased problem-solving ability (see page 117), and many six-year-olds love to try to work things out for themselves and so become more interested in books, magazines, factual programs, and the world around them. Encourage this interest whenever you can.

Speech is normally very clear by age six, and you should be able to understand everything your child says. Grammar may be confused, but he will mimic what you say, so it is important to speak correctly. Although language skills are developing rapidly, his written language may still be rudimentary. Children are often encouraged to read at an early age. However, cognitive changes that need to occur in order for a child to learn to read normally manifest themselves somewhere between six and six-and-a-half, and this is when children are capable of reading.

Remember:

▌ It is common for six-year-olds to reverse their words and/or letters—their visual development isn't always sufficiently advanced. This is not necessarily an indication of dyslexia (see page 121).

▌ Pushing a reluctant reader to read when he isn't ready (see page 89) will do nothing but alienate him.

"Reading should always be pleasurable, so keep it light-hearted. He'll soon want to do it on his own."

Learning to spell

Many children find spelling difficult, and the frustration it causes can undermine your child's enjoyment of reading and writing. For this reason, it is important to make spelling fun and easy.

Spelling mistakes are common at this age, as six-year-olds often learn to read phonetically and apply the same principles—for example, spelling "rough" as "ruf" and "chicken" as "chikin." While it is a mistake to constantly correct your child's spelling, as it can dampen enthusiasm, it is important to show him where he is going wrong. Practicing incorrect spellings can cement them in a child's mind, and it can be hard to relearn the spellings later.

To make spelling easier and fun:

★ Use refrigerator magnet letters to encourage your child to put together words and sentences. Remove letters and ask him to replace them to complete the word.

★ Play word-finding games with his books. Give him a list of words to find. Then try the same verbally—he will have to work out the spelling from what you say.

★ Play word games using rhyming words and then ask your child to change them by adding a different letter—for example, changing "cat" to "mat." Find as many combinations of words as you can from the same beginning and ending letters.

WRITING SKILLS *Make learning to write fun by encouraging activities that involve learning about words and the shapes of letters.*

Encouraging reading and writing

Developing your child's enthusiasm for reading and writing will provide him with the skills he needs throughout school, and also give him hours of enjoyment as he loses himself in books and learns to express himself in writing. The best way to encourage a love of reading and writing is to read to your child daily, and plan activities that promote literacy skills while having fun at the same time.

To help your child:

▶ Ask your six-year-old to help with your shopping list—encourage him to add his own ideas, and when it is complete, read through the list together.

▶ Label the people and objects in your six-year-old's pictures—for example, "house," "girl," "dog," and "tree."

▶ Create a scrapbook of pictures and label them with cut-out words—encourage him to copy the words himself below the labels. When a child is familiar with letter shapes and sounds, words become "friendly."

▶ Ask your child to dictate a story to you and then write it all down for him. Point out the key words.

▶ Keep pens, paper, and pencils handy in easily accessible storage, so that he can use them when he wants.

▶ Help your child to make a picture/word journal.

▶ Look for books you both love. Spend time together in the library or bookstore, read books that form a series, and suggest books as presents when it is your child's birthday.

▶ Remember that your six-year-old's reading and listening levels are different. When you read easy books, beginner readers will soon read along with you. When you read more advanced books, you instill a love of listening to stories and motivate your child to read for himself.

▶ Encourage letter-writing, which shows that writing has a purpose. Ask your child to write a short letter to a friend or family member and mail it. Ask for a reply, and your child will soon be involved in the fun of correspondence! Even more useful, encourage him to write short thank-you notes for his birthday presents.

Dyslexia

"Dyslexia" comes from a Greek word meaning "difficulty with words." This condition affects reading, spelling, writing, memory, and concentration, and sometimes math, music, foreign languages, and self-organization. Some people call dyslexia "a specific learning difficulty." It tends to run in families, and can continue throughout life. If your child is dyslexic, you are far from alone. At least 10 percent of the population is dyslexic, 4 percent severely.

People who are dyslexic may have many creative and practical skills, and can be extremely bright, which makes the condition all the more frustrating. There are many ways to diagnose dyslexia at different ages.

In young children, look for:

★ Family history of dyslexia.
★ Speaking clearly later than expected.
★ Jumbled phrases—for example, saying "teddy dare" for "teddy bear."
★ Use of substitute words or "near misses" such as saying "hairbrush" instead of "haircut."
★ An inability to remember the label for known objects, or mislabeling—for example, calling a lampshade a lamppost.
★ A lisp—for example, saying "duckth" for "ducks."
★ Confused directional words—for example, "up/down" or "in/out."
★ Excessive tripping, bumping, and falling over for no apparent reason.
★ An aptitude for constructional or technical toys, such as bricks and puzzles.
★ A lack of interest in letters or words, despite an enjoyment of being read stories.
★ Difficulty learning nursery rhymes.
★ Difficulty with rhyming words, such as "cat, mat, fat."
★ Difficulty with odd-one-out—for example, "cat, mat, pig, fat."
★ A history of bottom-shuffling rather than crawling as a baby. Around 70 percent of dyslexics never go through the crawling stage, which some believe is required to develop the correct reflexes.
★ Difficulty with sequences—for example, a colored bead sequence.
★ Appears particularly "bright."

If you are concerned that your

GOOD AT DRAWING *Although dyslexic children struggle with reading and pronouncing words, they are often highly artistic. This is because the right side of their brain tends to be larger than in non-dyslexics.*

six-year-old may be dyslexic, talk to your child's teacher or doctor, who can arrange an assessment.

To help a dyslexic child:

★ If your child finds it difficult to remember left and right, put a blue band on his right hand and a red one on the left.
★ Teach nursery rhymes and encourage your child to repeat them; they will help him understand rhythm, rhyme, and repetition.
★ Teach your child songs that have sequences, repetition, or fill in the gaps, such as "Row, Row, Row Your Boat." Change the words to the song to see if your child notices.
★ Read as often as you can. When children become familiar with the patterns of words, sentences, and stories, they are more adept at using them themselves.
★ Learning to follow instructions and to listen is important, particularly since many dyslexic children have trouble with their attention span. Games like "I Spy" encourage children to listen carefully.
★ Computers can be helpful in developing reading, spelling, and number skills. Choose games that are fun, and avoid those that have a strong competitive element or short time limits. Encourage your child to hit numbers and letters on the keyboard and see them appear on the screen.
★ Ask him to memorize a shopping list, or a series of landmarks.

Emotions and personality

Your six-year-old will be starting to assert himself, forming likes and dislikes and expressing them clearly. He will no longer go along with all your plans and may resist them quite firmly. For the first time, you may find yourself arguing with your child as he tells you exactly what he thinks.

Words can hurt, and your six-year-old may use harsh statements when he is angry. "I hate you" is cutting but might come from an irate six-year-old who has been told "No" or asked to do something he doesn't want to do. It is vital that you take such announcements as an expression of anger, not as a statement of truth. Your child understands that these words hurt, but he is not aware of the power of the word "hate"; he is just letting you know how much he dislikes your request, not you personally.

The most calming reply is to say, "I'm sorry to hear that, but I still love you." It is wise to hold back on negative replies such as, "Well I don't love you, either." This sort of response is not only immature coming from an adult, but may also be taken seriously by your six-year-old, who will worry that he has permanently lost your love. At age six, your child is still not fully socially aware, so when at someone's house, he might say, "I want to go home, it's boring here." You may be embarrassed, but he won't be; he has not learned to keep thoughts to himself.

BEING OBSTINATE *He will make it known when he disagrees, but he should usually give in first.*

Your fickle child

At six your child will be unpredictable. Food can be a battleground as his preferences alter from day to day. One day he may enjoy sausages, but then reject them when they are served again. If he has a sweet tooth, you could be pestered for candy. You will notice the start of negotiations, too, as he bargains for treats, perhaps promising to be well-behaved at home to get his treat in advance. There is nothing wrong with giving your six-year-old rewards—stickers and praise work well—but only after he has shown you the behavior you want. If you reward him in advance, he is less likely to keep his promise.

Avoiding favoritism

Your six-year-old will have developed a strong sense of fairness and will want to be treated the same as his siblings. Spreading your love and attention between all your children and avoiding favoritism is not easy, but strive to do it to avoid resentment building between siblings. If your six-year-old feels constantly picked on and compared to a sibling, it may lead to spitefulness and misbehavior just to get attention. Favoritism can create problems between parents, too; when one parent sticks up for a child against the other, conflict can arise.

Not all comparisons are harmful; some can be realistic and useful. For example, when you have been to a parents' night, it is reasonable to talk as a family about the strengths of each sibling and the challenges they face. For example, "Sam is doing well in history and he needs to work on science; Liam, you're getting good grades in math and we're going to help with your reading now." This way achievements can be recognized for all siblings. Unhelpful comparisons, however, can put down one child. For example, saying "Why can't you be neat like your sister?" plays one child off the

> "He will want to be treated fairly and will be sensitive to how you treat him in relation to his siblings."

Listening to your child

You are your six-year-old's most important confidante—he relies on you to hear and meet his needs. Being a good listener is a skill you can learn even if it is not a natural talent. Try opening your ears, but not necessarily your mouth. If your six-year-old wants to talk, try to stop what you are doing, make eye contact, and sit down so you are on the same level. Make sure you keep your attention on him; don't let your mind wander.

How he communicates
Your child will communicate with words, tone of voice, and body language, so tune in to this. For example, if he says he feels happy yet looks sad, give him time to say more. Encourage him to speak, conveying that you are listening by leaning toward him, and saying "yes" or "mmm-hmm" at intervals. Try not to interrupt him.

Mostly your child simply wants you to listen so you can share his world and be proud of him; this helps to build a strong relationship between you.

other, builds resentment, and rarely motivates a child to improve. Another way to avoid favoritism is to apply the same house rules to everyone. When your child is treated fairly, he is more likely to cooperate; if he feels you are stricter with him, he may be tempted to rebel. It is impossible to be fair all the time, but trying is a good first step.

Disciplining your six-year-old

By age six, your child will know how you expect him to behave. He will have a clear sense of family rules—for example, to be kind and gentle with others, to be polite, and to share and take care of toys and property. However, he may be quite impulsive and unable to contain his emotions, so he won't be able to stick to these rules all the time. When you react consistently and calmly to misbehavior, you will get the best results. Shouting angrily can escalate a problem rather than solve it.

Remember:

▶ For many parents, the most effective way to teach good behavior is by paying positive attention to it.

▶ Manage misbehavior right away by giving a small consequence. For example, if your six-year-old has scribbled on the walls, get him to help you clean it up, or take away his crayons for five minutes.

▶ Avoid long-term consequences, such as grounding or not allowing computer games for hours at a time. These consequences become meaningless to your six-year-old, who has quickly forgotten why he received the punishment in the first place.

Most six-year-olds do not like to be scolded and are sensitive to being singled out for bad behavior. This sensitivity is helpful, as it motivates children to do as they are asked. It can backfire, though, if your child is frequently reprimanded and never praised. Misbehavior can become a pattern, with punishments an accepted part of everyday life. If you feel your six-year-old is starting a pattern of disobedience, especially in school, do something about it right away. Meet his teacher and work out how your child can be given a chance to show his cooperative side, perhaps through taking on small errands in school. This way he will understand that the adults in his life have faith in him, expect him to behave well, and are prepared to help him show his worth and praise him for it.

"Consequences that last a long time can build resentment and don't give your child a chance to show you he can behave."

Emotional health

Resilience is your six-year-old's ability to feel good about himself and bounce back from setbacks. A child who is resilient has good self-esteem, feels he can influence his life, and can solve problems. Resilient children tend to cope better and recover more quickly from difficulties. Helping your child solve everyday problems will help build resilience. When he faces a challenge, support him in working things out for himself before you step in. For example, if he is struggling with homework, ask questions such as, "Where do you think you could look for the answer to that question?" rather than jumping in and finding the information for him.

Having a positive but realistic attitude is important. Your six-year-old will face times when things don't go his way. For example, maybe he wasn't made team captain as he had hoped. It helps if he has the attitude that it is still worth trying, perhaps by adjusting his aims. For example, if he can't be captain, perhaps he will make a great goalie. This way he can accept disappointments, but balance them with achievements.

A sense of accomplishment

Whether it is a project for school or crafts at home, your six-year-old will love to have something to show for his efforts. Foster this desire by supplying materials, space, and assistance.

The importance of praise
At age six, your child is aware of his achievements and will gain a sense of pride when his work is displayed. You will see him glow with satisfaction when you admire his work at parents' nights or point it out to visitors at home. Remember to focus on the positive when you comment on his project; it is the effort that went into the work that counts more than perfect detail. For example, say "That's beautiful—you've made the colors so bright," rather than "Too bad you didn't color it neatly."

Don't, however, overpraise your child, as this will devalue what you are saying.

ENCOURAGING CREATIVITY *Painting and coloring give your child the freedom to be creative. Comment positively on her ideas for pictures and use of colors, and display her artwork with pride.*

Your child's emotional health can be deeply affected by your reactions and those of other important adults, such as teachers. He will take as the truth any comments you make about his abilities, even if spoken flippantly. For example, a child of six who is told he is not good at something will assume this is true and cannot be changed. So it is essential to avoid specific statements such as "You're just not cut out for sports" because your child might give up on developing his sporting ability completely.

Playtime and friendships

SAME-SEX FRIENDSHIPS
At this age, children tend to play with friends of the same gender. Girls tend to have one or two close friends.

Your six-year-old loves games with rules, as he likes to know where he stands and wants everyone to play fairly. This is an extension of his need for security and predictability. Boys tend to spend most playtimes in a large group, enjoying physical activities, and their games are likely to be competitive. Your six-year-old daughter, however, will be less competitive in her play and will probably concentrate on one or two close friends. At around age six, teasing between boys about being a sissy will have started; to avoid name-calling, your son will be motivated not to seem girlish.

Common behavioral concerns

▶ **My six-year-old son bosses everyone around, including me. How should I handle this?**
Your son probably just lacks a few social skills. Explain to him that it is not always pleasant to be harangued. Explore with him how he might feel if, for instance, someone spoke to him the way he often speaks to others. As ever, make sure you lead by example, and always say "please" and "thank you" and use a pleasant tone. Of course, there will be times when you need to tell your child what to do, but try a little subtlety sometimes.

Your child might be bossy to gain power, so give him choices, such as "Would you like me to read your bedtime story now or in five minutes?" Praise him for appropriate behavior, and tell him when he has been helpful, for example.

▶ **My six-year-old daughter is very clingy. What can I do to help her feel more secure?**
Many children of six appear insecure, while others seem brimming with self-confidence. If your child is clingy, it's because she needs the security that you provide. So be there for her, and try not to brush her off or make fun of her neediness. Inevitably there will be times when you must be apart. On these occasions, make sure you always say goodbye before parting, and always return when you said

you would. It's often better if your child can move away from you rather than the other way around. At school, wait until she runs inside, instead of dropping her off and dashing to work.

No doubt you will already be aware if anything is likely to be upsetting your daughter, such as a new baby, a death in the family, or a house move. It is also worth exploring if there is anything amiss at school; ask her if she is worried or sad about something.

▶ **My son wants certain toys that his friends have. How can I help him resist this peer pressure?**
This is a tough lesson to teach a young child, but it's an important one. When your child asks, for example, for the same allowance money, haircut, or jeans that his classmates have, explain to him that families don't all do or have the same things. When feasible, offer your child choices. Perhaps he could have the bedroom furniture he wants, but not the new bicycle as well.

Point out that he has some things that not all his friends have. Perhaps it's a grandma who speaks Polish, or your family's new puppy— you may need to think laterally! Don't succumb to peer pressure, and do be aware that some of the things your child says about his friends (for instance, their bedtimes) may not be accurate.

▶ **How can I handle my son's frequent mood swings?**
Make sure he's getting enough sleep, and that when he erupts, he's not hungry or thirsty. Peak times for mood changes are when blood-sugar levels fall—for instance, right after school—in which case a drink and a snack will help.

Praise him when he is in a good frame of mind, and he may make an effort to stay that way. When he feels low, or explodes with a fit of temper, don't overreact. Try to calmly assess why he's behaving like this, without asking repeatedly what's wrong. Keep communicating: this will become more vital when your child reaches the emotional peaks and troughs of adolescence.

MOOD SWINGS *Your child's mood may change in an instant, but there is usually an underlying reason for it. The better you communicate with him, the easier it will be to help him and make him happier.*

Your child's life

As your child develops more of a life of his own, with friendships and activities, things will get busy. A routine is crucial to ensure that everyone gets what they need from family life. At this age, your child really can begin to play his part in helping the household run smoothly.

Building friendships

Your six-year-old's friendships are likely to be well developed by now, both in school and in your neighborhood. There will be the occasional disagreement, but this is normal. At this age, bonds can weaken or strengthen depending on shared pastimes and the amount of time children spend together. To expand your six-year-old's pool of friends, enroll him in after-school activities where he will meet children with similar interests, and invite children over to your house to play.

If your child struggles to make friends, enlist the help of his teacher, who can encourage bonds to develop at school—for example, through pairing your child up with another on a class project or field trip.

Developing concentration

There is great variation between six-year-olds in how well they can concentrate; temperament and motivation affect each child. Most six-year-olds have trouble paying attention in some situations, as they are still very active and impulsive. Your six-year-old will concentrate best when he is interested in a subject and if it is neither too hard nor too easy.

Don't judge your child's attention span on his ability to watch TV. Focusing for 30 minutes or more on a favorite TV program does not tell you how well he can concentrate in school. For a few six-year-olds, the ability to pay attention can be affected by ill health and by being upset. If your child has concentrated well in the past and then starts having difficulties, check whether he is unwell or emotionally stressed. Children who have attention deficit hyperactivity disorder (ADHD) (see page 60) may have a short span of attention and be unable to sit still for long.

ATTENTION SPAN
Playing games can encourage your child to concentrate and complete an activity— an important skill for school success.

To encourage your child to concentrate:

▶ Play simple games such as spotting the difference between two slightly different pictures—this will help your child notice detail. Prompt him by asking him to look carefully at an object in one picture, then checking for differences in the same object in the other picture.

▶ Do jigsaw puzzles together as this activity requires attention to detail and persistence to finish the task, and gives a sense of achievement. Promoting concentration works best when you choose puzzles showing something your child likes, such as characters from his favorite movie or TV show. Make sure the puzzle is not too hard or he may give up.

Cooperation and teamwork

Working together to get household jobs and other responsibilities done teaches your six-year-old important life skills. One way to do this is to agree to consider everyone. All members of the family have things they want to do or achieve in a week. Your six-year-old might want to see a movie, invite a friend over to play, or go swimming. You, and the rest of the family, will also have ideas about how you want to spend your time. Agreeing in advance on what is happening when, and perhaps listing all activities on a whiteboard, can make life simpler. If everyone manages to

"One of the most important elements of successful family life is developing a 'team' mentality."

First nights away from home

Your six-year-old may start spending the occasional night with relatives. Plan ahead to help him feel as comfortable as possible on these overnight trips.

To make trips successful:

★ Prepare your child by explaining how long he will be away and when you will pick him up.

★ Help him pack and make sure he has included some games, a book, and a comfort toy to help him sleep. He may want to take his own pillow along.

★ He may want to speak with you before bed each night or at breakfast, so arrange a brief phone call if needed.

★ If your child seems particularly anxious, let an adult in your relatives' home know exactly how he feels, and share ideas with that person on the best ways to handle any distress.

Staying the night

At age six, your child is probably not old enough to sleep away from home under supervision by adults he doesn't know well, but will probably jump at the opportunity to go and stay overnight with a grandparent, for example.

Staying overnight with friends, or having one or two friends stay over, may be something your child wants to do when he is older.

LITTLE HELPER *Your child will enjoy small jobs at this age. Give him real, meaningful tasks, and praise him for being so good and helpful.*

get the leisure time they want, it is then time to divide up some household responsibilities. A six-year-old can have regular jobs to help out and feel involved (see below). If this is all done in the spirit of fun, your child will feel included and valued in the family. Make it clear to your six-year-old that you value him as a team member, and praise him for being cooperative.

If family teamwork becomes the norm, your child will develop an understanding of what it takes to run a busy home. Make it clear that you will respect his relaxation time, just as he should respect yours. So if you are, for example, talking on the phone, expect him to give you space. It is all about mutual respect, which can be taught by you respecting your six-year-old as well.

Allowances and jobs

You may want to start giving your child some small tasks around the home, but if you don't feel he is ready yet, wait until he is older. He may need your help to do some of them. If you do want to encourage him to play a role, you could offer a little incentive in the form of an allowance. Most six-year-olds enjoy purchasing small toys or candies, or saving for things, and having money of their own teaches them the value of things. Some families offer a weekly allowance, with the expectation that everyone will do certain chores regularly, but don't be too strict about this with your six-year-old. View allowance money as a reward for a job well done, and positive reinforcement of your child's role in the household.

Let your child choose from the following:

❱ Sorting laundry, and redistributing it after washing.

❱ Helping to prepare food by, for example, cutting up vegetables and grating cheese. Always supervise your child when he is using a knife.

❱ Helping to set the table.

 ▶ Making his own bed.
 ▶ Keeping toys and belongings neat.
 ▶ Feeding the family pet.
 ▶ Raking garden leaves and helping with weeding and planting.

Moral development

By the age of six, your child will understand the rules of home, school, and the broader community. He will also know the basics of right and wrong— for example, that it is not okay to hurt another person or to break things deliberately. He will see these rules as being set by the authorities, such as the police, and will tell you that the rules cannot be changed. In later years he will begin to understand that rules are made by people and can be debated and altered.

At age six, he is more likely to do the right thing to avoid punishment, rather than because he is motivated by kindness or generosity. So, for example, if he finds some money, he will hand it to an adult if he thinks he might be punished for keeping it. He will also be motivated by your approval, and the admiration of his friends. He can tell the difference between rules that are there for routine purposes, such as "always hang your coat up," and those that are about moral values, such as not stealing. If your family behaves with generosity, charity, and tolerance toward others and shows a respect for the law, then your child will develop his values along these lines, too.

"When you praise him for honesty and care of others, he will develop positive values."

Body image

Your six-year-old will be naturally curious about his body and the differences between males and females. He is likely to ask questions quite openly, such as "Why don't you have a willy, Mommy?" Incorporate discussions about your child's changing body, and the way we all differ, into regular conversations, and use books, magazine articles, and advertisements to broach the subject. Try not to show embarrassment about the body; and don't be afraid to use the proper terms, such as "penis" and "vagina." Key to the discussion must be the idea that bodies are beautiful, and come in all shapes and sizes.

Body image is developed at an early age, and your six-year-old will quickly pick up negative remarks, even if made in jest.

Your 7-year-old

14
13
12
11
10
9
8
7
6
5
4
3

YEARS

"He may begin to have very specific interests and hobbies, and will know his own mind."

A LOVE OF BOOKS Your child may be able to read alone by now, but she will still enjoy storytime with you, too.

STAYING IN SHAPE Finding an outlet for your child's boundless energy is essential to his health and physical development.

FRIENDSHIPS "Best friends" are common at this age, but be prepared for occasional differences of opinion!

Growth and development

Your seven-year-old child is likely to be highly energetic and will need a healthy lifestyle—a balanced diet, plenty of exercise, and a good routine—to support this. All children develop at different rates, and girls faster than boys, so try not to compare your child's growth to that of her classmates.

Physical development

Most seven-year-olds are extremely physical and love a range of challenges that test their strength and agility. Climbing is a natural urge but will, of course, sometimes result in injuries. Unfortunately, fractured bones are all part of childhood (see page 188).

Improved strength and hand–eye coordination mean that your child may be able to bat a ball and that handwriting may at last become legible, especially for girls. Backward letters will hopefully be righting themselves by this stage. If you are aware that other children are racing ahead with reading and writing, while your own child is struggling to make sense of letters and numbers, discuss this with her teacher. It important to distinguish between learning difficulties and dyslexia (see page 121).

Precocious puberty

Although your child is still "little," it is worth your while to be informed about puberty, as it can happen early. Puberty means the physical changes that happen to allow the body to reproduce. When this process starts and stops, and how long it takes, varies widely between children. It is not a single event, and the changes that take place in a child's body also include rapid growth and an increase in strength and endurance. Partly because children are larger than they used to be, puberty is arriving earlier than it once did, and occasionally children reach puberty at an extremely young age. Normal puberty starts as early as the ninth year in girls. If it occurs before the eighth birthday, it is called precocious puberty and may need to be investigated by a doctor. In boys, puberty occurring earlier than age 10 would be considered precocious.

GROWING UP *She is growing up fast and may become body-conscious. Be positive about her looks, whatever her size.*

"Some 'tall' children may turn out to be smaller than their shorter friends, whose bodies have not yet shown any sign of puberty."

A boy's testicles and penis may enlarge, and he may grow pubic hair. His voice could deepen, and he may develop acne (see page 274). Girls with precocious puberty usually develop breasts and pubic hair. They may start menstruating, too, but this is usually a late change. If you suspect that your child is going through puberty too early, it is best to get medical advice as soon as possible. If puberty starts a year or so before expected, it is not usually a cause of major concern, except for the fact that being very much taller than her peers, and having signs of puberty at an early age, may have psychological implications.

There may also be concern that the final height reached by a girl with early puberty will be unacceptably short as she will have less total "growing time." This means that a girl with early puberty will be taller than her friends for a while as she shoots up in height, but will stop growing earlier. If puberty starts this year, your daughter will need to see a pediatrician for tests to find out why it is so early. Precocious puberty needs expert medical help to slow down the process, so see your health-care provider without delay and ask for referral to a specialist.

Seek medical advice if:

❱ Your child is showing signs of puberty (see above) at less than eight years old for a girl or nine for a boy.

❱ You are worried that your child is growing too slowly or too rapidly.

❱ You are worried that your child is significantly underweight or overweight (see page 52).

The dangers of over-exercising

Some children of this age will be sports enthusiasts, and exercise should be applauded—it helps strengthen muscles and bones, benefits the cardiovascular system, and helps maintain a healthy weight. However, it is possible for children to over-exercise, and sports such as gymnastics can put too much stress on joints and muscles, which may lead to problems such as joint pains.

Sometimes children become exercise fanatics to keep themselves thin as part of an eating disorder (see page 138), and as a result, their pubertal development may be delayed.

If you think your child is doing too much exercise at this or any other age, encourage her to reduce the amount and do other, less active, pastimes. If necessary, seek medical advice.

Your child's lifestyle

Being prepared for the next few years means focusing not only on diet but also on the amount of sleep your child gets—the rapid growth and change your child's body will go through in the next few years means it needs to be treated with respect.

Lack of sleep will result in fatigue and also poor concentration. Every child is different, but most seven-year-olds need around 11 hours of sleep; having constant late nights will eventually take its toll.

Vegetarian children

Some youngsters grow up in vegetarian households. Others choose to turn vegetarian, often around the age of seven, when they fully appreciate how meat is produced and are upset by the idea of eating it.

It is perfectly possible to grow up fit and healthy on vegetarian fare, though harder on a vegan menu, because dairy products contain so many valuable nutrients, among them iron, vitamin B12, and calcium. Choosing to become vegetarian is not just admirable ethically. It can also bring long-term health benefits, especially for the heart and blood pressure. Don't make fun of your child's lifestyle choice or force her to eat meat when she doesn't want to.

If your child is a vegetarian, try to offer:

◗ A good variety of different meals, even if these take a bit more planning and preparation. Don't just fill your child's plate with bread, potatoes, and other starches in place of the meat portion.

◗ Protein sources such as legumes, nuts, tofu, cheese, and eggs. It is important to combine proteins because single plant foods don't have all the amino acids your child needs. If you combine them, a complete protein is provided. It is easy to make meals that combine proteins—for example, eggs on toast, or beans and rice.

CALMING HER DOWN
Reading will help your child wind down. A routine is important at this age to ensure she is in bed on time and has adequate sleep.

Your child's health

It is important to keep track of your child's weight and continue to provide a nutritious diet, so make sure her snacks are good-quality, healthy food. While eating disorders are more common in older children, the seeds can be sown at this age. Bedwetting may also be an ongoing issue.

Eating disorders

Eating disorders, such as anorexia and bulimia (see page 297), are more common in older children. However, at age seven, many children already feel the pressure to be thin, start worrying about their weight, and begin talking about dieting. This generation, though so young, is bombarded with images of how they should look and behave, and many of these notions are linked with early sexualization, too.

You can help prevent weight from becoming an issue by:

▌ Encouraging an active lifestyle.

▌ Serving a healthy range of meals.

▌ Eating together as a family whenever possible.

▌ Not discussing emotive topics at mealtimes.

▌ Being discreet if you are watching your own weight. It may be best to avoid mentioning diets and dieting in front of your child.

If you are concerned about your child's eating, see your doctor without delay. Even if the eating disorder is not serious enough to endanger a child's life now, it can have serious long-term effects, including lifelong eating problems, trouble conceiving for females (this is a problem for very overweight or very underweight women), and even osteoporosis.

Warning signs of an eating disorder can include:

▌ Irritability because of hunger and a low blood-sugar level.

▌ Preoccupation with portion sizes or calories.

▌ Distorted ideas of her own body size and weight.

▌ Weight loss or weight gain.

▌ Weighing herself often.

▌ Surreptitious snacking.

"Girls are more prone to having an eating disorder, but boys aren't immune."

▶ Toying with food at mealtimes.

▶ Watching others eat before digging in herself.

Healthy snacks

Snacking is good for your active seven-year-old, as it will prevent her
blood-sugar levels from dropping drastically, especially when there is a
long time between meals. A nutritious snack can help keep your child
from becoming grumpy or listless after school, and a timely snack can stop
a child from overeating at the next meal. Your child may enjoy helping
to prepare her own snacks, too, and can make up her favorite food
combinations. Suitable snacks can include: cereals, fruit, a mug of soup,
crackers, cheese, a sandwich, celery or carrot sticks, yogurt, a hard-boiled
egg, a milk shake, or a fruit smoothie.

Handling bedwetting

At least 1–2 percent of seven-year-olds wet the bed, and boys are more
likely to do so than girls Sometimes bedwetting runs in the family, with
one or both parents having a history of acquiring nighttime bladder
control later than other children. Some seven-year-olds may just sleep
so deeply that they can't recognize and act on signals of a full bladder.
Whatever the reason, at this age, both you and your child are likely to
consider bedwetting a problem.

To help your child:

▶ Reduce carbonated and caffeine-containing beverages—they can irritate
the bladder and make your child pass urine when her bladder isn't full.

▶ If your child was dry at night, but now wets the bed again, take her to
your GP to make sure a urine infection isn't the cause of the problem.

▶ Don't get angry with your child, as stress makes bedwetting worse.

▶ Use a waterproof undersheet, and bed linen that is easy to wash.

▶ Alarm systems that use a pad and buzzer can really help if you persist.

▶ Consider reward systems, such as using a star chart, to help to increase
the number of nights your child is dry.

▶ There are several types of medication that can be prescribed. They rarely
cure the problem, but they can help in the short-term, especially if your
wants to sleep away from home—at her grandparents' house, for example.

DRINKING PLENTY
*If she wets the bed,
make sure she drinks
plenty of water during
the day. This helps her
respond to the feeling
of a full bladder.*

Understanding and skills

Your seven-year-old may have made real progress in the last year, and you may notice that she is able to concentrate for longer and think more logically—skills that together enable her to solve sometimes complex problems. Encourage her hunger to learn by doing activities with her.

While hands-on learning is still key, your seven-year-old may also spend a lot of brain power pondering more abstract matters. Her approach is likely to be more systematic, and she will, for example, enjoy working out similarities and differences between things. She may have access to a computer at school, if not at home, and use it to play games and maybe even access the Internet to look things up, with your help.

However, some children, often boys, aren't reflective by nature and may need to be encouraged to stop and think about options instead of rushing headlong into things.

Number skills

Your seven-year-old has a growing grasp of numbers and, as well as counting confidently now, she may be able to do some basic addition and subtraction. She might even do a little multiplication and division if you keep it simple. She may begin to learn more complex mathematical concepts, such as geometry, at school, but you can help, too: when your child can fit a square brick into a round jar, that is geometry at work. Help her measure and compare items, and encourage her to find similar shapes and repeating patterns in everyday objects.

Make counting and sums relevant to her world: for example, for counting and measuring, make a treasure map where she has to look "10 steps to the left" to find a clue, or give her a box of candies and ask her to share it equally among four people, to help her learn division.

At seven, the use of calculators is controversial, as children should learn to do arithmetic without one. Later on, calculators tend to be used most intelligently by children who are good at math.

EARLY MATH *She will be able to do simple sums, but the best way to encourage number skills is to make them fun, relevant, and useful.*

Collecting things

Seven-year-olds tend to love collecting things. It is probably their way of creating sense and order out of the world around them. At this age, they tend to collect an eclectic range of objects, which can include stickers, stamps, coins, erasers, shells, model planes, or toy pigs—you will find that your child's bedroom soon fills up.

It is best to let your child collect what she wants, as long as it is reasonably hygienic and affordable. Your child won't appreciate your throwing her treasures away, but she may like a hand with arranging them or keeping them safe. For instance, you could help her make a box with compartments for different pebbles.

CARD SWAPS *It can help children to bond if they collect the same things. Trading items such as cards will also give them an early lesson in negotiation skills.*

Learning through exploration

While your child will be learning plenty at school, hands-on learning at home and from everyday experiences is still best for your seven-year-old, so teach her and discuss matters with her whenever you can. Broaden her horizons by taking her to different types of places for outings, and a range of destinations if you take vacations as a family.

It doesn't matter if activities you do at home with your child also take place in the classroom. For example, if your child has already planted seeds at school, she will enjoy showing you exactly how it is done. Give her a chance to show you, or at least ask her if she knows how to do something.

Enhance an understanding of nature by:

) Going to the zoo or visiting a farm.

) Collecting leaves and making leaf-print pictures.

) Finding animal or bird footprints in the park or backyard.

) Picking up acorns or pebbles.

) Visiting the same places at different times of year, perhaps taking photos each time so that you can discuss what has changed.

) Growing and caring for plants—there are easy-to-grow seed packets suitable for children.

"Help your child think through her ideas, and, when discussing matters as a family, try to show her that you value her views."

THE SCIENCE OF COOKING *Measuring ingredients and cooking will teach your child some basic mathematical and scientific concepts.*

◗ Going for country walks. Take time to stop to observe your surroundings.

Enhance an understanding of science by:

◗ Using a tape measure to compare the size of rooms and everyday objects.

◗ Letting her help you with—or watch you do—home repairs and other chores. Let her try simple tasks with your supervision.

◗ Letting her watch you pump up or change the tires on a bike or car.

◗ Encouraging her to build things herself, perhaps using more complex materials, such as wood and glue. For example, she could make a marble run using empty toilet-paper rolls that she has stuck together.

◗ Giving her the materials to learn to sew— this will give her a great practical lesson in measuring and judging sizes.

◗ Preparing food together and letting her watch you cook—she will also learn about nutrition and biology.

◗ Recycling at home, and perhaps visiting the local recycling center.

Speech and language

The developmental leap in speech and vocabulary between the ages of six and seven is immense, and many seven-year-olds are confident readers, no matter what age they started formal education. You will notice a difference in your child's speech patterns; gone are the "baby" consonant mix-ups, such as "abble" for "apple." Your seven-year-old may be adept at working out meaning, and be able to find words to explain differences and opposites; for example, blunt and sharp or sweet and sour. She will also understand terms such as "alike," "different," "beginning," and "end"— and start to use them regularly. Encourage this by asking your seven-year-old to explain what she is feeling, and help her find the words to describe things. For example, if she doesn't like a food, ask her why—is it too salty, too spicy, or too chewy? Adjectives will be creeping into her vocabulary,

The effect of TV

Watching an hour of TV each day won't harm your child, but it is better if you can watch and discuss a program with her. This way she will learn something from it. Watching TV can encourage language skills, as well as the development of critical thinking and understanding. Educational programs can be stimulating, and those designed to entertain can teach factual information and moral lessons.

The problem comes with too much TV viewing, which has been associated with poor educational achievement and reading comprehension. Studies have found that when a child watches a lot of TV, there is often a lack of interaction with parents and few books in the home, and that the child lacks the basic skills needed to start school.

and you can encourage this new language skill by using as many as you can yourself. Don't be afraid to use new words, as this is the best way to expand her vocabulary. Take time to explain what they mean.

If your seven-year-old's vocabulary is expanding rapidly, you may be surprised that her use of grammar takes a swift downturn. As she becomes familiar with tenses, as well as plurals and matching verbs to first and second person, speech becomes more complicated and mistakes are likely to be made. Your child may confuse tenses, and pick up speech patterns from others. Don't discourage her from expressing herself; just gently repeat it correctly. Model appropriate language; one study showed that children can develop grammatical rules without explicitly being taught them.

A love of reading

Children who are read to regularly and who are given the opportunity to explore books tend to develop a love of reading. If your child isn't an avid reader, encourage her by searching out books she might enjoy. And be prepared to think outside the box! For example, some children may eagerly read about their favorite sports teams, but refuse fiction. The key is to give her what she wants to encourage reading in any form.

You can take it one step further by looking for fiction that encompasses interests; for example, a ballet-loving seven-year-old girl might love stories about dance; a soccer-crazy boy might like stories about a boy who became team captain. Model the behavior you want, too. If you

"Encourage your child's natural curiosity and give her the words to describe what she sees and feels."

read a lot and clearly enjoy it, fill your home with books and talk about what you have read. Lots of children (boys in particular) show little interest in extracurricular reading, but it is worth persevering with a bedtime story (or an audio CD), and talking about the parts of the books that your child has enjoyed most.

Learning a musical instrument

If your child shows enthusiasm for learning a musical instrument, encourage it. It is a skill she will maintain for life. Conversely, if your child shows no interest, forcing her to learn will cause misery for the whole family. Start by choosing an instrument not only for how it sounds, but also for whether it is easy to transport and comes in a small enough version for your child. If possible, borrow an instrument until you are sure your child is going to continue with the lessons. There is no way around it—you will have to sit with her while she practices, ideally for 10 minutes a day at this age, if you want her to learn quickly and succeed.

Answering children's questions

You may find that the regular barrage of questions from your seven-year-old is exhausting, but don't underestimate the importance of your response.

According to Dr. Robert Sternberg, a professor of psychology and education at Yale University, answers can be categorized into seven levels, in terms of encouraging higher levels of thinking. He believes that the more you aim for the higher levels, the better your child becomes at critical thinking. The most important thing you can do is to answer questions as fully as possible and encourage further thinking. The more your child is persuaded to think, the better she will become at doing so.

★ **Level 1**—Rejecting the question ("Because I said so, don't ask me any more questions!").

★ **Level 2**—Restating the question ("Why do you have to eat your vegetables? Because you have to eat your vegetables").

★ **Level 3**—Admitting ignorance or presenting information ("I don't know, but it's a good question"; or give a factual answer).

★ **Level 4**—Encouraging a response through authority ("Let's look it up. Who might know the answer to that question?").

★ **Level 5**—Encouraging brainstorming and giving alternative explanations ("Why does our dog have fur? Does she have delicate skin or require warmth?").

★ **Level 6**—Encouraging alternative explanations and evaluating them. Consider your answers and look them up in a book or on the Internet.

★ **Level 7**—Following through with your evaluations. Looking things up together, talking through some possible answers, and deciding which one makes the most sense.

Emotions and personality

Now that your child has a greater understanding of—and control over—her emotions, you may find that she begins to use them to get what she wants. While she will definitely be more independent now, don't be fooled by the bravado— she needs you more than ever.

Handling your child's sensitivity

Your seven-year-old is ready for a little privacy. Her increased body awareness will mean she may want to bathe and change in private. You will also notice signs that she is sometimes embarrassed by your behavior, especially when she is with friends. She will be motivated to conform to fit into her peer group and will be sensitive about your appearance and behavior. She won't be as keen on public displays of affection from you, and she may beg you not to wear certain clothes, act "loudly," or generally be "embarrassing." It is up to you whether you tone down to avoid criticism. Be aware that her feelings are real, so don't set out to challenge her desire for conformity. She will make up for public rejection of you by wanting affection when you are at home together, and she will be fiercely protective about you to others. The harshest verbal bullying at this age is often a negative comment about a parent.

Understanding emotions and self-control

Your seven-year-old will now have a wide vocabulary, including labels for the most common, and some complex, emotions. She may be able to describe jealousy, for example, as well as joy and anger. She will also hide her emotions. For example, she may pretend not to care if you take away a toy when she has misbehaved. This may be to persuade you that the punishment hasn't worked and to tempt you to give up on it. Your seven-year-old can't keep all her emotions under control; strong feelings will still break through, especially anger and distress.

Being able to think about her feelings and those of others, and to keep some thoughts private, are rapidly developing skills in your seven-

PERSONAL SPACE *Your child's bedroom and belongings are likely to become more important to her as she begins to want more privacy.*

year-old. She is no longer at the mercy of every emotion, and pure expressions of feelings are now under more control.

A battle of wills

Negotiating and bargaining will be your seven-year-old's specialty. Her verbal skills will be developing rapidly and she will be able to argue her point of view, especially to get what she wants. She is likely to take a pragmatic approach, asking for something on the off-chance that you will give in, and then debating the issue as if her heart will break.

While the skills to form an argument are part of your child's continuing social and language development, it can be tiring if every request is challenged. Encourage her to voice her point of view, asking her for preferences on simple decisions. However, for most everyday decisions, you must make the final choice. You know what is best for your child most of the time. Reduce arguments by being clear when she can have a say and when she must do as you ask, saying, for example, "Please choose your cereal, and then after breakfast you have to brush your teeth."

BEING PROVOKED *Don't engage in arguments, but do stand your ground. Eventually she'll only argue when she has an important point to make.*

Spoiling your child

It can be a delicate balance knowing how much to give your seven-year-old and when to hold back. Many parents worry about spoiling their child by giving them too many possessions or too few responsibilities. While having a range of different toys is good, it is a concern if your child has too many to compensate for other things, such as a lack of time with you. Remember that at this age, your child will still crave your attention and your involvement in her play.

Sometimes children can be spoiled by always getting what they ask for. It is best not to give in every time your child pesters you to buy something. Instead, explain about saving up. Waiting to get what she wants is a crucial life skill that will help her to manage both impatience and money.

"Giving your seven-year-old affection and attention and telling her how much you care is not spoiling. Children thrive when they know they are genuinely loved."

Encouraging decision-making

Seven-year-old children vary greatly in how much attention they pay to everyday choices. Depending on their personality, some have favorite clothes, foods, and drinks, while others go with the flow and put on the first garment out of the drawer or eat whichever meal has been set in front of them.

Being able to make a careful choice is a useful life skill as your seven-year-old faces ever more decisions at home and school. Many choices are simple, such as which book to read or what kind of sandwich to eat, but each choice is a chance to develop decision-making skills. Help your child by practicing with her and talking about how she reaches decisions. For example, ask her to choose where the family goes for a day trip. Limit her to considering three places, and then get her to talk about the positives and negatives of

Role models

The strongest influence on your seven-year-old is you. It can be disconcerting to know that she is learning more from the way you behave than what you say to her. For this reason, be conscious of how your actions must look to her.

She will view your relationship with your partner as a blueprint for her own relationships in later life. Your communication style will influence her; she will copy your problem-solving methods, perhaps learning to get agreement by talking calmly or by showing anger. She will also model her values on yours, so if you value education and hard work, she will too. However, although your child looks up to you, this doesn't mean you need to be perfect all the time.

PARENTAL ROLE MODELS *Boys will generally model their fathers and girls their mothers, but this is not a hard-and-fast rule.*

each. Finally, get her to come to her decision, then abide by her choice. One of your tasks as a parent is to encourage your child to be as independent as possible.

Remember:

▶ If you feel like a servant to your seven-year-old, then you are doing too much and she is not practicing the skills she needs to become a well-organized and self-sufficient individual.

Being self-critical

The desire to be first, best, and right is strong in your seven-year-old and may lead her to be highly self-critical. She will want to do well, but may see winning as her goal, rather than putting in her finest effort. The way you react can help your child see the value of trying, even if she is not always "the best." When you notice how hard she has worked and make comments on the care with which she has created a story, for example, then she will glow with pride.

It is very common for a child of seven to be distressed by not doing as well as she had hoped. At these times, she needs comfort, reassurance that no one comes out on top every time, and a reminder of her other achievements. This way her resilience is built up and she will learn to put disappointments and successes into perspective.

Party excitement

Having a party will be so exciting for your seven-year-old that she is likely to become overwhelmed, and she may even have a tantrum if things don't go her way.

If you see her getting overexcited, simply taking her aside for a hug can solve the problem, or distract her by getting her to help you with a small job. If she does misbehave, take her aside and let her know her behavior is not acceptable. Don't scold her in front of her friends; this can make her feel ashamed and may lead to defiance instead of good behavior.

Careful planning

Whether you have a party at home or elsewhere, your child is old enough to enjoy planning it with you. At this age, inviting 8–10 children, led by two adults, is about right. Set a time limit of around two hours. This is plenty of time for playing games and eating without causing the children to get overexcited.

Arrange plenty to do, and try to leave at least some presents to be opened after the party is over, when your child can properly appreciate them.

Common behavioral concerns

▶ **What can I do when my seven-year-old insists on dressing like his classmates and doing all the same things they do?**
Now that your child has some established friendships, don't be too surprised if he suddenly wants to look and be like his peers. Children dislike being different, so looking and being like their friends is usually really important to them.

If it is possible and desirable for your child to dress in a style similar to his classmates', it's worth complying. If it's clearly silly or too expensive, then use your discretion. Make sure he is confident in who he is as an individual and that he understands that it's okay to be and look different. Your child's job is to use pester power (see page 92), but as the parent you are the final arbiter, and there's no need to feel guilty for saying "No" to something.

▶ **My daughter gets so frustrated sometimes. Is there any way I can help to defuse these negative feelings?**
Seven-year-olds can often visualize only too clearly what they want but, for one reason or another, find they can't have it. Frustration can build up, and your child's temper can become frayed.

Ask your child to name her feelings and tell you about them. Move her attention to a task she can complete successfully, then give her some support to tackle the difficult one. In extreme cases of frustration, help her clear her head and relieve any tension through physical activity or just a walk outside in the fresh air.

▶ **My daughter has "best friends," but some of them don't last long. How can I help her when she's upset about a friend no longer wanting to play with her?**
You're right not to underestimate the sadness that children can feel at the end of a friendship. There are many reasons why friendships end, but whatever the cause, your child deserves reassurance that she

FRAGILE FRIENDSHIPS *Friends are important to your seven-year-old, so take the arguments she has with them seriously, even if the matter seems trivial to you.*

will be okay. It is usually unwise to tell your child not to be silly, or to point out where she went wrong. After losing a friend, your child needs you to bolster her fragile self-esteem and tell her, directly and through your actions, that you think she's a great person.

Sometimes relating your own experiences of friendships can give comfort as well as hints for the future. Bear in mind that at this age, broken friendships are usually short-lived.

▶ **My rebellious seven-year-old often does exactly the opposite of what I tell him. Why is this?**
Defiant behavior is a common way for seven-year-olds to assert themselves. Be positive rather than negative in your instructions, and be firm without getting irate. This will help reduce your child's need to rebel. For example, saying to him, "It's safer to walk on the sidewalk" may be more effective than saying, "Don't let me catch you walking in the street again." When your son misbehaves, show him that you are disappointed rather than angry. Getting angry tends to raise the emotional temperature all around.

Make sure any instructions you give him are clear, and give a straightforward reason for them. Praise your son when he cooperates. If he doesn't, he may respond to a small consequence.

Your child's life

Many seven-year-olds are very busy! Apart from being at school and having homework, there are extracurricular activities, family time, and playtime to fit in. But you are undoubtedly busy, too, so it will help to encourage your child to plan her time and become more self-sufficient.

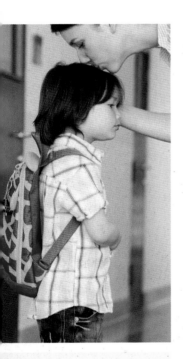

BEING SELF-SUFFICIENT
Your child should now be able to get himself ready for school and for family outings, and know what time he is expected to do things.

Sit down with your child on the weekend, look through all her commitments, and plot everything out so that she realizes what has to be achieved and learns how to prioritize. Although it can be tempting to leap in and do things for your child, it is important for her to learn the basics of taking care of herself and her belongings.

To help your child:

▶ Establish a routine where she sets out her clothes for the next day and does any homework at a set time.

▶ Write a list of everything that should be in her bag at the beginning and the end of every day. Tape it inside her bag, and encourage her to check it before leaving home and when she returns. If she is not a strong reader, use a combination of pictures and words.

First school tests

Your seven-year-old may experience her first tests at school and may feel pressured. There are several ways to deal with this. First, if your child doesn't need to know about the tests, don't tell her! Most tests at seven are designed to find out where your child stands, and pinpoint weaknesses and strengths. While it may be tempting to offer help with studying, in the long run this does your child no favors, as she will come to rely on extra help to achieve the same result.

If your child knows about the test, play down your expectations. Make it clear that you will be happy with her very best effort. If she is expected to study at home or prepare for a test, make it low-key and fun. The less pressure you apply now, the better your child will be able to face taking exams in the future.

Handling sibling conflict

As your child reaches age seven, she is likely to become more possessive about her belongings, not wanting her siblings to touch or borrow her toys or enter her bedroom.

To help your child protect her belongings:

❯ Allow your seven-year-old to have some private space for her most precious things. This might mean her room is out of bounds for siblings, or she has a toy cupboard that she can lock.

❯ Start a household rule about borrowing, along the lines of, "We always ask permission before we borrow someone else's belongings."

❯ Help children stick to the rules by giving them reminders and praising them when they do ask beforehand.

Gifted children

Some children have a very good memory, and may be able and eager to learn simple math, science, and social studies concepts. They may develop an all-consuming interest in one particular topic, such as historical periods, science, or animals, and have an extraordinary understanding and knowledge about the subject.

Gifted children may:

★ Use advanced vocabulary.
★ Be observant and curious.
★ Retain a variety of information.
★ Have periods of intense concentration.
★ Be able to understand complex concepts, perceive relationships, and think abstractly.
★ Have a broad and changing spectrum of interests.

★ Be good at critical thinking and be self-critical.
★ Be unusually alert in infancy.

If your child seems far ahead of her peers and meets the above criteria, speak to her teacher about seeing an educational psychologist to assess the best way forward.

Try to give her the tools she needs to investigate her interests, and remember that a gifted child might struggle to conform if she is far beyond her peers. Encouraging activities that other children do can help to support healthy interactions, and widen your child's interests. Beware of obsessions and perfectionism, which can take over. Encourage realistic expectations, and set time limits on projects she is interested in.

SPECIAL TALENT *Gifted children usually demonstrate talent at an earlier age than other children, and this is particularly noticeable in the arts.*

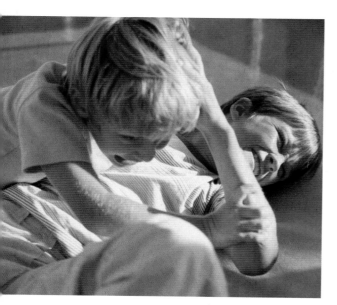

SIBLINGS AT WAR *The slightest dispute can get out of hand. Break up fights quickly and separate your children until they calm down.*

▶ Decide what to do if rules are broken. If an item is broken, siblings may be asked to contribute allowance money toward a replacement, though most toys are broken by accident. If something is taken without permission, it should be returned immediately.

Courtesy and manners

Good manners help your seven-year-old get ahead in life. She will get a positive reaction from people if she is pleasant and polite. She will already be copying your good manners and responding well if you expect her to say "please" and "thank you." At age seven, she is ready to show her manners in a more active way, perhaps by giving up her seat on a bus to a senior citizen, or offering food to someone else first. You may need to actively teach these expressions of selflessness. Take the time to explain why manners are a sign of respect for others. At first, explain what your child can get in return. As she develops her social skills, she will be able to understand that being considerate means caring for others without expectation of a direct gain.

Teaching morals

Your seven-year-old has been learning values and morals for a long time, because you have been teaching her by example, perhaps without even realizing it. She has also known for years that there are rules of various kinds. What is different now is that she can apply logic to the rules she comes across, and to the discussions you have together about boundaries, morals, and values.

At seven, she should readily see, for example, that killing someone is wrong. It is also a good idea to teach her explicitly that lying and stealing are both wrong. As a more general guide, you could use a dictum along the lines of "Treat others as you would like them to treat you." This underpins ethical values in most cultures, and is a useful and simple moral compass in new situations that your seven-year-old comes across.

Sooner or later, your child will realize that grown-ups lie, usually in social situations. This can be tough to rationalize to your child. However, there may be explanations that you can give her. "Maybe I lied a bit when I said Aunt Mabel looked great, but it's not nice to hear that you're unattractive, is it?" Again, "Do as you would be done by" covers that situation.

Talking about death

Straightforward, honest communication with your seven-year-old is the best approach when someone dies. She is able to understand that death is final and that she will never see the person again, and will benefit from clear, calm statements such as "John is dead" rather than "John has left us" or "John is in Heaven." It is possible to confuse and worry your seven-year-old if you tell her, for example, that someone died because they were ill. Your child may assume all people who are ill die. If you use euphemisms for death such as "She went to sleep" your child may worry about sleeping herself. It is normal for your seven-year-old to worry that you might die, too, so be prepared for this question. Some parents find that an answer such as, "Yes, but not for a very long time" can reduce fears. If your beliefs permit it, let your child attend a memorial ceremony or funeral to take part in the grieving process and show her feelings freely.

"Your child will have a natural curiosity about life and death and need an explanation when someone dies."

Racism and mixed-race children

Children can be very racist. Sometimes this attitude is "caught" from their parents; sometimes it occurs because parents shy away from ever discussing race and other differences. Children do like to classify people, but they need to be taught by adults that differences aren't deficiencies.

Help your child to avoid racism by:
★ Being a good role model.
★ Explaining race issues simply.

★ Choosing books and TV programs that can open your child's mind to other cultures. This is especially important if most of her friends and acquaintances come from only one background.

Mixed-race children
Children who are of mixed race can have a particularly bad time, as they may get abuse or bullying from "both sides" of a racial divide.

They may also feel torn between two cultures and struggle to find their own identity. Racist abuse is cruel and against the law in most of the developed world.

If your child is a victim of racism:
★ Make it clear that it is others who cause the problem, not her.
★ Approach your child's school and discuss the problems your child is facing. Ask to see the school's policies on racism and on bullying.

14

13

12

11

10

9

8

7

6

5

4

3

YEARS

Your 8-year-old

"You will notice your child becoming more mature and at ease with herself."

LETTING OFF STEAM Giving your child plenty of opportunities for physical play will help minimize boredom and bad behavior.

ACADEMIC ABILITY Your child may begin to show a particular interest and talent for certain subjects.

BEING THE BIGGEST As your child begins to compare himself to his classmates, his height may start to become an issue.

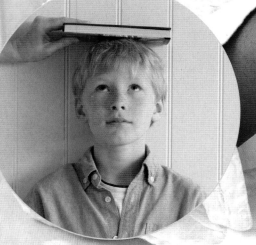

Growth and development

Your eight-year-old's stamina will increase along with his competitive spirit, and he will get a great deal out of physical play. There can be a real difference in the size of children at this age, as growth spurts happen at different times, but one thing they often have in common is a high turnover of shoes!

Body weight and shape

Before the pubertal growth spurt, which can happen at varying ages, some previously slim children develop "baby fat," which is quite normal and nothing to worry about. It is vital not to draw attention to this, particularly in girls, as an insensitive comment made to a vulnerable girl can result in the start of eating disorders (see page 297). Girls as young as eight can become upset by what they perceive as chubbiness, and, sadly, a number of them may start eating very little or exercising excessively (see page 136) to maintain their prepubertal shape.

Some girls begin the stages of puberty (see page 186) earlier than others, and if your child goes through puberty relatively early, she may start developing breasts and hips. Whenever her body shape begins to change, it is essential to reassure a young girl about her burgeoning womanliness.

Nutritious food

Good nutrition is essential to prepare your child for all the changes that are about to take place in his body in the coming years. Make sure that as a family you are eating a healthy diet, and avoid filling your cupboards with tempting high-calorie snacks. Parents who complain that their children keep helping themselves to cookies and bags of chips can easily stop this by not buying them.

It is easy for a child to slip into a sedentary lifestyle, so look carefully at how much exercise your child is doing and aim for at least 30 minutes, but preferably an hour, per day. This should be varied and could include swimming, playing soccer, going for a walk, or dancing. If you think your child is over- or underweight, seek medical advice. Your child's height and

DIFFERENT GROWTH RATES *Don't worry if your daughter is much smaller than her classmates—she'll catch up when she starts puberty.*

weight will be plotted on a growth chart (see page 22). If your child is significantly underweight, the reasons may be ill health, unhappiness, or, less likely at this age, an eating disorder (see page 297). If you suspect any of these, take him to your doctor for a checkup.

If a child is significantly overweight, there is unlikely to be a medical cause for this, but an assessment by your doctor may be helpful to rule out endocrine problems, such as an underactive thyroid gland or the overproduction of the body's natural steroid, cortisol. You will also be able to talk through the ways in which you can help your child achieve a healthy balance between eating and being active.

Handwriting ability

There is usually a real improvement in handwriting at this age, and some schools will introduce ink pens. This is sometimes the age when it becomes clear that a child is dyslexic (see page 121). If your child is writing his letters backward, struggling to read and write, and either you or his teacher are concerned, he will need a formal assessment.

Wearing glasses

It can be hard to spot that your child is near- or farsighted. Sometimes a teacher notices that a child can't see the blackboard if he is at the back of the classroom, or you may realize that he is squinting at the TV. If you have any concerns about your child's eyesight, or if you have a family history of needing glasses in childhood, take your child for an eye test at least once a year, and more frequently if recommended by your optometrist.

If the time comes that your child requires glasses, he may need some encouragement to get used to the idea. There are many attractive and affordable styles of glasses for children, so you should be able to find a pair that both you and your child agree on. Prime the rest of the family to say how cool he looks in them, as they must be worn.

BEING POSITIVE *Glasses can look very attractive, and your child must be made to feel good about wearing them, especially at school.*

Electronic games

Whatever your view on electronic and computer games, they are an integral part of leisure time for many children. It can be reassuring to know that they can help fine-tune your child's fine motor skills (see page 24), but it is up to you as a parent to decide on an acceptable ratio of physical games to computer games. Your child will have lots of energy at this age, and it is important that he gets ample opportunity to burn it off. Walking to school, if this is feasible, is one way of achieving some of his daily exercise (see also page 105).

Your child's brain

Although your child's brain has done most of its growing by age eight, it is continuing to lay down pathways (see page 21) that will become permanent. Some people describe the brain at this age as being like a sponge, and it is true that children learn new ideas rapidly, including languages, so now is the time to capitalize on this.

TECHNOLOGICAL SKILLS
Electronic games require good hand–eye coordination and quick responses, so they can enhance some aspects of development, when played in moderation.

To stimulate your child:

 Teach him how to play board games that require him to use logic and make decisions. Play them with him, but encourage him to problem-solve for himself.

Introduce the idea of noncompetitive teamwork, such as doing a large jigsaw puzzle or building a model together.

Find activities that require accuracy, patience, and good hand–eye coordination, such as sewing, knitting, beading, and detailed cutting-out of pictures to make collages.

Cook with him; encourage him to choose a recipe he wants to try, read it with you, and measure out the ingredients.

Encourage him to write by producing a scrapbook or a journal, and to read by giving him access to plenty of books.

Talk to him and ask him questions about how things work. Always help him find the answers to something he doesn't know.

Your child's health

With more outside influences, you may notice your child becoming anxious, and it is important to take action so this does not have an impact on his health. As his life gets busier, make sure he gets enough sleep and takes care of himself—he may, for example, rush tasks such as brushing his teeth.

"Make sure your child sees you taking good care of your teeth, and he's likely to follow suit."

Teeth and gums

Your child acquires on average four new teeth a year. Now that he is eight, he will have about 12 permanent teeth (though he won't get all his molars until he is 12, and wisdom teeth only emerge at the age of 18, or later). He should be brushing his teeth independently, at least twice a day. Many youngsters skimp on tooth-brushing, or even skip it altogether because they forget or they don't feel like doing it. But these teeth are important, even more so than your child's milk teeth.

To keep your child's teeth and gums healthy:

▌ Brush your teeth together every so often to make sure your child is using the correct technique.

▌ Try giving your child dental disclosing tablets. Made from vegetable dye, these chewable tablets reveal plaque and help pinpoint where more thorough brushing is needed.

▌ Treat your child to a new toothbrush often, at least every 3–4 months, as bristles get worn quickly.

▌ An electric toothbrush can be an added incentive to brush. The brush head will need to be replaced regularly.

▌ Make sure your child has regular dental checkups. These should be every six months, or more often if recommended by your dentist.

▌ Never delay taking your child to a dentist if he has a toothache or bleeding gums. Gum health is vital for tooth health, and even for general health, as diseased gums can harbor harmful bacteria.

▌ Poorly aligned permanent teeth may need braces. Full orthodontic treatment is unlikely to be needed at this age, but check with your dentist if you are concerned about the appearance or position of your child's teeth.

Eating whole grains

Your eight-year-old will enjoy snacking, so make sure the foods on hand are healthy. As well as enjoying plenty of healthy fruit and vegetables, you can also introduce whole-grain foods. Your eight-year-old's digestive system can now easily cope with the extra fiber found in whole grains. As well as fiber, whole grains contain B vitamins, the elements iron and magnesium, and several antioxidants, such as vitamin E and the mineral selenium. They are also rich in carbohydrates for sustained energy and growth. The health benefits of whole grains include lower cholesterol levels, and a reduced risk of obesity and diabetes.

"Whole grains" means grains such as wheat, corn, rice, oats, and rye when they are eaten in their whole-grain form—in other words, the whole grain kernel. Technically this includes the outer bran as well as the inner germ and the endosperm (which feeds the germ). Whole-grain foods can be processed, and include some breads, cereals, and even popcorn, so there is plenty of scope for tempting your child.

A LIGHT BITE
Snacks should be nutritious but not too filling, so that your child can still eat his next meal without feeling too full.

Physical effects of anxiety and worry

Children may not have the same level of responsibility as adults, but they don't always have a carefree existence. Your eight-year-old may worry about friendships, school, tests, and perhaps upheavals at home such as a house move or parental conflict. Anxiety and worry can cause physical symptoms, often as a result of activation of the body's stress mechanisms. These make the adrenal glands pump out hormones, such as adrenaline (epinephrine) and cortisol.

Common stress-linked complaints include:
- Headaches.
- Other aches and pains, especially stomachaches.
- Loss of appetite.

SIGNS OF STRESS *Your child may become withdrawn when something is worrying her. Get her to open up, as sharing her concerns can reduce physical symptoms.*

▶ Nausea and vomiting.

▶ Diarrhea.

▶ Trouble sleeping.

▶ Grinding the teeth.

▶ Nervous tics and spasms such as frequent blinking.

Many of these symptoms can have other causes, too, so if they persist, always take your child to the doctor for a checkup.

Sleep disorders

Eight-year-olds don't always sleep as well as younger children. Sometimes, anxiety may keep your child awake. More often, it is just excitement, or a desire to stay up later to watch TV, play games, or just be with you. Around 10–11 hours' sleep each night is the average your eight-year-old needs after a whirlwind day. He may lobby for a later bedtime as he matures, perhaps claiming that all his friends go to bed later than he does. Stand firm against pestering for a later bedtime.

Your task is to adjust your child's bedtime according to his age, while making sure he gets enough sleep. The nighttime routine will be changing, too, as your eight-year-old is increasingly independent and may want to read himself to sleep. You can't force a child to sleep, but your child can be in his room, preferably in bed, by a certain time, and it is reasonable to set a time for lights-out. For example, if your child is in bed by 8:15 pm, that gives him half an hour for reading before an 8:45 pm lights-out. If he is awake by 7 am, then you can be sure he is getting a good night's sleep. You are the parent, so it is up to you to decide and stick to a bedtime routine for your child.

Some children wake very early in the morning. There is not much you can do about this, but you can impress on your child the need to keep quiet and independently amused. If he is capable of making his own breakfast, this may prolong your own time in bed on weekends.

"If your eight-year-old doesn't get enough sleep, he will be grumpy, find concentrating at school more difficult, and be more likely to exhibit bad behavior."

Asthma (reactive airway disease)

Asthma is a chronic lung condition that causes attacks of coughing, wheezing, and/or shortness of breath. It can start at any age. Asthma is often mild, though it can be severe and must be controlled.

Controlling asthma is vital to your child's health, growth, and his learning, too—nights interrupted by coughing or breathlessness make for a tired child the next day.

Symptoms and triggers

All the symptoms of asthma are caused by narrowing of the airways. In asthmatic children, the airways are unusually sensitive, and can become inflamed and narrow in response to various triggers, such as cold air, infections, pollen, house dust mites, feathers, and animal fur. Sometimes even laughing can set off an attack. There is a link between asthma, hayfever, and eczema (see page 115), but asthma can also occur on its own.

A child may be asthmatic if he has a recurrent cough, especially at night, or if he wheezes after exercise, especially in cold weather. Sometimes there is a cough only and no wheezing. Symptoms are often worse during the night.

A modern illness

Asthma has become much more common. Nowadays about one schoolchild in every seven has it. The rise is partly due to doctors diagnosing it more readily,

especially in mild cases, but there is no doubt that there has also been a real increase, and this may be linked with the general rise in allergies. Air quality matters too, with passive smoking being a major risk factor.

Genetics are important, so asthma often runs in families, but not always. Even with identical twins, one child may have asthma while the other doesn't.

Diagnosing asthma

There is no single test for diagnosing asthma, but using a handheld device called a peak flow meter can help, by measuring how

PREVENTING ASTHMA ATTACKS
You can help minimize the number of asthma attacks your child has by eliminating or reducing known triggers, such as feather pillows and house dust mites.

fast a child can breathe. X-rays are sometimes needed, mainly to rule out other causes of breathing difficulty.

Prevention and treatment

Asthma cannot be cured, but it is possible to relieve symptoms dramatically, usually to the point where a child can lead a completely normal life. Avoiding your child's known triggers (see left) is a good start. A flu shot in winter is advisable for children with asthma.

Treatment is usually given via inhalers. Some are symptom-relievers, while others have an anti-inflammatory action that helps prevent attacks in the first place. There are also other drugs, some taken by mouth, that can protect the airways and reduce the number of attacks. A child should be allowed to keep an inhaler at school where he can easily access it. He may need to take an extra puff of his inhaler before gym class, for instance.

For an acute attack, your child's dose of inhalers may need to be increased. Antibiotics seldom help, because bacterial infections rarely trigger attacks. Always get medical help urgently if your child is too breathless to speak, is distressed, or turns blue.

About half of all children outgrow asthma. But if your child still has asthma symptoms at 14, then he may have a tendency to experience attacks of it as an adult.

Understanding and skills

Your eight-year-old will appear mature and more organized, and have a good understanding of the world and how it works. He will be eager to discover the reason for things and, although he still needs information and clues from you, he will be prepared to think things through for himself.

Your child's interests

It is important not to judge your child by the same yardstick as others. His talents may lie in creative writing, art, drama, music, science, math, or in some field of sports. At eight years old, it can be hard to know in advance what your child will be good at, until he has tried it, and this applies to academic subjects as much as to extracurricular activities.

There will be subjects and activities he takes up that he has little enthusiasm or skill for, while others may lead to a lifelong passion.

To help your child:

▶ Encourage your child in areas that are right for him, not just the things that appeal to you. Don't expect your child to have the same inclinations as you, his siblings, or his friends. Every one of us is an unpredictable mix of nature and nurture.

Problem-solving games and puzzles

Many different games, puzzles, and activities can entertain your eight-year-old as well as enhance his problem-solving skills.

Try the following:

★ Tic-tac-toe.
★ Checkers.
★ Chinese checkers.
★ Connect 4.

More strategic games include chess and backgammon, both of which can be very satisfying if your child shows an interest in them. However, your child may not have the maturity to play a whole game, or play it with other children, especially if it involves losing many pieces.

Card games, such as solitaire, may appeal to your child, too. There are also many board games that require problem-solving skills. Clue, for instance, is suitable from eight years onward. There are versions of Sudoku, the logic game using number grids, that are especially designed for children.

▶ Allow your child to sample different activities. After-school and vacation clubs can offer samples of drama, chess, or tennis, for example.

▶ Give praise when your child does well at something.

▶ Make sure your child knows it is okay not to be good at everything.

Fear of failure can begin around now. Sometimes this is a downward spiral, unless you and his teachers take steps to stop it. It is important for your child not to adopt a defeatist attitude just because he doesn't always fulfill expectations (his or yours). Your child cares what you think. He might say "I can't play football" after his team loses. Try to encourage him, and help him keep the loss in perspective.

Encouraging individual thinking

Your eight-year-old will like to be part of a group, and do as his friends do, but encourage him to think for himself.

To encourage spontaneous and individual thought:

▶ Ask your child to think up new uses for, say, a shoebox.

▶ Praise him when he makes something for you rather than buying you a card or a present.

▶ Pose "What if...?" questions, such as "What would we do if the stove broke?" or "How would we cope if there was a power outage?"

▶ Ask him to design or draw a machine that does two different things, perhaps preparing breakfast and sweeping the floor at the same time.

▶ Suggest that he makes up a recipe using certain ingredients.

QUESTIONING THINGS
As your child reads, ask him why he thinks a character behaved in a certain way, or what might have happened differently in the plot.

Helping with math

By this age your child is likely to add and subtract confidently, and he may know how to "borrow" and "carry over," so he can add up columns of numbers. He may be able to multiply and divide, and understand simple fractions as well as pie charts and bar graphs. He can understand geometry better than before, and this will help him with everyday tasks, such as fitting his books on his bookshelf or toys in his toy box. Geometry is a skill that is vital to every field, not just math.

You can help your child with math by demonstrating its relevance to his immediate world. Also, approaching the subject from more than one angle enriches and deepens his understanding.

You could encourage your child to:

- Add up prices together when you are shopping.
- Explain measurements when cooking or doing repairs.
- Work out how many stamps a thick envelope might need.
- Add up the numbers on car license plates.
- Ask which house or bus numbers can be divided by, say, two or five. This exercise may not be useful, but it can be fun.

If you are not sure how your child is learning math at school, ask his teacher if you can borrow some books or worksheets to acquaint yourself with the methods and materials.

Speech and language

By the age of eight, with some schooling under his belt, your child will undoubtedly exhibit a huge developmental leap, conversing at almost adult level, and correcting himself when his grammar is wrong. He may be more interested in using words creatively, telling stories, acting out dramas, making up rhymes, and anticipating the endings to stories.

Many eight-year-olds are confident and extroverted, believing in themselves and their capabilities. They may dislike being corrected, and set high standards for themselves. As your child's thinking is more organized, his questions will be clearer. Many eight-year-olds also take a great interest in reading, as they can normally master appropriate books with ease. All this means that you can expect leaps forward in speech and language. Your child will undoubtedly ask the meaning of words, and you can encourage this by playing word games and conversing with him—he will learn new vocabulary from you and how to express himself in a more mature way.

Creative writing

Your eight-year-old will likely have a great imagination, and a somewhat dubious grasp of the difference between fantasy and reality. At this age, it isn't lying as such—more wishful thinking! Directing your child's blossoming vocabulary and language skills, as well as a vivid imagination, into creative writing is an excellent way to make the most of his interests and abilities. If your child is reluctant to write thing downs, encouraging him to make up stories is a good way to begin.

BEING INQUISITIVE

As your child thinks more logically and her vocabulary widens, she will begin to ask more intelligent questions.

To help your child:

❱ Ask him to dream up new adventures for his favorite characters.

❱ Read him simple poems and ask him to add an extra line.

❱ Ask him to make up a background—a family history, a home, and interests for his favorite toy.

❱ Ask him to describe something he sees outside, or finds interesting or beautiful, such as "How does snow make you feel?"

❱ Help him to find alternative and associated words—for example, "hot" could be linked with being sweaty, thirsty, or feverish.

Learning cursive writing

It is not easy to switch from printing to cursive writing, so be positive and encouraging. Not every eight-year-old's fingers are dexterous enough, and if he is left-handed, he may face extra hurdles. Let your child choose a pencil of a hardness and length that suit him. There are templates for practicing cursive writing and your child may use these at school.

At home, encourage him to write things in the new way. He may find it easier to manage short runs of words, as in a shopping list, rather than a complete sentence, which could be dispiriting if he doesn't write well yet. Perhaps he can then work his way up to short thank-you notes and letters. Praise him for his efforts at every stage.

Minimizing the use of slang

With the advent of peer pressure and a natural instinct to conform, many children adopt the grammar and speech patterns of friends, and you may not always be impressed.

To deal with this, ask the meaning of a slang term, and encourage your child not only to understand what he is saying, but to find alternatives that can be used in appropriate company.

You can't change the way your child speaks with his friends, but you can stress the importance of communicating clearly, fluently, and correctly at home. Explain that slang is often offensive, and can be difficult for some people to understand. It has a time and a place, but it is a good idea to correct him (quietly and gently) every time he uses a lazy word that has a more suitable meaning. So if, for example, he says, "I ain't gonna do it," correct him with "I'm sorry, I can't do it."

Rather than undermining or criticizing him, the aim is to present him with speech options that can be used in appropriate situations, and give him an understanding of how correct speech and grammar work.

Emotions and personality

Your eight-year-old's relationship with you is the most important in his life, rating seven times as influential as those with friends. Even though he is more independent, your love, attention, and confidence in him affect his happiness and self-esteem every day.

"Try not to give your child 'over-the-top' praise or you may find he's more embarrassed than pleased."

At age eight, your child's personality is well established; he may be outgoing, prepared to talk to almost anyone, or quiet and less sociable, or somewhere in between. He may be easy-going, or he may have a challenging, questioning manner. What is common to most eight-year-olds, though, is the ability to plan ahead, reason things out, and express themselves more clearly than in previous years, as their cognitive and verbal skills advance in leaps and bounds. He will be able to enter into more complex conversations and be interested not only in facts but motivation, such as why people act the way they do.

Although it is important to your child's self-esteem to give him praise, you may need to adapt the way you give it. At this age he will prefer you to be less gushing, but still genuine, when you notice his achievements.

Dealing with impatience

Even though your eight-year-old can reason and plan, and his impatience is no longer as immediate as when he was a toddler, he will still have difficulty waiting. You may get a barrage of requests, such as, "When's dinner?", "Please turn on the computer," "Can you find my football helmet?" before you can respond to even one of them. This is because your fast-thinking eight-year-old always seems to have a plan for the next few hours. For example, he has worked out that if he has dinner now, then he will have time for 30 minutes on the computer before football. He won't be too pleased when you gently say you can't comply with all his requests right away. He is unlikely to articulate what is motivating him, so ask what he is planning and then find a solution to suit everyone. Your calm reaction to his demands can help him manage his impatience.

The need for independence

By the age of eight, your child will be independent in most of his self-care, such as washing and dressing, although he may need reminders to use soap. His most pressing drive at age eight is to do things outside the home without you, such as running errands or visiting friends. Only you can decide when you are comfortable letting him go off on his own. Take into account both your child's maturity and your neighborhood. If you have a mature eight-year-old, aware of staying safe, you will give him more independence. If he tends to be impulsive and doesn't recognize risks, then more limits apply. Living near a busy street or where there are no local stores can also affect your decision.

When your eight-year-old does start to leave home alone, give him small tasks, perhaps taking something to a neighbor's house, so he can practice independence without being too far away from home. With each success, your faith in your child will build and so will his confidence. Remember, you must always know where your eight-year-old is going, who he is with, and when he plans to be home.

Fears and anxieties

By the age of eight, your child has probably outgrown his fear of ghosts and monsters and will be more concerned about being scolded or failing—for example, at school or at a sport. These concerns mirror your eight-

SETTING HIM FREE *Many of his activities will take him outdoors, and it is important to allow him some freedom.*

Early sexualized behavior

Sexual curiosity is common among eight-year-olds, with about 40 percent of children between the ages of six and nine reporting sexual exploration. Common behavior between similar-aged children is kissing and hugging, showing off, or comparing or touching their own or friends' private parts. Most children find these experiences interesting, but a small number have negative feelings, and it is important that they feel confident to say no, leave the situation, and tell a trusted adult.

Sexualized behavior is a cause for concern if it seems inappropriate for a child's age or if those involved are older, and when it causes a child to be distressed or fearful, or feel coerced.

If you are worried about your child's sexual behavior, seek advice immediately from a professional who has child protection experience.

year-old's awareness of himself as an individual and his need to be seen to do well. The most effective way to address these worries is to assist your child in getting prepared. For example, try setting a study or training schedule if he has an upcoming test or event, and talking through the most worrying situations so he can air his concerns.

While you are helping with these practicalities, make sure he knows you will be proud if he does well, but that the most important thing to you is the effort he puts in, not whether he wins or loses.

Boys and girls at play

At age eight, girls are likely to be loyal to one or two best friends and spend time in smaller groups of children at playtime. Boys at this age tend to hang out with larger groups of friends and play in teams and competitions. They usually have more boisterous fun than the girls, who may be a little less high-spirited in their activities.

Your eight-year-old is more likely than ever to play primarily with children of the same gender; more than three-quarters of play at this age is boys with boys and girls with girls. Between the ages of 8 and 10, girls' games are less competitive than boys' games and involve more turn-taking.

GIRL TALK *Girls tend to stick together and, although they may have an aversion to the boys at school, they might talk and giggle about them.*

Criticism and self-belief

Your eight-year-old is highly conscious of success and failure and may be discouraged easily, or have his pride hurt, if he feels he has been unsuccessful. Many of his worries may seem minor, but to him they are immediate and distressing.

To help your child:

▶ When you listen well, react calmly, and take the issue seriously, your eight-year-old will respond by calming down, too. If you dismiss the problem, he is less likely to open up to you in the future. Keeping worries to himself may exacerbate the problem.

▶ Be realistic in building up your child's self-belief. Talk with your eight-year-old about what interests him, his strong points and talents, as well as identifying areas where he struggles. Work out a plan to tackle topics in which he is less confident. Tutoring or extra practice might help.

▶ Avoid falsely complimenting your eight-year-old to try to make him feel better. Stick to praising what he does well and the effort he puts in, and reassure him that he can't excel at everything.

Dealing with shyness

Your eight-year-old may be shy because he is naturally quiet, lacks confidence, or is copying you in his dislike of social situations.

To help a shy child:

▶ Try bringing him in more frequent contact with others. Seek out clubs or teams that appeal to your child, where he can meet others who share the same interests. This works well if there is a cooperative or teamwork element—for example in scouting, sports, or drama.

▶ Work on his self-confidence by praising his social successes. When he realizes his fears are unfounded, he will be more willing to try new things.

▶ Being alone for long periods will reinforce his anxiety about being with people, so limit the time he spends on solitary activities such as watching TV in his room or playing on the computer.

▶ After school and in the evening, gently prompt him to play with friends or family and spend time with others.

▶ Seek help from a health professional if your eight-year-old's shyness seems to be increasing, or if it is affecting his ability to go about daily life.

"Always take your child's concerns seriously—they are real to him—and don't tell him he is being 'silly.'"

Common concerns

▶ **I think my son is being bullied at school. What should I do?**
Ask your child what is happening so that you are clear about the situation. Let him know you are contacting the school to address the problem. Schools have a legal duty to protect your child, and should have a written policy on bullying. Work with the school staff to investigate and take action. As part of their anti-bullying policy, the school should have an action plan to address bullying; make sure you are aware of this and how it is being applied with your child and the bullies involved.

High-risk times for bullying are recess periods and traveling to and from school, so make sure there is additional adult supervision at these key points. You can help by encouraging your son to respond assertively. For example, practice loudly saying "Stop, don't do that. I'm going to tell an adult." Do not advise your child to hit back, as this can escalate the problem.

Unfortunately, some children are targeted—for example, those who are shy, lacking in confidence, or have difficulty making friends. If this is the case for your son, build his self-esteem and support him in making new friends.

▶ **My daughter seems so worried all the time. How can I help her?**
Some children worry a lot, perhaps taking after their parents, though a few children can be worriers even if their parents are happy-go-lucky. Try to find out what your child is concerned about. It may be something imminent, such as a test, or something less likely but still possible, like the threat of war. Children can get very involved in what they see on the news. Talking through possible courses of action and outcomes can reduce anxiety.

Make sure your daughter knows that you're there for her, no matter what happens. It's not always possible to allay all of a child's fears, and despite your reassurances, sometimes she may lie awake worrying. Sometimes a silly rhyme brings light relief and reminds a child what to do—for instance: "I take off my cares when I take off my clothes. Then I lie on my back, so I don't bump my nose."

▶ **I caught my child cheating when he was playing a game with another child. Is this normal?**
At age eight, your child's moral development is such that he'll decide whether or not to break rules, depending on whether he thinks he will be caught, punished, or disapproved of. He's got winning on his mind at age eight, and may be tempted to cheat to finish ahead on a game or get the advantage over a competitor. Common tricks include moving pieces of a board game or giving the dice an extra roll when no one is looking. To encourage fairness, talk about your values. Emphasize that doing well has to be based on effort, and that any achievements attained through deceit are worthless.

Any time you're sure your eight-year-old has taken an unfair advantage, pull him aside and let him know that you disapprove. If you are unsure, then avoid interrogating him about it and tell him that if he has cheated, he should own up. Just raising the issue makes cheating less likely to happen in the future.

▶ **My son is very conscious of being shorter than his classmates. What can I do to help him improve his body image?**
Children can become body-conscious at a very young age. Boys are also quite competitive by nature, so your son is bound to compare himself to his friends. Explain to your child that real people come in all shapes and sizes. The ideal physique to which he aspires may not be realistic, so don't tell him he will be tall one day, because it may not be true. Instead, find successful role models, such as actors and sports stars, who are short, and tell your child about them. Most important of all, help your child feel valued for all the good qualities he does have, and reaffirm those qualities as much as you can.

Your child's life

Friends are increasingly important to your child now, and school is likely to be the center of his social life, as well as a place of education. He will want to socialize with his friends outside of school, too. The ups and downs of friendships, plus lots of other distractions, can sometimes affect learning.

Relationships with friends

Your eight-year-old may argue with his friends over trivial conflicts such as mild negative comments. However, it is often the case that, by the next day, all will be forgotten. Your best strategy, if your eight-year-old does come home feeling rejected, is to be consoling and supportive, but wait to see what happens before you go into overdrive to help him make new friends. However, be aware that sometimes disagreements between friends can be more serious. Where a group of children hang out together, one child may be left out or bullied in some way. It is normal for one or two children to dominate in a group. If your child is being repeatedly left out, physically or verbally attacked either by individuals or gangs, and feels hurt and distressed, then this should be treated as bullying and action must be taken as soon as possible (see left).

BEING INCLUDED
At the age of eight, many children are eager to be popular and join a group to get that feeling of belonging.

Struggling academically

There are a host of reasons why your eight-year-old might be struggling with schoolwork at this age. Perhaps he has missed vital lessons through illness, the work is too difficult, or he has been experiencing specific problems such as dyslexia (see page 121). For some children, bullying, depression, or prolonged sadness (see page 216) can get in the way of learning, too. Take action to help your child if you notice a negative reaction to school such as resistance to homework, rushing schoolwork to get it over with, or reports from teachers about unhappiness, lack of concentration, or disruption of others.

To help your child:

▶ Get your child's point of view about why he is not achieving at school; he may be able to explain the problem.

▶ Next, make an appointment with his teacher and enlist his or her help to improve the situation. Perhaps changes such as adjusting the level of the work, tackling bullying, or some extra support for homework could boost your eight-year-old's enjoyment of learning.

▶ Once these solutions are in place, keep checking that things are improving. If there is little difference, then ask school staff how your eight-year-old can be assessed for specific learning issues.

The benefits and dangers of the Internet

The Internet provides a wonderful resource for your eight-year-old, and he will use it for homework, computer games, and contacting friends. But this use comes with some potential safety issues including cyber-bullying, access to adult sites, or contact by adults who intend to harm. For greater safety, it helps if you have a working knowledge of the Internet, are able to set parental controls, and know how to check the search history. You need to be able to supervise your child, so locate the computer in a busy family room, rather than a bedroom.

Chat rooms and instant messaging mean your eight-year-old can be in touch with friends, but may also be vulnerable to people who might cause harm. Supervise this sort of computer use closely and explain clearly that people stop feeling like strangers if your child has been chatting to them for a long time, but they may not be presenting themselves honestly. Set a rule that you must be told immediately if your eight-year-old is asked for personal details or a face-to-face meeting by someone you don't know.

"Protect your child from the dangers of the Internet by supervising use and becoming computer literate yourself."

Allowances

You may feel that your child is too young for an allowance, but it is worth considering. It can help your child make choices, work out how to save up for things he wants, and even help him with his math. Even a small amount will make your child feel trusted and is an important step toward independence. The most important issue for your eight-year-old will be how much he gets. The amount needs to be affordable for you and could be a set amount each week. You will also need to decide where your child keeps his money. If he is saving up, then a bank account might be a good choice. If the money is kept at home, then help him pick a safe place.

You may want to lay down rules—for example, limiting the amount of candy that can be purchased, or insisting that some money is saved. Whatever your view, make this clear to your eight-year-old so he knows where he stands. Sometimes withholding the allowance is used as a way to manage misbehavior. If you do this, avoid confiscating all of the money; this can feel the same as someone taking away your whole paycheck.

Common concerns

▶ **My daughter often makes excuses for staying home from school. What should I do?**
Refusing to go to school is your child's way of telling you she is afraid, and it may be expressed as mild physical symptoms such as stomachaches (see page 81). Common causes include not wanting to be separated from a parent, concerns about bullying (see page 172), struggling with work, or fearing a test.

To resolve these fears, work together with the school staff to ensure that your child is safe from victimization. Solve test and learning issues through extra support, including a teaching plan tailored for your child. It is a priority to return your child to school as soon as possible, as anxieties will become worse the longer she is away. A small number of children are school-phobic. This is a strong reaction, including deep anxieties and physical reactions. If you are worried that your child has a school phobia, seek professional assistance.

▶ **My husband and I are separating. How can I explain this to my son?**
There is no easy way to tell your son that you are separating. Simply be straightforward and tell him clearly what is planned and when things will happen.

Give your child plenty of opportunities to ask questions and express emotions. Explain clearly that the separation is not his fault. He may be worrying about this without daring to ask you. During and after the separation, keep the rest of his life as unchanged as possible—for example, remaining in the same area, the same school, and attending clubs as usual.

You too will be dealing with strong emotions. Although it's hard, try not to involve your son in these, and encourage him to keep mementoes of the other parent. This bridges the gap between visits and can be reassuring. Even when the separation is mutual, children can feel divided loyalties. Minimize this by communicating directly with your partner, and avoid giving your son messages to carry between the two of you.

REAL-LIFE QUESTIONS

9–11 years

"She will be curious about the world and begin to think and act more independently. The greatest challenge will be finding a balance between her need for family and her desire for freedom."

DOING SPORTS *Your child should have access to sports through school. Encourage him to join clubs and teams that will keep him active.*

Getting the basics right

The preteen years mark a period of intense growth and development in advance of puberty and adolescence, and you may be surprised to discover that your child suddenly requires more food and much more sleep. As always, it will be up to you to ensure that all his basic needs are met.

Good nutrition

Physical growth occurs more rapidly during this period than at any time since infancy, and this development requires fuel. Your preteen is likely to experience the first surge of the adolescent growth spurt at this age, and it is normal for children to gain weight and shoot up in height. For this reason, caloric needs are high, and your child requires good-quality, regular meals, representing all the food groups (see page 17), at least three times a day—with plenty of healthy snacks in between.

If your child is active, don't be alarmed by a sudden surge in appetite; as long as he is eating properly, with plenty of fruit and vegetables, and a low intake of fatty or sugary junk foods, his weight will remain stable. Preteens need plenty of:

Foods from every food group—this will ensure that your child gets all the nutrients he needs. For the most part, nutrients aren't shared between the groups; one group will be high in one nutrient, and another in something else. For example, dairy foods are higher in calcium than any other group, and fruits and vegetables are higher in vitamin C.

A good-quality vitamin and mineral supplement—at this age children are often picky eaters, and will snack incessantly rather than eat proper meals. Their food choices are often affected by peers. If you have a daughter, choose a supplement for women, containing extra calcium and iron.

Plenty of calcium—40–45 percent of an adult's skeleton is built during the preteen and early teen years. Your preteen should be getting 1,200 milligrams of calcium each day, which is equal to four glasses of milk, or the equivalent. Substitute yogurt, cheese, soy, or calcium-fortified juices and cereals if your child doesn't like to drink milk.

Protein—this is essential for growth and development on all levels, so make sure your preteen eats a healthy mix of animal and vegetable proteins (see page 137).

Iron—this is important, not only for girls starting menstruation (see page 186), but also because both boys and girls require more iron due to the expanding blood volume associated with growth. Leafy greens, dried fruits and vegetables, and lean meats are good sources.

Folate—preteen girls are more likely than boys to be anemic because of menstruation. This causes them to be deficient in folate, a B vitamin needed for cell division. Folate levels are high in dark green leafy vegetables, seeds, beans, and orange juice.

Many preteens, especially girls, begin to entertain the idea of dieting, which can compromise their nutrient intake. Keep a close eye on this. While you can't force a child to eat healthily, and may only encourage rebellious behavior by doing so, you can fill the house with healthy food only, which limits choice. Preteen hormonal swings may begin around this time, and you can help keep your child's moods a little more even by reducing sugary, additive-filled foods.

Healthy sleep

Most preteens will be adamant that they should stay up later than before; however, research confirms that 9–10 hours per night is necessary for optimum health, growth, and development. Computers, televisions, and video games should be turned off at least an hour before bedtime, and ideally should be kept out of the bedroom altogether. Try to make your child's room a sanctuary that is conducive to relaxation and sleep. If he has loud music playing constantly, homework and clothing strewn everywhere, and his computer on all the time, it is unlikely to encourage relaxation and healthy sleep patterns. Encourage him to clean up his room at the end of every day, although, admittedly, this is easier said than done!

Exercise and leisure

Once again, an hour of exercise each day is ideal. As your child becomes more independent, he may have clear ideas about how he wants to spend his leisure time, and that may mean he favors hanging around shopping

WELL RESTED *There is a direct link between sleep and growth. If your child is not getting adequate rest, it will adversely affect her well-being.*

malls with friends rather than enjoying active pursuits. The best way to work this out with your child is to add up the hours of exercise he gets at school and from hobbies, how much walking he does, and then strike a balance. Allow occasional "hanging out," as long as he also exercises.

Changing schools

This period also marks one of transition for many children—changing schools, making new friends, and taking up new interests and hobbies. Studies show that the transition from elementary school to middle school is one of the most stressful events of a child's life. Some children go to schools in different neighborhoods, often traveling by bus, and many find themselves without their childhood friends.

The best thing you can do is to be supportive, and listen to your child's concerns. The more you talk and plan, the easier this transition will be for your child and for you. Be reassured that he will probably be settled in within a couple of weeks.

"When your child is going through changes, keep talking, and if he has concerns, look for solutions together. If he gets your support and understanding, he is more likely to turn to you when the going gets tough."

To help your child adjust to a new school:

▶ If possible, involve him in after-school and summer break activities where he will meet a different set of friends altogether, giving him more continuity when the change occurs.

▶ Make sure he is prepared for the first day at his new school, with the appropriate clothing and equipment, and that he understands that the workload will probably increase.

▶ Work out strategies for meeting new people, and for dealing with the "unknown" (such as finding his locker in an unfamiliar building), and look for ways to get your child involved in the new school (through sports, music, or drama, for example) as this will make integration easier.

Your 9-year-old

"Although friends are important, your child will need quiet time doing activities alone."

BOISTEROUS PLAY Boys can be loud and unruly in their play at this age, but it is usually harmless fun.

CONFIDING IN YOU She may have some secrets now, but if you have a good relationship, she'll tell you if she's worried about something.

GREAT PALS She will be happy to spend time with close friends and look forward to seeing them at school each day.

Growth and development

Your child is growing up, and she may begin to be more curious about her body and sexuality, especially as she develops a growing awareness of the opposite sex. Some girls may be going through puberty and will need to be prepared for the many changes that will take place.

Sex education

All humans, whatever age, are sexual beings. It is just as important to enhance your child's sexual growth as it is to enhance her physical, emotional, and cognitive growth. As a parent, you have a responsibility to help your child understand and accept evolving sexuality.

At this age, children tend to prefer to socialize with their own gender almost exclusively and maintain a fairly rigid separation between males and females. Your child will now have a strong sense of self. She will already be aware of the social stigmas and taboos surrounding sexuality, and if you, as her parent, are nervous about the subject, she will be less open about asking questions. There are lots of books available to help if you need a refresher course in biology, and you can use them to supplement what you tell your child.

Many children will have a fairly good idea of where babies come from by this age and may ask their friends about intercourse, particularly if parents have not been forthcoming with information. They may engage in same-gender sexual exploration. Parents are often unsure about how much to tell their children and when; sex is a subject which leaves many parents strongly divided, with some preferring total honesty about topics such as sexual preferences and abortion, while others prefer to "protect" their children from the adult world for as long as possible. As parents, you need to agree on your approach, and it is preferable to answer all your child's questions honestly. Explain that there are different types of families and all have equal value. Acknowledge that while most people will have romantic feelings for people of the opposite gender, it is normal for some to have feelings for members of the same gender.

WEARING MAKEUP
A girl may show an interest in wearing cosmetics, but should be made aware of her natural beauty.

"Becoming a woman is an exciting time. When talking to your daughter, try to be matter-of-fact, informative, and positive."

Being prepared for menstruation

You might think that your child's ninth birthday is a tad too soon to worry about periods, but anything between the ages of 10–16 is a normal time for menarche (the onset of periods), and some girls begin menstruation before this. So it is not too soon to start discussing it.

It can be difficult for a girl if she is unprepared for her period to start, and so it is important that your daughter knows what is to come and is neither shocked nor embarrassed when it happens. Many schools will run a program to talk to children about changes in puberty, but as parents you shouldn't rely on this alone. You should at least be prepared to back up the school's session by answering questions when your daughter comes home. It can be difficult for parents of either sex to open the conversation, but saying something like "Do you know about periods?" is a suitably bland starting point. You may need to give your daughter information in digestible chunks over a period of time.

Remember to deal with all of the following:

❭ Sanitary protection (see right).
❭ How to cope with stains and accidents.
❭ The erratic nature of periods when they first start.
❭ Pain relief (see page 228) if necessary.
❭ Other possible symptoms, such as pain and irritability before a period.

Stages of puberty in girls

The process of puberty tends to happen in the following order in girls:

★ The appearance of tiny breast buds, which in the following four years develop into the typical adult-shaped breast. This process may happen more quickly (over as little as 1.5 years) or be drawn out as long as nine years.

★ Soon after the breast buds appear (and sometimes before they appear), the first sparse pubic hairs are seen. Over the next 2–5 years, pubic hair grows steadily until it reaches adult distribution.

★ Underarm hair usually appears later, at an average of 12 years old, and takes about 1.5 years to become adultlike in amount.

★ There will also be less attractive aspects of puberty, such as body odor and acne (see page 274).

These changes are triggered by a surge in estrogen, which also causes an increase in growth. A girl who has until now been growing at 1½–2½ in (4–6 cm) per year will shoot up at a rate of 4–5 in (10–12 cm) per year for 2–3 years.

A tendency for early menarche and early puberty (see page 135) can run in families, so if your periods began before you were 11, your daughter may well start hers around this age too. On average, periods start two years or so after the breasts start developing, but not invariably. Poverty and poor nutrition are thought to delay first periods in some girls.

Sanitary protection

Tampons are less conspicuous than sanitary pads, and can enable a girl to stay more active, which is useful for sports. Girls can use tampons from an early age, but they may find it difficult to insert them at first. You should stress the importance of changing a tampon frequently to prevent infection and the rare, but potentially fatal, complication called toxic shock syndrome. At this age, sanitary pads may be easier, but do make your daughter aware of tampons, as she might like to try them, at least for days when she expects to be more active.

Your daughter needs sanitary pads that are absorbent enough to cope with an unexpectedly heavy flow, yet slim enough for her young frame. Forget what you once used: nowadays there is a wide range of pads and panty liners available. You can choose two or three products together, and your daughter can decide what she likes best.

Teach your daughter how to dispose of used sanitary pads. Also ensure that she has a wrapped pad in her school bag and a change of underwear handy in case she gets caught out by an unscheduled period.

Staying in shape

Your child will become better at jumping, throwing, and running. With an increasing need to get children into good exercise habits that will last a lifetime, one option is to take your child to a gym that runs programs for children. It is important that the child is initially assessed by a professional coach and shown how to use each piece of suitable equipment. She should have a program geared to her age and level of fitness, and should be discouraged from using any apparatus that places too much stress on joints or muscles. Children as young as nine should be aiming to improve their cardiovascular fitness, not to develop big muscles, and there should always be an emphasis on having fun.

PLAYING SPORTS
Your child is more likely to stay in shape if she finds a sport she enjoys. Make sure she tries a few different activities.

KEEPING CLEAN *Your child should be capable of showering and bathing at this age, but for safety the bathroom door should remain unlocked.*

Your child's health

Whether or not your child is prepubescent, it is worth instilling some good personal hygiene habits at this age. Puberty may also bring extraordinary levels of clumsiness and accidents as children get used to their new body shape and strength.

Personal hygiene

Your nine-year-old should be able to keep herself clean, but children vary in how conscientious they are about bathing, washing their hair, and brushing their teeth. As your child approaches puberty, hygiene is very important, as her skin may become greasier and she will sweat more.

You could encourage good hygiene by:

▶ Providing clean towels.

▶ Letting your child choose shower gel and shampoo that she likes.

▶ Suggesting she choose a deodorant with you (there are many that are mild, and that appeal to younger users).

▶ Getting her an electric toothbrush.

Being accident-prone

As your child's body changes shape, becoming more muscular, she will develop greater performance in sports that require muscle power. Each new piece of equipment—such as roller blades or skateboards—comes with its own risks. Injuries happen far more frequently during vacations than when school is in session, probably because schools are safety-conscious and because many children are more active during vacations.

Reasons to seek medical attention:

▶ An injury that may need stitching. Some cuts can be dealt with quite quickly and painlessly, with glue rather than stitches, and it is best to seek medical help as soon as possible.

▶ A possible fracture (broken bone).

▶ A burn. Immerse the burn in cold water for at least 10 minutes before going to your nearest emergency department.

▶ An injury where there is a chance that a piece of glass or metal or a small stone has been left in the wound; an X-ray may be needed to check this.
▶ A head injury that has caused loss of consciousness, several bouts of vomiting or drowsiness, or any other neurological changes.

Technology and your child's health

Technology makes a child more sedentary, and even modest levels of use can affect your child's fitness and increase her risk of obesity (see page 112), especially since many children snack while viewing TV. The average child watches about three hours of TV a day, but research from the British medical journal *The Lancet* suggests that children who watch even two hours a day are more likely to become young adults that smoke, are overweight, and have high cholesterol levels.

There is also the possibility that watching violent programs may increase violent behavior. While that has not been proven, it is fair to say that watching violent programs and playing violent games are activities that are unlikely to benefit your child much.

To reduce the amount of TV watching:
▶ Plan plenty of activities for you and your child.
▶ Don't interrupt physical activities to watch TV. Instead, record a program to view later—your child may not even bother watching it.
▶ Reduce the time spent in front of the TV by making a habit of watching programs together.

> "At some point your child is bound to need a trip to the hospital for an X-ray or some stitches."

Ready for orthodontics

Up to 70 percent of all children may need some sort of orthodontic treatment at some point. This can be to straighten crooked teeth, or to treat overbite or underbite, where there is a problem in how the upper and lower teeth fit together, affecting biting or chewing.

Orthodontic treatment works best and is least painful between the ages of 8 and 14. At age eight or nine, the jaw is growing fast, and it is a time when some children will need orthodontic treatment to expand the jaw and reshape the mouth. However, there are still a number of permanent teeth to come through (see page 160), so these children may need braces both at nine and then again at 12–14 when the permanent teeth are in. Other children will only need braces once the permanent teeth have come through.

Understanding and skills

While she is still very much a child, you will find that your nine-year-old has a substantial intellect. She may be good at categorizing things, and able to use reference books with increasing skill. She is likely to use the Internet at least as fast, if not faster, than you can.

Sophisticated thinking

At nine, your child has a growing capacity for abstract thought, and she may become intrigued by concepts, such as life, death, and spirituality. Or she may want to know how the universe began, what the largest number is, or why there are so many different countries. She may be concerned about such things as justice and fairness, and have high standards of right and wrong. She will understand that rules exist, and knows that it is important to follow them. Around now, some children become fascinated by the police, the government, and even politics. Although your child will be inquisitive, you may not always have the answers to her questions, but you can have an open discussion.

DEBATING ISSUES
When discussing something with your child, don't be afraid to give your opinion, but be ready to listen and value what he has to say, too.

You might, for instance, explain to your child that different nations arose because of things that happened long ago, and talk about how the world began. Your own background and faith will obviously affect your answers. Whenever possible, try to give some answer other than "just because." The way in which you answer can impact greatly on your child's approach to problem-solving (see page 144).

Doing projects

Your child may become immersed in a hobby or project now that she is more able to follow complex step-by-step instructions, and is less distracted by diversions and interruptions. This often depends on a child's personality: many nine-year-olds are perfectionists, while others are more casual in their approach and may be engrossed in a project, then suddenly drop it for something more interesting. Around this age, many children leave several unfinished projects in their wake.

Speech and public performance

Many nine-year-olds write fluently, and speak confidently to their family, but freeze when required to "perform," even if it is just a "show and tell" session in the classroom. Confident speech is an important element of language development; throughout their lives, children are called on to "think on their feet," improvise, debate, negotiate, put views across, and exhibit knowledge.

Confident self-expression is not only the key to successful communication, but will also encourage your child to seek out words to clarify thoughts, which expands vocabulary and develops cognition.

To help your child:

❯ Encourage her to join a local drama group or sign up for the school play.

❯ Express your belief in her ability to perform and to speak publicly, and encourage her to hold plays or recitals for family members.

Dealing with dishonesty

Some children lie more than others, but you can be sure that your nine-year-old will lie at least occasionally. She may be lying deliberately, or she may simply be exaggerating for effect, but either way, she is likely to be aware that she is not telling the truth.

There may be other occasions when your child takes something that doesn't belong to her, like a few coins that were lying on the table. She may think there is nothing wrong with this, but needs to understand that it is improper.

Owning up

It is important to make it easy for your child to own up. As with any other misdemeanors, immunity from punishment usually provides an excellent incentive to confess.

When your child admits her dishonesty, you can explain why what she did or said was wrong. Usually, putting herself in the other person's shoes is enough to show her the right way next time. If your child finds it hard to admit to lying or stealing, you could try asking, "Were you crossing your fingers just then?" or perhaps "Was it a teeny-tiny lie?" Naturally, you need to be a good role model for your child, which means avoiding blatant (and not-so-blatant) dishonesty.

"Drama helps shy children learn to let go of fear, open up, and feel more positive, while outgoing children find an outlet for creativity and energy."

▶ Ask her to read aloud to you regularly.
▶ Always praise her efforts, and help as much as you can with her diction and delivery.

Language and literacy

Nine-year-olds tend to have established some favorite routines and leisure activities, and in many children, reading becomes a great interest. Not only will your child be able to choose and read a huge number of books independently, but she will develop preferences for authors and genres.

Give your child opportunities to visit the library or bookstore, and take advantage of this crucial stage to develop a lifelong interest in reading, and also to improve her language and literacy. Your nine-year-old may also show interest in project or "how-to" books, which will encourage her cognitive development further.

Your child will have a growing vocabulary, and feel confident using more complex sentences. You may find that she adopts the speech patterns of parents and teachers, particularly if she is passing on important

Considering private tutoring

Some children struggle with certain academic subjects, sometimes because they missed the teaching of the foundations, or because they suffer from learning problems.

Dyslexia (see page 121) is a relatively well-known condition, but there is also the less well-known dyscalculia, in which there

is a difficulty with numbers, and dysgraphia, in which there are problems with writing. Some children with learning difficulties respond to extra tutoring, to help them learn the basics in a less stressful environment. Other children just need a little guided practice to improve.

Pressure to learn
Don't be tempted to tutor a child to get her up to a higher ranking or to take an entrance test for a new school, unless she is border-line. If she is struggling, she will lose confidence in her own ability, and you may have to continue tutoring to keep up a standard.

information; you will also find that she will most definitely employ careless enunciation as her grasp of the language becomes firmer. Grammar and spelling will improve naturally through schoolwork, but don't be surprised or concerned if it slips.

Helping a reluctant reader

Not all nine-year-olds are natural readers, but don't despair. Some children just need nudging. Look out for books or comics that reflect your child's interests—these might be biographies of pop singers, historical memoirs, humorous books, even comics. It only takes one or two good books for a child to develop even a grudging interest, and you can build on that.

But don't push too hard. If your child genuinely shows no interest, leave some books around, read to her when you can, even if it is just snippets from a book of funny stories. Purchase audio CDs or tapes to play while you are driving in the car, for example, or take her to the bookstore and let her browse. Unfortunately, many children of this age are discouraged by school curriculum reading and have no idea there is such a wealth of interesting books out there.

FACT FINDING *In his thirst for knowledge, your nine-year-old may be drawn to factual books on subjects that are of particular interest to him.*

Dealing with swearing

Nine-year-olds often begin to use colorful language in an attempt to shock, but most of the time they are just repeating what they hear at school, on the street, and on TV. Don't overreact, as this simply gives your child something to bait you up, and also "cements" it in her brain when it might otherwise be quickly forgotten!

Make it clear that you expect her to show respect, and that swearing is disrespectful. Some families penalize children with a "swear jar," making them hand over some of their precious allowance money for every slip-up. Always model the speech you want. If you swear yourself, you can't berate your child for doing the same.

Emotions and personality

Your child's advancing social skills will make her good company, although you will probably find yourself competing with her friends and favorite activities for attention. How you handle your child's behavior at this stage will depend very much on how well you communicate with each other.

Firm friendships

DON'T TELL! *Keeping secrets can cement your child's friendships. It reflects her awareness that she can hide thoughts from others, and shows her loyalty.*

Having a best friend or group of good friends is very important to your nine-year-old, as the ideals and approval of peers are a strong influence on her. Your child will form friendships based on common interests and shared values. For example, she is more likely to be friends with someone who has similar attitudes about whether it is acceptable to cheat. By the age of nine, your child will be more aware of a range of complex feelings in others and be able to suppress her own opinions in order to be polite. For

example, she can wait as you speak with other adults without complaining of being bored, realizing that negative comments may be hurtful.

Being secretive

By the age of nine, your child will enjoy the sense of power she gets from knowing a secret. While it is healthy for your nine-year-old to be able to keep some secrets, there are others that should always be told. Help your child understand the difference between good and bad secrets: a good secret might be that Mom is organizing a surprise party for Dad. This is an acceptable secret because it is positive and the surprise makes it fun. Your child should be taught never to keep secrets that could harm herself or others; these should always be told to a trusted adult. Point out to your nine-year-old that, if she is threatened with harm for telling, then it is even more important to let an adult know. When you teach this lesson, think about how you react to hearing secrets. For example, if you ask your child to let you know if she has been hurt but then criticize her for tattling, you aren't being consistent and future secrets may not be shared.

Screen time

Using a computer and electronic games is fun for your nine-year-old and allows her to play with friends and meet challenges. However, these games can be a source of conflict when it is time to turn off or share, and they can become compelling. Watching TV and DVDs can also become a favorite activity at this age and needs monitoring to make sure the content is appropriate for your child's age.

To help your child:

❯ If children are sharing electronic and computer games, use a timer for each turn to avoid squabbles.

❯ It is wise not to permit game-playing before school, since fast-paced games don't help your child prepare for the slower speed of classroom learning and she is more likely to become bored in class.

❯ Turn off electronic games 1–2 hours before bed so that your child has a chance to wind down.

❯ It is advisable to limit screen time to a maximum of two hours per day, including time for TV, DVDs, and electronic games. This gives your nine-year-old time for other leisure activities.

SETTING LIMITS
Electronic games are designed to be compelling, making them hard to switch off. That's why your child needs limits set by you.

Communicating with your child

Healthy communication with your nine-year-old starts with listening, which isn't always easy when you have so much to do. But each day, try to make some time to give her your full attention. This way you will be aware of issues in her life and be better able to understand her perspective.

Communication works best when you sit down with your child, make eye contact, and look attentive rather than distracted, worried, or angry. Avoid bossiness; your nine-year-old is ready to work things out with you rather than be told what to do. She will also appreciate it when her views are taken into account, even if the outcome is that she still cannot have things her way.

"Be sure your nine-year-old explores a range of interests, so that if one is unsuccessful, she has others to pursue."

Encouraging resilience

The basis for your nine-year-old's resilience is probably already in place and includes a close bond with you, good self-esteem, and an awareness of her strong and weak points. A threat to her resilience at this age might be focusing too heavily on one or two talents at the expense of weaker areas. When there is reliance on just one or two skills, there is little to fall back on if difficulties arise. For example, if your child has focused on a key talent such as basketball, and then cannot continue playing, she may lack other avenues to gain that sense of accomplishment. Your attitude helps as well. If you concentrate on enjoyment and effort rather than winning or losing, then your child will adopt that mind-set, too.

Teaching positive thinking

Looking on the bright side of life is a habit your child can learn. It is an attitude that will enable her to seek an upside in difficult situations. Thinking this way contributes to your child's resilience by giving her an optimistic outlook. The best way to teach positive thinking is to practice it yourself and bring it to her attention. For example, if the car won't start, a pessimist might say, "This always happens when we're in a rush," but an optimist might say, "I'm glad it didn't stall somewhere dangerous." When you ask your child to identify positive aspects of difficulties, this can become ingrained in her. There are some serious situations, such as illnesses, when optimism isn't appropriate, but in general, positivity helps you and your child hold a more pleasing view of life.

Solitary activities

While your sociable nine-year-old will probably be busy with friends most of the time, the chance to relax by herself will be a welcome change and should be encouraged. Being able to occupy herself alone, without complaining that she is "bored," is a helpful skill for your nine-year-old; it increases her self-sufficiency and reduces reliance on you.

Promote solitary play by ensuring that she has somewhere she can play or think without interruption, and encourage her to turn off distractions, such as music and the TV. She may want to simply read or pursue a hobby, such as painting, so make sure she has the materials she needs to go ahead with it independently.

Common behavioral concerns

▶ **My nine-year-old son has become so rebellious lately. How can I tackle this?**

Defiant behavior becomes more difficult to deal with as your child grows up, if only because it gets harder to send a child to his room, or institute time-out and other simple punishments. Try to be firm with your child, but do not get angry or shout. If necessary, count to 10 to calm yourself.

It should go without saying that spanking is unproductive as well as potentially harmful. Research shows that, contrary to what some older generations may believe, children learn nothing positive from physical chastisement.

Do, however, tailor the punishment to the crime. For bad behavior, you could consider restricting the use of something that your son really likes, such as his computer. Always make sure your child knows what's expected of him, and preferably why. He is old enough to understand now, so avoid giving "just because" reasons. Remember to praise good behavior, and always listen to your child when he talks to you.

Finally, reassure yourself that you can't totally eliminate conflict or misdemeanors from the family home. It's within the home that children learn the way to behave, and they also learn a lot from disagreements and the way in which you handle them.

▶ **My daughter is quite sensitive. How can I help her?**

Whether it's receiving a criticism of schoolwork or being called unkind names, your sensitive nine-year-old will take it to heart and turn to you for reassurance. Offer the comfort of a hug, then listen, and show you understand her feelings—for example, by saying, "You look very upset. It sounds like your friends were pretty rude."

Build your child's emotional vocabulary by helping her label each feeling. For example, while there may be sadness at being left out, there could also be hurt pride. Labeling feelings helps your nine-

BEING UNDERSTANDING *It's unrealistic to expect your child to be happy all the time. Accept that, just like you, she will have down times, and find ways to help her express her emotions.*

year-old understand that many emotions can be triggered by one event. Her ability to name and express her emotions means she is less likely to act them out in spiteful actions.

Try not to talk your child out of feeling sad; this dismisses her emotions and means you have no opportunity to teach her how to express herself.

▶ **I hear my nine-year-old daughter and her friends constantly talking about others, often maliciously, and I'm worried she does this at school too. What should I do?**

Gossiping is pretty common among nine-year-olds—more often girls, but boys gossip too. You could point out to your daughter that the classroom is not the right place for it (as she should be paying attention to the lesson). You can also explain that those who gossip often end up being the target of not very nice talk themselves.

Of course, you should try setting a good example yourself—avoid gossiping about your new neighbor or a friend's bad haircut, at least in front of your child.

Remember, you can't entirely stop children from gossiping and, while it can waste a lot of time, if it's not malicious, it does have some value. It means that at least your child is communicating and forming opinions!

Your child's life

Most nine-year-olds are well established in full-time schooling, and becoming more confident of their abilities as their cognitive development increases. Their interests become wider and more varied, and they may begin to be competitive and genuinely interested in doing their best.

DOING HOMEWORK
It can help to give your child a set time to do his homework. Don't interfere, but stay nearby in case he needs your help.

While some competition among peers is healthy, some children become obsessed with being the "best," which can affect their social life and lead to anxiety. Not all children are academically proficient; some have skills in other areas. We all want our children to master the important elements of academic life: being numerate, literate, and able to express themselves, with an understanding of the world around them. Some children find this easy, and thrive in an academic environment; others struggle and need constant encouragement from home to meet requirements.

Be realistic about your child. If she is bright and achieving all grade As, then celebrate. If she is bright and bringing home Cs, then work together to get things on track. If your nine-year-old struggles, yet manages a reasonable pass on her spelling test, that is cause for celebration, too. Everything that shows effort is an academic achievement.

Encouraging healthy study skills

Most nine-year-olds have a small amount of homework. Reinforcing skills learned during the day, such as math, languages, or reading, are often given as homework, as well as projects. No matter how little homework your child is given, it is advisable to set up a firm homework routine, as good habits are easily established at this age, and they will serve your child well in the years to come.

To help your child to study:

▶ Break the sessions into 15-minute slots (the average attention span of a nine-year-old) with a five-minute break in between, and a reward when the job is done—perhaps half an hour of watching TV.

▶ By all means, help your child if she needs it, and help with quizzing before a test if she thinks it would be useful, but otherwise, leave her to it.

Practice makes perfect

Your child may be doing extracurricular activities that require regular practice, such as learning a musical instrument. She may be reluctant to spend her hard-earned spare time with more "work," so make this practice a part of a regular routine, and keep it short—20 minutes is plenty for a nine-year-old. If it is an extracurricular activity, your child may be adamant that she doesn't "have" to do it, so it can help to use a star chart with a reward for regular practice. Sometimes it can help to stand back and let her be. It only takes one poor performance in front of people for many children to realize that practice might be important after all.

Types of parenting

There is no single best parenting method; you will make your choice about the way you express love toward and discipline your nine-year-old. But certain parenting styles are more effective than others. For example, a

ENJOYING HOBBIES
Playing the recorder is a good introduction to learning music. A child can then move on to more complex instruments.

Signs of bullying

Children don't always admit they're being bullied, but there are some telltale signs to watch for:

★ Returning from school with unexplained injuries.

★ Coming home with missing or damaged clothing or equipment.

★ Having lunch money stolen, or returning home hungry.

★ Reluctance to go to school (see page 175), or playing truant.

★ Vomiting in the mornings on school days.

★ Doing less well in class.

★ Mood swings.

★ Poor sleep.

If you suspect your child is being bullied, then she probably is.

Many children receive some abuse during their school lives, and the bullying can be verbal, physical, or by email/text message. Try to talk to your child, and also make a point of talking to the school as well. Schools have a duty to keep your child safe, and an obligation to have a policy on bullying.

warm, assertive style provides your nine-year-old with affection, clear boundaries, and predictable reactions from you. Assertive parents are warm and loving, set simple, fair rules, and are consistent in applying them. They manage misbehavior quickly and calmly and give small but meaningful consequences when needed.

One of the least effective parenting styles is being harsh, which includes showing less affection or praise and managing misbehavior by shouting, put-downs, physical punishment, or serious consequences such as removing possessions for days or weeks at a time. This style may leave nine-year-olds feeling worthless, frightened, or angry.

Being inconsistent or uninvolved with your child can also be unhelpful. Inconsistent parents are unpredictable in how they behave, sometimes being loving, at other times harsh. Common pitfalls include not being aware of where your nine-year-old is or what she is doing, or setting rules but only applying them some of the time—for example, specifying a time when your nine-year-old should come in from playing, yet not always doing something about it if she is late. This style of parenting leaves your nine-year-old uncertain and potentially insecure, as she is not sure when or why she will next receive affection or punishment.

Teaching responsibility and accountability

Taking greater responsibility for herself is a key step toward independence for your nine-year-old. You may have started teaching this skill by giving her regular chores. The next step might be to develop other helpful habits such as getting herself ready on time.

To encourage independence:

◗ Break the task down into smaller parts, such as when to wake up, when to eat breakfast, and when to leave the house.

◗ Plan with her what she needs to do and give her some help. For example, she will need an alarm clock and a lesson in how to set it.

As she completes each step, your nine-year-old will gain a sense of achievement. It can be a difficult transition, however, from relying on you to get her organized to doing things for herself. Remember, your child won't get this right every time, so do intervene to help if she occasionally gets distracted and doesn't get ready on time.

MANAGING TIME *Your child should wear a watch by this age so that she can take responsibility for doing things on time. Let her choose her own watch if possible.*

Common lifestyle concerns

REAL-LIFE QUESTIONS

▶ **My nine-year-old has always been a good eater, but now she's suddenly picky about everything I put on her plate. Why is this?**
At nine, your child may be buying her own snacks, and choosing her school lunches, too. She may become very picky—for instance, cutting every trace of fat off cold cuts of meat, or perhaps refusing to eat anything that doesn't have mayonnaise on it. Some children develop an aversion to certain foods, with complaints such as, "You *know* I don't eat eggs!"

Sometimes fads are related to friends' tastes in food, but often the reasons are completely inscrutable and seemingly illogical to all but the child herself. If your child's food intake is still more or less balanced, then let it be. It won't last anyway. Try to encourage her to try a little of what everyone else is eating—not least to save you from having to cook lots of different meals—and let her eat her current favorites occasionally as an extra, but in moderation.

▶ **My nine-year-old wants her ears pierced. Is she too young?**
Strictly speaking, your child is still a minor and therefore needs your permission before a piercing. In practice, many youngsters go ahead anyway, and sometimes pierce their own ears or get a friend to do it. Clearly, it's better to have a piercing done hygienically rather than furtively in a pal's bathroom with a needle, thread, and raw potato.

You're the parent, so it's really your decision as to how to play this. Nine years of age is still a little young in most cultures for pierced ears, but you may want to consider that an earring in one or both lobes is a fairly innocuous kind of piercing. You may be able to buy some time and persuade your child to wait a bit longer—for instance, by pointing out that fancy earrings won't be allowed at school (girls may be permitted small plain studs, while in some schools boys are forbidden from wearing earrings at all). Explain that the more years you wear earrings, the more likely the earlobes are to become misshapen, with a piercing that

PIERCED EARS *Your daughter is more likely to want to have her ears pierced if her friends have theirs done. You could compromise by buying her some pretty clip-on earrings instead.*

resembles a vertical slit rather than a tidy hole. Offer your child ear-piercing and a nice pair of earrings as a future present—for instance, on her thirteenth birthday.

▶ **Because he isn't a good communicator, I have no idea how my son is doing at school day-to-day and whether he's enjoying his time there. What can I do?**
As a typical nine-year-old, your son will probably not be forthcoming about schoolwork, particularly if he aims to do as little homework as possible. Familiarize yourself with his schedule and try to strike up a good relationship with his teachers. Many schools offer a contact book in which both teacher and parent can write down concerns. Some schools also encourage email communication, so use this to keep in regular contact and find out if your child is keeping up with his homework.

Rather than asking your son every evening what he's done at school, ask him over the weekend, perhaps when you are out for a walk or in the car. This more relaxed approach may get him to open up to you. Reassure him that you won't be angry if he's doing badly in a subject; if this is the case, ask where he thinks he's going wrong, and encourage him. Supportive home environments are proven to produce children who perform better and go on to higher education.

SURFING THE NET She will be skilled at using the computer, but you will need to monitor her use.

14

13

12

11

10

9

8

7

6

5

4

3

YEARS

Your 10-year-old

"He will be eager to master new skills and is becoming more confident in his abilities."

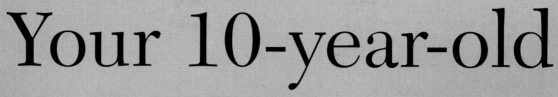

A QUESTION OF TRUST He is old enough for some freedom now, but he should be required to come home at agreed times.

IN THE CLASSROOM As your child nears the end of her elementary school years, there will be more expected of her.

Growth and development

Your child is gradually becoming more physically able and, even if he isn't athletic, he will enjoy being active and playing outside. Although boys are unlikely to have started puberty yet, it is worth being prepared for the changes that will happen in the years to come.

Strength and endurance

With progress in puberty comes muscle development. This applies to both girls and boys, although it will happen later in boys. The adolescent growth in muscles is not directly paralleled by an increase in their strength. Maximum strength in boys appears more than a year after their maximum growth rate—in other words, after their growth has begun to plateau. Strength and performance improve for several years into the twenties, so a boy will look grown-up before he has reached his adult strength.

Boys and puberty

Now is the time to prepare yourself for the changes that will take place in your son over the next few years. The start of puberty in boys depends on the production of the hormone testosterone, which will cause his body to change not only in shape but also in strength and endurance, and eventually enable him to reach his full reproductive capacity. In some boys this can happen as late as 14.

Signs of puberty in boys:

▶ The first sign of puberty in boys is usually enlargement of the testes, followed by growth of the penis (see page 252), with further enlargement of the testes and changes in the skin of the scrotum.

▶ Pubic hair appears shortly after this process has started; underarm and then facial hair appears much later.

▶ Unlike girls, whose growth spurt starts at the same time as the first sign of breast development, boys don't have their growth spurt until puberty is well established, usually between the ages of 12 and 14. They will continue to grow at a rate of only 1½–2½ in (4–6 cm) per year, so it is quite

"Be open with children about how their body will change during puberty and initiate a conversation if they don't ask questions."

Healthy bones

During a growth spurt there is a rapid increase in bone length, and good nutrition and exercise are vital to ensure that your child's bones attain maximum strength. A diet and lifestyle that build healthy bones at this age will help prevent osteoporosis in later life.

Calcium is a mineral that is a vital component in the formation of bones, and vitamin D supplies one of the hormones that controls it. Both vitamin D and calcium are essential in the diet. Vitamin D is also formed in the skin when sunlight falls on it. People with dark skin who live in countries with little sunshine, or who keep their skin covered, need to eat a diet rich in calcium and vitamin D.

Good sources of calcium and vitamin D include milk, soy, oily fish, beans, and green vegetables. Children on a dairy-free diet need to eat other sources of calcium, and many need a supplement.

Although rare, low levels of vitamin D and/or calcium can result in rickets, where the bones become soft and deformed.

CALCIUM INTAKE *Encourage your child to eat dairy products, such as yogurt, which is high in calcium.*

> "Your child's face will slowly change and take on a more adult appearance."

common to see boys who are shorter than girls of the same age.

▶ If your son is showing signs of puberty before the age of nine—known as precocious puberty (see page 135)—contact your health-care provider.

Physical changes

Most children put on fat from about eight years (see page 157) to adolescence, but the rate decreases when the growth spurt starts. The rate of fat gained reaches a minimum at the same time as the rate of growth reaches its maximum, and in boys fat is actually lost. In contrast, increase in muscle thickness is greatest at this stage.

Limbs in boys become thinner during the growth spurt, while a girl's limbs will become fatter, although they do so more slowly during the growth spurt than before or afterward. In other words, boys become taller and thinner and girls become taller and more shapely.

There is significant growth of the forehead due to the development of the brow ridges and frontal sinuses. The lower jaw also grows at this time, so that the jaw projects more and the upper jaw also grows forward.

Your child's health

Your child may begin looking like a teenager as he adopts the familiar slouch, but there are reasons why good posture should be encouraged at this age. He may not be keen on sleeping and eating well, but this could be to the detriment of his health and well-being, so take action if necessary.

Poor posture

At age 10, a preteen slouch is so common that you could consider it almost universal. You are entitled to suggest that your child should try to sit up straight, especially at the dinner table, or in family photos. You could also explain, because it is true, that sitting badly weakens the muscles around the spine, with possible long-term problems. However, constant nagging about posture (or anything else) is unlikely to be helpful. The slouch at this age is often because children want to appear casual and "cool," or because they are self-conscious about their bodies—this is particularly true of girls when they start to develop breasts. Occasionally, scoliosis (curvature of the spine), a condition that can run in the family, starts around now. It usually improves without any drastic treatment, but seek medical advice if your child's spine is noticeably curved, or he seems unable to sit or stand up straight.

Sleep patterns

Not all 10-year-olds need nine hours' sleep a night. If your child wakes easily on school days and seems alert (barring an initial 10 minutes or so of grogginess), then he is probably getting enough sleep. However, don't feel bad about making sleep an issue if you are concerned.

HEAVY SCHOOL BAGS
If your child overloads his school bag, it may be too heavy and cause him to slouch. Check what he is packing.

To help your child sleep:

▶ Ensure that his bedroom is comfortable and welcoming, and neither too warm nor too cold.

▶ Cut out caffeinated drinks in the evening, including tea, coffee, cola, and other soft drinks.

▶ Restrict TV in the late evening (this is easier if your child does not have a TV in his room).

▶ Try to help your child deal with any anxieties that may be causing insomnia.

▶ Ensure that your child has enough physical activity in the daytime.

▶ Make sure he has time to unwind before bedtime. Like adults, children find it hard to go straight to bed after excitement or activity. If your child's sleep is disturbed during the night, you may want to make sure he has no medical problems.

TIREDNESS *Your child may find it difficult to concentrate at school and do his homework if he is not getting adequate sleep at night.*

Nocturnal emissions

Boys can ejaculate during their sleep in the time prior to puberty. While this is unusual at age 10, it can happen. It tends to ease off as adolescence progresses. These emissions can reflect erotic dreams (so-called wet dreams), or can occur for no obvious reason, which can be startling and worrying for a young boy. Your child may or may not be troubled by involuntary daytime erections at around the same time. Be calm and matter-of-fact about nocturnal emissions. Show your child how to change the bed, and use lighter-colored bed linen, which is less apt to show semen stains. Many boys fear they have wet the bed, so reassure your son that the wetness is not urine. Do explain to him at some point that the liquid contains sperm, as this is an important biological fact.

Maintaining a healthy weight

Although your 10-year-old will do games and PE at school, it may not contribute much to his fitness. Try to pursue physical activities as a family to help your child maintain a healthy appetite and weight.

Your child will be naturally active, but it is all too easy for a child to become sedentary, so your enthusiasm and participation are really important. Try to be positive about being active yourself to encourage this same attitude in your child.

Without making a big issue of it, provide healthy meals with plenty of protein, carbohydrates, and fiber but not too much fat. This should ensure appropriate weight gain, which is particularly important in the preteen years when many children gain a little weight (see page 157).

Weight can also drop in some preteens, especially if your 10-year-old skips meals. Girls in particular can become very figure-conscious, and there is little doubt that eating disorders (see page 297) can begin around now. If you are worried about your child's weight or eating habits, ask your health-care provider for more guidance.

Allergies

Allergies are an increasingly common problem in children. Some disappear with time—for example, milk allergy, which is often gone by age two. In contrast, peanut allergy is usually (but not always) a lifelong problem.

Your health-care provider can advise on whether blood and skin tests are appropriate. All tests have their limitations, so if you observe a worrisome reaction after your child eats a certain food and the test comes back negative, you should still avoid serving that food until your doctor can arrange for your child to try it in a safe setting, such as a hospital.

Take your child to a conventional pediatrician or an allergy specialist.

Food allergies

These can be life-threatening by causing anaphylaxis—a rapid response to the ingestion of a substance such as a peanut, including swelling of the face and tongue, difficulty breathing, and collapse. A less severe response is a rash or hives.

Treatment involves avoiding the allergen and, if the allergy is potentially life-threatening, carrying an EpiPen (prefilled syringe containing epinephrine, which can be injected into the muscle). All anaphylaxis sufferers need a management plan. As well as an EpiPen, this may also include an inhaler, an antihistamine, and steroids. The school should hold a copy of the plan and have a trained member of staff who can administer the EpiPen. While anaphylaxis appears to be on the increase, death as a result is rare in children.

Allergies to inhaled substances

Pollen or house dust mites can cause wheezing, allergic rhinitis, and/or hayfever. One treatment for hayfever is antihistamines. Treatment for wheezing includes inhalers and steroids. Also see "Asthma" on page 163.

Skin reaction

An allergy to certain substances contacting the skin can cause a rash or, in the case of latex, can also cause anaphylaxis (see left). The trigger should be avoided.

Understanding and skills

By age 10, most children are confident about their abilities, taking pride in doing things well. Your child will show interest in and concern about personal capabilities, and be eager to master new skills—particularly if there is someone in his peer group who can do something better.

"Your child will be more focused on his interests, having a clearer notion of what he likes rather than taking a stab at everything."

Self-awareness

Children at this age begin to compare themselves to others, and it is essential to developing self-esteem that you encourage self-awareness. This means helping your child recognize his strengths and weaknesses, set appropriate goals and take appropriate risks to achieve those goals, and learn from mistakes. When a child understands himself, he can better understand the world around him. If there is one thing that will encourage healthy self-understanding at this age, it is to let your 10-year-old make mistakes and help him find solutions. This will help him to become resilient and develop coping skills when things don't go as planned.

All children need to feel good about themselves. Your 10-year-old will be more body- and appearance-conscious and may begin to compare himself unfavorably to others, especially role models such as sports stars and pop stars. Therefore it is increasingly important that your child recognizes and takes pride in his good points, feels comfortable in his

Talk, talk, talk

Most 10-year-olds are a fountain of information and chatter, so remember that your child is learning important communication skills, and testing out his speech, language, banter, jokes, and ideas on a willing audience—you!

So try to give him plenty of time, and lots of feedback.

Remember:

▸ The more you talk, the more your child will talk.

▸ The more you listen, the better developed his listening skills will be. And that is the art of communication.

Be open to discussion and ideas, correct or challenge incorrect thinking and grammar with explanations, and get your 10-year-old thinking for himself.

body, is aware of his achievements, and has a good self-image. Take the opportunity to point out some of these things. For example, you might say, "You're so good at making that salad—can you make it for the picnic on Saturday?" Keep it honest, though. Children can tell the difference between false praise and a genuine compliment, and you will only make your child feel cheapened if you don't tell the truth. This isn't just about emotional health; it is about developing understanding.

Your child and the community

Now that your 10-year-old is able to think logically, in a more sophisticated way, and has better problem-solving abilities than before, he can be entrusted with more freedom, and relied on to undertake jobs around the home and in the community. These are all responsibilities that should be encouraged, as he develops confidence, learns important life lessons, and becomes aware of the world outside.

Your 10-year-old will be capable of helping out and taking an interest in what is going on outside his front door, his neighborhood, and even his country. The earlier you involve your child in the community, the greater his understanding will be.

He could become more responsible by:

▶ Helping those who need it, such as someone who is ill or less able.
▶ Thinking about the planet and its resources. For example, make it your child's responsibility to turn off the lights in empty rooms or sort the recycling into different bags or bins each week.
▶ Considering people who have clearly defined needs. He could, for example, set up a charity booth or take part in a sponsored event. The idea is to create understanding through positive endeavor.

Language and literacy

Your child's vocabulary will be wider, with adjectives featuring heavily— there may be a real sense of drama in much of what he says, and because he believes it to be true, it is important to take it seriously. A good sense of humor will be developing, so he will tell jokes. Don't underestimate this. While it should be light-hearted fun, children learn a great deal about language from the use of rhymes, puns, and silly words.

HELPING OTHERS
Simple tasks, such as helping a neighbor with gardening, will give your child a sense of responsibility to others.

"He may have the negotiation skills of a car salesman, managing to get what he wants by striking at the right time and hitting the right notes."

Teaching negotiation

You may be astonished to find that your 10-year-old is a smooth operator when it comes to getting what he wants. If these skills are honed, they will serve him well in the future. So instead of listening to a tantrum, stop, sit down, and make it clear that you will only discuss the issue if your child is willing to explain his position clearly, without anger. Listen carefully; agree or disagree, but not without stating your reasons and allowing him comeback. Keep an open mind. Listen carefully, and if he presents a valid case, congratulate him and move on. Your child will learn that reasoning, debating, and negotiation are valuable skills.

Modern etiquette

Literacy and the creative use of language have been sadly compromised by the electronic age. Most children no longer send letters. However, all is not lost. Traditionalists might be up in arms against new technology, but there is no doubt that it can be used positively, and to a child's benefit. There is nothing wrong with thanking someone by email or text. As long as your child realizes the importance of appreciation and courtesy, it is possible to use technology successfully. The important thing is to encourage your child to say more than "thank you," and explain why he liked a gift, and to invite further correspondence.

Encouraging comprehension

Your child lives in a society where short-term interests are easily satisfied. Because he will probably be accustomed to dipping in and out of TV shows and the Internet, he may develop a poor attention span and be less able to absorb and comprehend what he reads in a book.

You can help by reading alongside your child and asking questions, or reading to him and asking him about what he has just heard. For example, "What did that word mean? Why do you think the ending was the way it was?"

It is possible to train children's minds to think differently—to reflect on what they have read or heard, and to ask questions when they don't understand. This is an important element of comprehension. Many of us reread passages that didn't make sense at first, and children need to be encouraged to do the same. When your child is reading, ask him to explain something. Gently challenge him if he gets something wrong, and guide him to the correct answer. If your child is not a natural reader, encourage him to pay careful attention to radio and TV programs and audio books.

Emotions and personality

Your 10-year-old will be aware of his own values and talents, and will have a sense of belonging to family and friends. His role with his peers is also taking shape—perhaps he is a leader, a follower, or the joker. Whatever the role he has carved, it is forming part of his identity.

Your 10-year-old's peer group will be increasingly influential as he seeks acceptance through shared values, interests, and appearance. He will want to spend more time with friends and less with the family.

While boys still tend to befriend boys, and girls' friendships are primarily with girls, there will be an increasing interest in the opposite sex. This happens alongside more awareness of intimate relationships and greater use of sexual joking and swear words. Conversation among same-sex friends may entail questioning about love or dating. This is primarily light-hearted, although tensions can arise if your 10-year-old has started to have crushes (see page 214).

SOUL MATES *At this age, your child will get much fun and pleasure from her closest friends. The strongest bonds usually develop from shared interests and experiences.*

Independence and freedom

Your freedom-loving 10-year-old will be pushing at the boundaries these days. He is naturally driven to be more independent and will strive to do things away from your watchful gaze. Knowing when to limit his freedom can be difficult: you may be torn between keeping him safe and letting him spread his wings.

Loosen your supervision a step at a time so he can show you how self-reliant he can be. Start with simple responsibilities, such as remembering to come home by a set time. It is perfectly reasonable, and vital to his safety, that you know at all times where your 10-year-old is, who he is with, and when he will be home.

Temper tantrums

Full-blown tantrums are rare at age 10, but there may be occasions when your 10-year-old loses his temper and sulks or slams doors. This is an age when your child will be more aware of his emotions and able to take into account other people's feelings and opinions, but he won't always be able to control his reactions. He will try to stay in control, and you may see him contorting his face in an effort not to cry or show anger. At these times, it is helpful to acknowledge how he feels. For example, if you've said "No" to a late-night event, add, "This is probably disappointing for you. Is that how you're feeling?" In this way, your 10-year-old can see that you have considered his feelings and have some idea what it must be like for him.

Remember:

▶ Prompting your child to talk about feelings helps him get a grip on his emotions and express them without being overwhelmed by them.

Crushes and early dating

Ten-year-olds are likely to be interested in the opposite sex, although they are much more likely to talk about this interest than act on it. In fact, many 10-year-olds would run a mile if the object of their affection actually agreed to a real date. Ambivalence about relationships is common as children are teased about love, yet for some it is a status symbol to claim to have a boyfriend or girlfriend. These contradictions reflect that children of this age vary greatly in their maturity.

When dating does happen between 10-year-olds, it tends to be a close friendship that may include some experimentation with kissing and cuddling. Even though these relationships are usually quite innocent, do supervise, to make sure you are comfortable with the level of intimacy your 10-year-old is displaying.

Sexual preferences

This can be a time of confusion about sexual preferences. Your children may play along with teasing and interest in the opposite sex while actually feeling something different. It is part of normal development to have same-sex crushes on people; for some this is a passing interest, while for others it represents a choice they will maintain later.

ALL TALK *Sharing ideas with friends about dating, sex, or the emotional buzz of having a crush allows your child the safety of exploring these ideas without taking action.*

Withdrawal and depression

Everyone gets a little sad sometimes, and your child is no exception. This is usually a reaction to an event such as a house move or a friend moving away. Such sadness is reasonable and will gradually pass. Depression, however, is more serious. It shows itself, for example, in a child losing interest in things he would normally enjoy, having too much or too little sleep, and possibly talking about death or suicide. If you notice signs of low mood or loss of interest persisting over two weeks, obtain guidance from a health professional. You cannot force your child to cheer up, but it can help to continue to give him opportunities to join in with the family and invite him to participate as much or as little as he wants.

Dealing with stealing

Talk with your 10-year-old about honesty and trust. Show your pleasure when your child is honest, and act quickly with a consequence if you know he has been dishonest. Try not to lecture, but ask him how he would feel if his friend took his favorite game or allowance money. When he imagines how it might feel not to trust his friends or to lose his things, it can help him see why stealing is wrong. Young children steal for a variety of reasons. Sometimes they just cannot wait to have something, or they may steal for a dare. Warn your child that he may be dared to shoplift by friends, and make him aware of why taking things from stores is illegal and does not live up to family values.

BEING REMORSEFUL
Your child knows the difference between right and wrong now. He should feel remorseful when he has behaved badly and know when he needs to apologize.

If you find out he has taken something, he should be made to return it or pay for it with his own money. He should also apologize to the person he has stolen from. This consequence gives him the message that he can't gain by stealing and that his action has caused upset to someone else. It may be tempting to threaten a visit to the police station, but this can backfire, as it is not always as frightening as expected.

Common concerns

▶ **Is my 10-year-old son too young to be left alone at home?**
Different cultures hold varying customs about leaving children home alone, and 10-year-olds vary greatly in maturity. However, in general your 10-year-old is not sufficiently aware of danger or able to manage an emergency on his own and therefore should not be left alone in your home.

You can, however, begin to prepare your child to be safely home alone in the future—for example, by talking about safety rules such as not opening the door to anyone, not preparing hot food or drinks, and staying inside the home. It is also not advisable to leave 10-year-olds in charge of younger children, as they are unlikely to cope with the care of others in an emergency.

▶ **I don't like the look of some of my daughter's friends. How should I handle this?**
You may be worried that your 10-year-old has made friends with others who trigger poor behavior. Rather than being judgmental, encourage your daughter's friends to meet at your home, and stay around to chat with them. If you still feel there is a problem, don't forbid your daughter to have these friendships, as this may have the opposite effect. Do talk about your concerns, perhaps asking how she feels about these friends, as well as

sharing your concerns. It is difficult to limit your child's contact with friends she sees at school. Talk with her teacher about your worries and ask if she can be encouraged to spend time with children who will be a more positive influence. If you work, ensure that she is supervised outside of school hours by enrolling her in after-school activities.

▶ **We used to be close, but these days my son doesn't tell me anything and I feel quite bereft.**
Your son is probably saving his juiciest stories and heartfelt hopes to share with friends, and you are

ON HER TERMS *You may find that your child opens up to you in her own time, rather than responding to your questions after school or around the dinner table.*

feeling left out. When he comes in from school and you ask about his day, he's less likely to regale you with playground tales, and more likely to mutter "Nothing" or "Don't know." This change comes naturally as his energy is increasingly focused on engaging with friends rather than family. It certainly doesn't mean you're not important, just a little taken for granted.

Don't give up on communicating. When there is a quiet moment at the end of the day, your 10-year-old will probably answer your original question in full.

▶ **I was really upset and got angry recently when my 10-year-old acted angrily toward me for the first time. She said some quite hurtful things. How should I have reacted?**
If your child says hurtful things, calls you names, or tells you you're a bad parent, keep your cool. Count to 10 backwards and then do it again. Take a deep breath and remind yourself that five minutes ago, your daughter was happy to be with you. If you can't stay calm, leave the room until you have control of your emotions.

Once your daughter's initial anger has blown over, ask her to tell you how she's feeling. When you react calmly, it will be hard for your daughter to maintain her outrage, and you're more likely to communicate positively.

Your child's life

With his increasing need for privacy and his developing social life, you may feel pushed out of your child's world. This is difficult, but it simply means he is growing up. However, although on the whole he will want to be independent, there will be times when he desperately needs your help.

School projects

At this age, your child is likely to have many school projects to do. These are an excellent way for him to develop research skills, work in an elastic time frame, search out answers and solutions, use creativity, and work independently. Doing a project can also be an ideal opportunity for your child to share knowledge and interests with you, and you can help by making positive suggestions and encouraging your child to have fun while learning. Try not to become overly involved, as this can disempower your child and reduce the learning elements of project work. Encourage him by offering advice, pointing out sources of information, and making sure he has everything he needs. Then stand back and watch learning in action!

"A child's project doesn't have to be the best in the class, and savvy teachers know whose has been done independently and whose hasn't."

Your child's room

Having personal space is important to your 10-year-old, and his bedroom will become his territory, a place to express himself with little interference. While posters of favorite baseball teams, for example, and his chosen color scheme are usually acceptable, it is the level of mess that may cause conflict. He may be the epitome of neatness, or have periods of disarray, then a massive clean-up, or he may be the kind of child who simply can't, or won't, keep any sort of order. If your child's room is a mess, do your best to ignore it. See this as his space to do with as he wishes. However, this can change if there are issues that you cannot ignore regarding health or cleanliness—for example, stale food, dirty clothes, or clutter that gets in the way of completing homework. Try to negotiate with your child to keep the floor clear, bring all dishes down once a day, and put dirty clothes into the laundry hamper. Although you can, of course, clean up his room for him, it is better to make it his responsibility—he is old enough to do this now. You might want to consider agreeing on rewards, if he keeps it neat. To avoid invading his privacy, perhaps agree you will check his room once a week, but give him advance warning.

The need for privacy

A strong desire for privacy will be influencing your 10-year-old's behavior at home. He will be more conscious of his body and will want to get dressed and washed without interruptions. He will also need time to himself for private thoughts and perhaps want to write a confidential diary.   Greater respect for privacy at home is easy to achieve with the help of bathroom locks and signs for bedroom doors.

Your child's once easy acceptance of parental nudity may now be replaced by requests to cover up. This is a function of his greater awareness of the body's sexual and reproductive functions and of his own development. Nudity at home is a personal decision, but it is worth considering each family member's view so that no one feels uncomfortable.

HER OWN SPACE
Encourage your child to keep her room neat, but don't be obsessive or label her as "lazy." She may simply not be as neat as you.

Healthy packed lunches

It is a good idea to involve your child in making up his lunch box, as it provides an opportunity to teach him about nutrition. Let your child choose the contents within an agreed selection of foods, making sure that salty, sugary, or additive-laden foods are off the menu. At this age, he can easily manage a thermos of warm soup or pasta. Add some fruit, raisins, a piece of cheese, and a bottle of water, and even a square of good-quality chocolate, for a perfectly balanced lunch. Or move away from traditional lunches by giving him raw vegetables, such as strips of pepper with dips, or even a piece of chicken, with salad.

If your child is teased for the healthy content of his lunch box, practice replies with him—for example, "You can't like your lunch too much if you're so interested in mine." Food swapping is common as children barter unwanted items. This is difficult to monitor, and you will have to rely on your child's awareness of healthy eating.

All about cell phones

The average age at which children get their first cell phone is dropping, and many children in the West now have one by the age of 11. They are a status symbol, and your child will undoubtedly pester you to have one. Because so much social interaction now takes place over cell phones, they do have a role in today's society.

The risks to children of using a cell phone are still an uncertain and controversial area. It is thought that as children's brains are still developing, they absorb more of the electromagnetic radiation produced by cell phones. There is also some research suggesting that this radiation could slightly raise the temperature of the brain. Whether this might be dangerous to health, though, is far less certain. There may be subtle long-term effects, but more research needs to be done.

On grounds of caution, it makes sense to restrict your child's use of a cell phone. Using a hands-free set can reduce the amount of radiation your child's head absorbs, but some argue that it could increase the amount reaching other parts of his body. Texting instead of talking is more protective, but bear in mind that texting a great deal can cause repetitive strain injury. Having a cell phone can give your child extra freedom and still keep you both in contact, but carrying a phone, and especially using it in public, could make your child a target for thieves. Make sure your child always uses his phone responsibly and doesn't "show it off" to other children. Like other technology, cell-phone use should be monitored and

PHONE USE *Texting is often cheaper than calling, but monitor the number of messages your child is sending to ensure that it doesn't get out of hand.*

Talking about body image

Your 10-year-old is beginning to be more interested in how he looks, while also being exposed to media messages about what is "normal." If he expresses concerns about his looks or his body shape, you can soothe his fears somewhat by being 100 percent positive about who he is as a person rather than his body. Put body image into perspective by talking with him about the qualities that make up a person: these might be physical, spiritual, emotional, and intellectual. Encourage him to have role models, such as TV personalities and sports stars, who are all shapes and sizes and not necessarily "handsome" or "beautiful" in the superficial sense.

For a small number of 10-year-olds, body image is a serious problem. If your child is being bullied because of his appearance, seek advice immediately.

subject to guidelines. For example, you might decide your child's cell phone shouldn't be on during mealtimes or homework time. Of course, the costs of using it also need to be considered; many parents choose "pay as you go" plans, or make children responsible for paying phone bills from their own allowance money.

Talking about alcohol and risky behavior

He may only be 10 years old, but there is no harm in talking to your child about the temptations he will face later. An upfront approach is best. Talk about why people like to take risks—for example, explain that they might feel excited by drinking alcohol. Be honest that these things seem fun at first, but afterward they will make you feel ill or get you in trouble.

Be ready to answer your 10-year-old's inevitable questions about your own risky behavior in the past. Prepare what you will say. It is your decision whether you tell him or keep it to yourself. Whatever you decide, avoid making risky behavior seem glamorous. If your 10-year-old is already drinking alcohol or breaking the law, seek professional help.

Common concerns

▶ **My daughter is starting to ask for help with homework, and I'm not confident about helping her with math. What should I do?**
Many parents balk at helping their children with math, and this is largely because numeracy is problematic for many people—not just children. The most important thing you can do is keep your cool. This means avoiding looking panicked when your child asks for help. Conversely, parents who are good at math should avoid being judgmental if their child is not.

If you really think your child is having ongoing problems, rather than a temporary glitch, speak to her teacher about how best to assist your child, given your lack of confidence in the subject.

▶ **I accidentally saw my 10-year-old son kissing his female friend. Isn't he a bit young for this?**
Curiosity about sexual relationships is growing in your 10-year-old, and it is common for children of his age to wonder how to kiss and what it feels like. It is normal for your son to experiment, so don't be too concerned. He may just have kissed another child to see how it feels. This is a very normal part of children's sexual exploration. Your reaction can help: if you are calm and accept that this is a playful practice of grown-up behavior, then you show acceptance of your 10-year-old's developing awareness. If you are horrified or punish your child, then he may see this intimacy as bad or forbidden and be less open with you as he matures.

Your 11-year-old

"As outside interests develop, your child will seem much more grown-up."

COMPUTER USE Your child will need to use a computer at this age, so make sure she does so safely and effectively.

THE OPPOSITE SEX This is the age when casual friendships between boys and girls may enter a more serious, preteen phase.

MIDDLE SCHOOL Most children will thrive on the new demands, different facilities, and changed curriculum of middle school, but it can take a while to adjust.

Growth and development

The physical changes that take place at age 11 are very much dependent on whether your child has started to go through puberty. Since puberty tends to happen earlier in girls than in boys, there are likely to be more noticeable differences in a girl's body than in a boy's at this age.

As your daughter begins to develop into a young woman, you will notice a gradual change in her body shape. She is likely to be self-conscious about these changes, and your tact and understanding will be needed to ease her through this transition. Boys of 11 often show no signs of puberty at all, and in some there will be no changes until as late as age 14 (see page 251).

Physical changes in girls

Breast development occurs at different rates in girls, but small breast buds may be changing to a more rounded shape as the area around the nipple, the areola, enlarges. The breast will continue to develop until it reaches a more adult shape. Bras are unnecessary until the breasts are almost fully developed, but your daughter may want to wear one as a sign of maturity. Camisole tops are often worn before girls need a real bra.

By 11 your daughter may have pubic hair in an early stage, or already have coarser hair that looks adult in distribution. Most girls will not have their full adult distribution until they are at least 12, and in some it may be as late as 18. It takes about three years for pubic hair to fully develop. The timing and rate of physical changes will vary depending on the child, but it is usual for underarm hair to start to appear a year or two later than pubic hair and 15 months for it to reach adult distribution.

Growing taller

The age at which girls reach their fastest growth rate ranges from 11 to 14, and at this time she will grow up to an incredible 3½–4 in (9–10 cm) per year. The rate of growth of a boy gradually slows until he reaches quite an advanced stage in puberty and then rapidly increases. At 11, therefore,

BEING OPEN *Having a relaxed attitude when talking about the physical changes that take place helps your child face puberty confidently and positively.*

most boys will be growing slowly. If your daughter has started to go through puberty, you may find it hard to keep up with her ever-increasing size as she no longer looks like your "little girl," but much to her delight, she will need new clothes and shoes more frequently. Don't panic if she is already wearing size eight shoes by the age of 11; her feet will reach their adult size before the rest of her body. Legs tend to have their growth spurt first, and the shoulders and hips widen at the same time that the trunk lengthens, with girls' hips widening more than boys' hips.

How puberty affects your child

Increasing levels of the sex hormones (estrogen in girls and testosterone in boys) will be playing a major role in the life of many 11-year-olds who are showing signs of puberty. Your bubbly, energetic, enthusiastic child

EMOTIONAL CHANGES *It can be a shock when your child becomes downcast and seems depressed, but this is all part of puberty. Try to take it in stride so that you can support her fully.*

may almost overnight become listless, struggle to get herself out of bed in the morning, and appear unable to concentrate or to remember anything you ask of her.

Her appetite may fluctuate wildly: there is often a huge increase in appetite, to allow for the growth spurt that occurs during puberty. Conversely, some children of this age may have a decreased appetite, if they are going through a period of slow growth before their teenage growth spurt. As they naturally begin to gain weight, girls may become more aware of eating healthily and exercising, but it is important to keep a close eye on teens who become obsessive about food intake and start to lose weight. If left unchecked, this attitude can all too easily lead to an eating disorder (see page 297).

Fluctuations in mood, concentration, and energy levels are normal, but if your child's behavior is affecting her schoolwork, talk to her teacher, who may be able to offer additional help, or at least be understanding.

Your child's health

Puberty is a normal process, but it can, unfortunately, bring with it some unwanted side effects, such as stress and sleep deprivation. Some girls of this age will also be starting to menstruate, and this can impact their everyday health and their lifestyle to some degree.

Dealing with stress

The emotional impact of puberty can cause many preteens to suffer from stress. Common symptoms of stress are headaches, stomachaches, and sleep disturbances, mostly caused by anxiety rather than an underlying condition. They are all very real symptoms and are due to overproduction of the hormones that are produced by the effects of stress on the body.

Sometimes reassurance that these symptoms are common and caused by stress is all that is needed to help them disappear. However, it is important to try to uncover the root causes leading to stress, such as bullying, before attempting to eliminate the symptoms.

Sleep hygiene

Sleep problems are common, with many pubertal children having difficulty falling asleep, which results in difficulty getting up in the morning.

To help your child get to sleep, improve her "sleep hygiene":

▶ Remove distracting items such as a television, computer, or electronic games from her bedroom.

▶ Make sure she finishes her homework at least an hour before bedtime to give her time to wind down.

▶ Try to get her to open up to you if she seems anxious. Talking about any problems, such as exam stress, will help her offload and sleep easier.

TIME TO CHILL *Help your child wind down at bedtime by encouraging activities such as listening to relaxing music and reading.*

"Your child is likely to be a late riser, so allow plenty of time in the mornings and get organized the night before to reduce some of the stress."

Side effects of periods

Most girls start their periods between the ages of 10 and 16, so by age 11, your daughter should be well prepared for what to expect. Although the normal menstrual cycle consists of bleeding for 2–7 days every 24–34 days, it is common for periods to be very irregular for the first few months or years. A first period is often followed by several months without any further bleeding. The following problems are common:

Menstrual pain Unless she is extremely fortunate, your daughter is bound to have menstrual pain. This is a normal part of menstruation, occurring when the walls of the uterus contract. It can be very uncomfortable, and many girls have to lie down and take painkillers; if the pain is particularly bad, they may have to miss school. Anti-inflammatory drugs, such as ibuprofen, work particularly well, and taking a warm bath and gently massaging the abdomen will help the muscles relax. Exercise also helps, and, as with most pains, distraction can be useful.

Heavy periods Many girls will get heavy periods (menorrhagia) at some point. This is bleeding that soaks through a sanitary pad each hour for a day or two, or lasts for longer than seven days. There may be large clots. If this happens regularly, it may be due to a hormone imbalance and treatment is available. Anti-inflammatories also work well for heavy periods. Frequent menorrhagia can make a girl anemic, so make sure she has plenty of iron-rich foods in her diet; a blood test may be needed.

Body exploration

Masturbation is a common way in which children as young as 2–6 explore their bodies, but it becomes more sophisticated and sexually motivated in teenagers. It is a normal part of development for both boys and girls, and it is nothing for them or you to be ashamed of. It is equally normal for children not to masturbate. As it is obviously a very private activity, you are unlikely to know whether your child masturbates. However, if you discover this, do not make a big issue of it. Make your child aware that it isn't acceptable to masturbate in public (although this is unlikely to happen at this age), but that there is nothing wrong with doing it in private. Masturbating in public sometimes happens if a child has learning difficulties and doesn't understand socially acceptable behavior.

"In time, your daughter will get used to managing her period, but to begin with she will need your support."

Understanding and skills

By age 11, most children have a firm grasp of their world and clear ideas about what is right, wrong, good, bad, and "normal." It is important to answer your child's questions fully, and to encourage debate and further learning so that she develops understanding.

A new way of thinking

It is normal for a child to become more irascible and sarcastic at this age, which is due to an improved capacity to handle more abstract thought. Along with an appreciation of sarcasm, your child is likely to understand irony and metaphor, and to show a more mature sense of humor.

With this new maturity comes a more logical, rather than haphazard, way of thinking, and most 11-year-olds (girls in particular) stop and think before doing something and consider the potential consequences of their actions. However, do be prepared for your child to use her logic against you. You may find the tables turned in many an argument, as your 11-year-old points out your inconsistencies and holds her own in lively debates. For example, asking her to keep her room neat may be met with a scathing comment about the state of your own bedroom!

You can also expect rebellion as she balances the need to be "cool," usually as the result of peer pressure, with the desire to please. For this reason it is important to give her an opportunity to vent her often confused feelings.

Problem-solving

If you are always quick to intervene when something goes wrong for your child, and even quicker to suggest a solution, your child will never learn to problem-solve for herself. This is

MOOD CHANGES *As she learns to think for herself, she may sometimes be stubborn and argumentative. This is part of growing up—she is not just being difficult.*

"At this age, there is a natural conflict between wanting to be 'good' to please important adults, such as teachers, and appearing 'too good' to peers."

an example of "overparenting." While you don't want to see your child go through difficulties, it is important to allow her to make her own mistakes and learn how to handle the consequences.

If your child can learn problem-solving and negotiation skills at this young age, recognize her weaknesses, and successfully communicate her needs, it will serve her well for the rest of her life. Stepping in and taking over may put an end to a problem your child is facing in the short term, but it will teach her nothing in the long run. In addition, there is a danger that you will undermine her confidence, self-belief, and self-respect. Solving a problem for herself will empower your child and give her a great confidence boost.

To encourage your child to problem-solve:

▶ Ask for her advice on matters such as planning a trip or prioritizing tasks. Your child can look at the task ahead and come up with solutions.

▶ Listen when she has a problem, and help her define it. Ask questions such as "What would happen if you tried to...?' This way you are guiding her toward a solution, rather than telling her what to do. Afterward, talk about what worked and what to try next time.

Encouraging interests and learning

Your child's interests will undoubtedly go in different directions from your own. You may feel awkward keeping up with your 11-year-old's newest passion, but remember that interests spark learning, which increases and improves understanding. Help her choose books from the library, find relevant websites, join clubs with like-minded friends, and actively seek out information.

Encourage her to "think outside the box"; for example, if your 11-year-old loves animals, why not encourage her to set up her own website with information about endangered species? Everything you do to feed an enthusiasm will spark her imagination. Try not to dismiss outlandish ideas; if your child thinks she can do something and it is safe, then let her try.

▶ Give her scope for negotiation. Clear limits are very important now, but your child needs the power to make a point, even if she seems to be "talking back." When your child starts thinking for herself, she will come up with reasons why your ideas are not acceptable, and it is very important that you listen. Clamping down and taking away her voice will limit her ability to think for herself, make decisions, put forward a reasoned argument, and solve problems.

▶ Offer opportunities for your child to take responsibility—give her a regular job such as taking the household garbage out on time. If, for example, she misses the pickup, she should figure out what should be done. These responsibilities help her to plan her time, work out solutions when things don't go as planned, and deal with her own mistakes.

Improving vocabulary

Several studies indicate that by the age of 11, vocabulary will be consistent with the amount a child reads; the acquisition of words increases according to the number of books read, especially when the books present a child with unfamiliar or specialized words. The more words your child learns, the greater her capacity to understand and use other unfamiliar words, and the greater her confidence in doing so.

TAKING RESPONSIBILITY
Give him tasks and he will learn from them. For example, if he doesn't change his bedding on time, it won't get washed.

There is no doubt that the average 11-year-old should be encouraged to read, and is capable of confident reading (in the absence of any learning disorders). Your 11-year-old will be able to use her burgeoning vocabulary to good effect in written work, using logic in arguments and combining oral, visual, and written material in school reports and projects. This is the age, therefore, where many children leap ahead, and sometimes, for the first time, problems become evident in those who are struggling.

If you are concerned about your child's ability to read and write, see her teacher first, and then look at some of the common features of learning difficulties such as dyslexia (see page 121).

Better literacy

Just as reading improves vocabulary, a 2007 study found that oral vocabulary is linked to a number of reading and comprehension skills. Researchers found that those with good oral vocabularies performed far better both in reading difficult words and in comprehension, while children with poor reading comprehension showed oral vocabulary weakness and read fewer difficult words easily.

To improve your child's literacy:

) Use unfamiliar words when you are talking to your child. Make sure you explain the meaning of those words and then encourage her to use them. This will have an impact on her ability to read well and comprehend what she reads, and translates into better writing skills.

) Play word games with your child. Ask her to come up with synonyms for common words—for example, you say "good," she says "great"; you say "excellent" and so on, through "superb," "superior," until you run out!

) When she is reading, ask her to explain difficult words, and try to weave them into conversations. Encourage use of a dictionary and help her with pronunciation.

) In written work, ask her to find alternatives for simple words such as "nice" or "good."

Guidance is the operative word when it comes to choosing books. Encourage your child to get help from her school and library and show her how to search for books on the Internet. If you are confident about your child's tastes, it is fine to choose or suggest something you think she will like, but don't turn your nose up if she enjoys something different from your own tastes. Remember that reading, whether it is a comic book, newspaper, or mass-market novel, all goes toward improving your child's creativity, imagination, and literacy.

INDIVIDUAL TASTES
It's important for your child to enjoy what he reads, so give him a free hand in what he chooses and refrain from being too critical about his tastes.

Understanding and expressing emotions

Encouraging an emotional vocabulary not only improves your child's "emotional intelligence," but can also be a useful tool for developing self-awareness and the ability to problem-solve and adapt to new situations. From a young age, it is helpful to provide your child with the words she needs to describe how she feels. As she approaches her teens, this is particularly important, because she will experience hugely conflicting emotions as she wrestles with peer pressure, budding self-sufficiency, independent thought, and the ability to understand and use logic.

Remember:

▶ Your child is learning to think for herself, and being able to identify and express her feelings is an important part of emotional development.

If your child can understand and "name" her feelings, she will have coping mechanisms to help her to control her thoughts and behavior. This gives her greater insight into her own responses and helps her choose positive outcomes and achieve her goals. You can help this process by talking about how others are feeling—for example, characters on television or in books, or people in news stories. Encourage your child to draw parallels to her own life; for example, ask her if that is how she felt when she didn't get invited to her classmate's party. Focus, too, on positive emotions, and use them yourself—for example, you might say, "This glorious sunshine makes me feel elated."

Correcting speech

Correct your child's speech by repeating the offending pronunciations and phrases correctly, but don't criticize. Children establish bad habits very easily, particularly with speech, and correcting these is much harder than tackling the problem on a daily basis. So, if she says "ain't," simply say "aren't"—no comments or rebukes, just a correction.

> "Helping your child to find the right words to express her feelings can be like teaching a new language."

Modeling respectful language

It is important to model the language you want to hear from your child. If you treat your child with respect, and speak politely to her, you can expect the same in return. This is important not just for courtesy, but also because it keeps your relationship on a healthy level and teaches her the skills she will need for adult life.

She is bound to lapse from time to time, but if your child knows how to speak politely to others, and how to interact appropriately, using suitable language and speech patterns, she can call on this life skill when required.

So don't swear when the plumber is late; don't lapse into slang yourself, or forget to show courtesy in every social situation.

Emotions and personality

From the time your child starts puberty, she may have an unpredictable nature as she goes through a roller-coaster ride of mood swings and identity crises. Switching between a mature persona and a frustrated, uncertain child is typical and will be challenging for you at times.

It can be difficult to be sensitive to a child who one moment wants your approval and the next is saying you are the meanest parent on the planet. You will be bowled over by how eloquent, thoughtful, and grown-up your child can be one minute, and then watch in amazement as a minor frustration sends her into a tantrum worthy of a toddler.

Caring about her looks

Image is not quite everything to your 11-year-old, but she is certainly likely to be interested in her appearance. Clothing, hairstyles, and makeup allow her to express her individuality or membership of her peer group. You may notice that she becomes choosy about clothes—for example, telling you she wants brand-name jeans, not the cheaper department-store label. She may want to wear favorite items of clothing over and over again, and have frustrated outbursts if they are in the wash.

Changing hairstyles and wanting streaks or colors will be a means of expressing individuality. Try to be as tolerant as you can about these quirks, but put a stop to extremes. If you think your child is dressed inappropriately for her age, avoid confrontational statements such as, "You're not going out in *that!*" This will only lead to resistance and rebellion. Talk it over with her calmly, say why you are concerned, then negotiate what is an acceptable look for school, leisure, and party wear.

Growing up too soon

Children are under plenty of pressure to act grown up. Magazines for "tweenies," those between childhood and adolescence, teach them about makeup, dating, and fashionable clothing. You may have inadvertently

PRIDE IN HER APPEARANCE *As she becomes self-conscious about her appearance, be understanding and don't criticize how she looks.*

reinforced this message yourself by demanding that your child "grow up." If you want your child to act her age, give her opportunities to be playful; at 11 years old, she should still be having plenty of childlike fun. Encourage leisure activities and help her live in the moment, rather than focusing solely on exams, achievements, and the future.

Getting the behavior you want

Until recently, you may have made the decisions about what is acceptable or unacceptable behavior and had the final say on family rules, rewards, and consequences. As negotiation replaces telling your 11-year-old what to do, hand over some responsibility to her to manage her own behavior.

Encourage your child to spell out what rules she wants—for example, speaking respectfully and listening to each other's point of view—and what would not be acceptable—for example, swearing, lying, or neglecting chores. Then she can negotiate with you her rewards for good behavior and consequences if she doesn't behave well. Her involvement in setting these standards makes them easier to apply, since your child will be more committed to them and can't claim not to know what is expected of her.

Friends and friendships

Friendships come under plenty of pressure as your 11-year-old makes the transition to middle school (the timing of this stage may vary). She may no longer share a class with her best friend, and her familiar crowd might split

HAVING FUN *She'll love to be silly with friends, whether it's pretending to be pop stars or doing each other's hair. Encourage this—she is still only a child.*

But all my friends are doing it!

When you say "no" to unreasonable requests from your 11-year-old, such as wanting to stay out late with friends, you're likely to hear a cry of "But all my friends are doing it!" Your first instinct will be to disbelieve your child, and assume this is a tactic to get you to relax the rules. Then doubt will set in, and you will wonder if you are a strict parent whose draconian rules stop your child from fitting in.

The key is to delay your response and check out whether a refusal is reasonable. Do this by calling trusted friends who have children of similar ages and ask what they usually do. Then weigh up this information with what you know of your child's maturity.

Once you've made your decision, explain your reasoning to your child, then stand firm against pressure to change your mind.

> "Young people with high self-esteem are less likely to worry about losing a friend or two by refusing to go along with risky suggestions."

up. It is helpful to your child, at least in the early days of starting her new school, to maintain relationships with friends from the old school. This provides stability while friendships are formed with her new classmates.

Having the skills to make new friends will make a difference to your child's relationships at school. Check that she is confident about asking to join in with an activity. Remind her that this approach won't work every time and not to be disheartened if sometimes she is not included.

Fitting in with friends

At age 11, fitting in is a major motivator for your child. She will be spending increasing amounts of time with friends and will want to be accepted. This may lead her to copy peers or agree to risky behaviors, such as shoplifting, as a rite of passage into a group or a way to blend in. Try to get across to your child that sticking to her principles and not joining in is often respected by peers, whereas appearing desperate to fit in is ridiculed. This can be difficult to accept for your popularity-conscious 11-year-old, but say it anyway. Keep building her confidence so that she can say "no." She will be confident that her views will be accepted and that she can find new friends if necessary.

Childhood crushes

All children develop at different rates, but some might start to form close friendships with the opposite sex at this age.

It can be difficult to know whether a first relationship is actually true love, a crush, or just physical attraction. However, any suggestion that this is not the "real thing" will be taken as a sure sign that you can't possibly understand her feelings. Whatever your opinion, treat the relationship as serious, avoid teasing, and be sensitive to the inevitable highs and lows. By gently asking how things are going and starting to include your child's boyfriend or girlfriend in family activities, you can monitor things without being invasive.

EARLY ROMANCE *Any relationship is likely to be relatively innocent at this age, but keep an eye on its progress.*

Common behavioral concerns

▶ **"You can't make me" seems to be our 11-year-old's response whenever we ask her to do anything. How can I get her to cooperate with us?**

This kind of challenge to authority is quite normal at this age, but it does need to be handled quickly so that being defiant doesn't become a habit for your child. However, before you start seeing this as misbehavior, check that your requests are well timed—for example, if you ask your child to do her homework in the middle of her favorite TV show, you're bound to get a negative reaction. Also make sure you are being reasonable. If, for example, you've been giving your daughter more than her fair share of chores, she might quite logically say, "It's not my turn."

If you're sure you are being reasonable and respectful and you still get a rude reply, give your daughter a consequence—perhaps take away a privilege by reducing her Internet access or reducing her allowance.

▶ **My son has been under a lot of pressure recently to perform well on his sports team. He now seems to have lost his confidence. What should I do?**

High levels of pressure may have resulted in your son's suffering from some physical signs of anxiety such as excess sweating, shakiness, or feeling dizzy. When this happens, a natural reaction is to try to avoid the situation that caused them. Unfortunately, this does not solve the problem, and your son can miss out on things he'd usually enjoy. Instead, help him cope with difficult situations by teaching him to relax his body as soon as he notices any signs of anxiety.

Negative thoughts are probably feeding his anxiety, so coach him to replace statements like "I can't do this" or "I'm going to let the team down" with positive thoughts such as "I can do this" or "This may feel scary, but I know I'll do my best."

If your child shows signs of anxiety that get in the way of everyday life and do not seem to be improving, then seek help from a health-care professional.

SELF-DOUBT *Starting a new school can reinforce a child's worries about his abilities, but these are inevitable given the challenges he faces in a new environment.*

▶ **My daughter always has to have the last word. How should I handle this?**

Your quick-witted 11-year-old will always want the last word in an argument, and this may come across as rudeness. Half the joy of back talk is the reaction it gets, so don't rise to the bait by demanding an apology or showing your irritation. Simply state, "That's not respectful," and then ignore your child until you have something pleasant to say to each other. Talking back could be an angry reaction to feeling that you aren't listening. Try paying more attention to your daughter's views, as this may result in less rudeness.

▶ **My 11-year-old has become very self-critical. Why is this, and what can I do to help him?**

At this age, a small mistake, such as doing badly on a school test, can seem like a massive error and cause a child distress. When this happens, sympathize with your son, even if the issue seems trivial to you. Help him get things back in perspective—ask, for example, "How many teachers or friends will remember this in a month?" Self-criticism can motivate your son to repair mistakes, so ask whether there is anything he thinks he could do to fix the problem, such as studying more. Taking action can help your child stop worrying and be positive.

Your child's life

Many 11-year-olds will face one of the biggest changes in their lives: moving from the familiar territory of elementary school to the larger and busier environment of middle school. Your normally fiercely independent child may be overwhelmed and need extra support in the first few weeks.

"Threatening your child with a punishment if she doesn't do well in school will not motivate her."

When your child starts middle school, she will have to familiarize herself with a different timetable, get to know new teachers, navigate a different environment, and handle more homework. Independent self-management is now required, particularly being able to read a schedule, organize her books and equipment in advance, and find her way between classes. Help her get organized by talking over the next day's schedule each evening and asking her to think about, and pack, what she will need for each class. Talk through some "what if" scenarios—for example, what she would do if she couldn't find her classroom. Guide her to work out what to do, and make sure she has the confidence to seek help if necessary.

Motivating your child

The most effective way to motivate your 11-year-old is by rewarding positive behavior with your approval, extra privileges, or treats. Typical rewards include extra allowance money or a points system, whereby she can earn credits to swap for extras, such as later bedtimes or her choice of DVD for a family movie night. The other motivation comes from gaining your positive regard. Even though she will have started to challenge your authority, and may not admit she wants your approval, she still wants to share her achievements with you. She will be secretly pleased when you see her work on parents' night or watch her perform in the school play.

Minimizing stress

Preparation is a big factor in reducing the stress of tests and homework deadlines. When your 11-year-old has a regular study time and sets a schedule for herself, she will feel in control of her learning.

To help minimize the stress of schoolwork:

▶ Provide a quiet place in your home for studying. Distract siblings so they are less likely to disturb your child when she is trying to concentrate.

▶ If she has lots of homework or needs to study, excuse her from chores.

▶ Remind her that you love her no matter how well she does on tests, and praise her for trying rather than offering big rewards for high scores.

▶ Show her ways to ease tension: tensing up and shrugging her shoulders, then letting them drop and relax; tensing her hands by making fists and then shaking them loosely; and taking long, slow breaths. Your child can even try some of these techniques during tests.

Brothers and sisters

If you are the parent of more than one child, you will undoubtedly witness a struggle between siblings, and this can be particularly obvious in the preteen years. Brothers and sisters have an unerring ability to

GETTING ALONG *Accept the ups and downs of your children's relationship with each other—one minute they will be friends, the next, foes. This is normal behavior.*

"Don't always intervene. Your children need to learn to sort out and resolve their own arguments."

push each other's buttons, provoking a fierce reaction. Sensitive parenting can, however, restore balance and help prevent serious rivalry.

Make each child feel special If a child thinks a sibling is held in higher esteem by you, jealousy will arise. All children need to be loved and accepted by their parents, and they have the right to express their feelings, receive respect, and be taken seriously.

Show enthusiasm for all your children's achievements You may be less excited about a younger child's milestones than you were with your older child because there is not the same novelty factor. If you do feel this way, try not to let it show.

Give each child responsibility Resist giving your oldest child all the chores or expecting her to take responsibility for younger ones. She doesn't have to do everything just because she is older; younger siblings can help, too.

Make kindness a family policy Children soon learn that it is easier to get along than to waste energy fighting uselessly.

Accept some conflict Children will lash out at each other from time to time. Teach them other ways of relieving anger, and make it clear that it is not acceptable to treat others in ways that they would not like to be treated themselves. Through her relationship with her siblings, your child will eventually learn tolerance of others. She will become more able to solve problems herself, through negotiation.

One thing that your child should be confident of is that you love her and her brothers and sisters unconditionally, without any hint of favoritism. She should know that although at times one child may need

Allowing more freedom

As your 11-year-old gets older and becomes more trustworthy, it is important to acknowledge her growing independence and be more flexible about what she is allowed to do. Therefore, consider offering more freedom when she is ready— for example, staying out slightly later with friends; a choice as to when she watches television, as long as she does other activities, too; more privacy and trips out alone with friends. Make your expectations clear when you give her more freedom, and also specify that if she is not prepared to stay within agreed boundaries, there will be consequences. This will help her to develop a sense of responsibility, and encourage healthy self-respect.

more attention than another, in the end, everyone will get their fair share of attention, and there is plenty of love to go around.

Extended family relationships

Many preteens begin to favor their peer group over family, and show little interest in family activities, particularly those with relatives. However, it is important to encourage your child to maintain these links. The family provides the optimum environment to learn everything from values, religious beliefs, family history, manners, respect, etiquette, and social skills through to responsibility, a good work ethic, relationships, and finances.

CLOSE FAMILY TIES *Try to keep relatives such as cousins in touch with your child. She will reap the benefits of close family relationships in years to come.*

We all want our children to have a positive experience of family life, and a respect for all family members, as this teaches them the importance of relationships. It is our families we turn to for help and advice, and who guide our values and choices. So instill family values in your child. Negotiate and compromise—perhaps she can bring a friend along to family gatherings, and miss one occasionally; however, stand by your policy of "family first."

Studies show that people with extended family support tend to be more literate and reach out for more education and better jobs. They are also at an advantage emotionally and are often more successful in their personal life. Both children and adults benefit from these relationships during times of stress, such as tragedy, death, or divorce, and reap rewards when there is a joyous family event. Some research shows that interaction with extended family can have a positive effect on life span and health.

"We are genetically wired to bond with family members, and, indeed, it is our memories of family life that form the foundation of our lives."

12–14 years

"This is a period of rapid growth on many levels. As a parent, try to embrace the change and enjoy watching your child grow into a wonderful and distinct individual."

Getting the basics right

Adolescence marks a period of intense and rapid growth and development—greater than at any other time since infancy. It is therefore crucial that your child gets "the basics" in terms of good nutrition, enough sleep, and plenty of exercise, in order to experience optimum well-being.

"Most children in this age group are ravenous, and are unlikely to turn their noses up at good, nutritious fare."

Nutritional necessities

Your child's diet is important to health and development and, while you will do your best to ensure that he eats well, you may be frustrated by the fact that he buys his own meals at school, is lured by junk food, pressured by his peer group to eat what everyone else is eating, and perhaps has become picky about certain foods, too. You can't control what your child eats away from home, but you can continue to teach good nutrition, and balance unhealthy habits by serving nutritious meals at home. These meals don't need to be "boring." For example, a thin-crust pizza with lots of vegetables and a blend of lighter cheeses will appeal to a preteen and is nutritious. Make healthy eating more likely by ensuring that he doesn't snack close to meals, and that snack foods aren't "meals" in themselves.

Your child doesn't have to be a social outcast to eat well with friends. Offer make-your-own pizzas for late-night meals with his friends, or homemade burgers and fries. Buy different fresh exotic fruit juices and sparkling water and set up a help-yourself drinks bar. Your child and his friends will have fun experimenting with concoctions and probably won't notice that soda isn't on the menu.

Eating habits

Improving eating habits among teens is crucially important for building strong bones and preventing obesity. The foundation for a lifetime of strong bones is built during the teens and young adult years, until about age 30. This represents your child's peak bone mass—the strongest his bones will ever be. Yet research indicates that teenagers are not getting nearly enough calcium to build strong bones (see page 252).

Maintaining normal weight is critically important, since obesity may lead to Type 2 diabetes, high cholesterol, and high blood pressure in later life. The best way to treat and prevent these is a combination of a healthy diet and exercise. In addition, positive eating patterns fostered during the early teens are likely to last a lifetime.

To encourage good eating habits:

▶ Teach your teenager that eating "healthier" does not mean giving up favorite foods altogether. For example, it can just mean cutting down on portion size and adding foods with nutritional value, such as having a smaller portion of fries along with an apple, or having fruit juice instead of a soda with a burger.

▶ Model good behavior—eat well, exhibit a healthy attitude toward food, display a good body image, and lead an active lifestyle yourself.

▶ Explain about key teen nutrients that may be in short supply, such as calcium and iron. Starting the day with a bowl of whole-grain cereal with milk is a great way for your teenager to get more calcium, and if he adds a handful of raisins, he will get iron, too.

Adequate sleep

You would be forgiven for thinking your young teen suffers from a sleeping disorder, but there is good reason for the sudden change in sleep patterns, which often include later nights and morning sleep-ins. Research indicates that teenagers appear to run on a different circadian rhythm than children and adults do. Puberty appears to cause a change in the mechanisms that trigger when the adolescent needs to go to sleep and to wake up. Forcing an adolescent to get up early does not seem to alter the cycle, and most young adolescents find it difficult to sleep before 11 pm. This makes getting up early for school quite a challenge. But sleep is important for your young teen, no matter how much he resists.

Teens struggle to deal with stress; irritability, lack of confidence, and mood swings are often common, but sleep deprivation makes it worse. Depression can result from chronic sleep deprivation, and not having an adequate amount of sleep can endanger the immune system, making a child more susceptible to illnesses. Sleep deprivation can also impair judgment, and given that many teens are being given freedom to make

FAVORITE FOOD
Fast food, such as pizza, is a fun option for occasional get-togethers with friends, and won't hurt in the context of a balanced, nutritious diet.

their own decisions, this can pose a safety risk. Encourage a healthy sleep routine, with no caffeinated drinks in the evenings, and no TV an hour before bedtime. Make sure weekend sleep-ins last no longer than three or four hours. Young teens need 9–10 hours of sleep, which means that a 10 pm or 11 pm bedtime is late enough, depending on what time your child needs to get up. Keep the television and the lights off when sleeping, and open the curtains when the alarm goes off in the morning. This can help create a more acceptable sleep/wake cycle.

Exercise and leisure

Many adolescents have little inclination to become involved in sporting activities, particularly if they are considered "uncool." Family outings may not hold the same appeal as they did, and you will need to find ways to keep your teen in shape. All children need a good hour of exercise a day, but think outside the box. For example, dancing is a good aerobic sport, and most teenagers like some form of music. Budget permitting, arrange courses in some of the more unusual sports—horseback riding, track and field, diving, archery, martial arts, or climbing, and look for any free activities offered in your community.

Life transitions

Quite apart from the huge number of physical and emotional changes experienced by your teen, he may face additional circumstances that can be stressful. He is likely to change schools, moving on to the next stage of his education, which can be daunting. He will undoubtedly demand new freedoms, but still requires solid boundaries to feel secure. Independence is an important part of preparing children for adult life, but it can be unsettling when they are used to having things done for them, and always have the security of a parent in the background. Continue to offer your support, and make changes in small stages, so that your young teen confidently masters each step before moving on to bigger things.

Overall, the early teen years are full of huge changes. Continue to respect your child and his choices, offer unconditional love, and keep the lines of communication open, so that you are aware of your teenager's concerns and can provide the support he needs at all times.

HEALTHY ACTIVITIES
Indoor climbing walls are widely available. This activity is great for muscle-strengthening, agility, and developing trust in others.

Your 12-year-old

"He will begin to think more deeply about things and have opinions, and he may start to challenge your viewpoint."

GIRL TALK She will have a great bond with her friends and tell them many private things that she won't share with you.

FEEDING HIS HUNGER Your hungry 12-year-old may be in and out of the cupboards and refrigerator. Provide healthy snacks that don't affect his appetite for meals.

BEST PALS Friends will be very important to your preteen, and she is likely to want to spend more time with them than with family.

Growth and development

While puberty is likely to be well underway in a girl by age 12, for many boys it is just beginning. It can help to be aware of some of the physical changes that are occurring. At this age, your child's brain is still developing, and the changes taking place can impact his abilities and emotions.

Most 12-year-old boys are still in early puberty and many will be showing no signs of adolescence yet. Many girls have already started to go through puberty by this age and have begun to develop a more adult body (see page 225). If your 12-year-old daughter is showing no signs of puberty, and is either very short or underweight, take her to your doctor. There are several possible reasons, including an underactive thyroid gland and Turner syndrome, where the ovaries are not properly formed. Another increasingly common cause is anorexia nervosa (see page 297), as a very low body mass index (see page 52) can prevent menstruation.

As puberty starts, most children naturally become more private, spending long periods of time in their room, for example, and being self-conscious about their bodies. For this reason, you will be unlikely to know exactly the stage of puberty your child has reached. However, you will notice a growth spurt, body odor and, undoubtedly, the mood swings.

HEIGHT DIFFERENCES
If your child is shorter than his friends at this age, don't worry— he is likely to catch up and may even end up being taller.

Physical changes in boys

At this age, a boy may have early pubic hair, but underarm hair, facial hair, and a changing voice are a long way off for most. The average 12-year-old boy will be about to launch into his growth spurt and will not reach his peak rate of growth until 14. A boy's growth rate gradually slows until he reaches quite an advanced stage of puberty and then rapidly increases. At this age, most boys will still be growing slowly, but there are exceptions.

Some boys will be noticing enlargement of their testes and scrotum, and for a few, the length of their penis will increase. The whole process can start as early as age nine and be complete by age 13, or start as late as 14 and be complete by 18. Both extremes are normal.

The stages of penis and scrotum development are:

1. The infantile stage.
2. Enlargement of the testes and scrotum with some reddening and change in texture of the scrotal skin.
3. Increased length of the penis with a lesser increase in breadth. Further growth of the testes and scrotum.
4. Considerable increase in the length and breadth of the penis with development of the glans (the bulbous tip of the penis). Further enlargement of the testes and scrotum with darkening of the skin.
5. The genitalia are fully developed.

Brain development

Although your 12-year-old's brain has done most of its growing, there will still be surges in the production of gray matter, which is responsible for thinking. Preteens in early puberty produce more gray matter in the frontal lobes, the part of the brain responsible for planning, impulse control, and reasoning. These lobes are not fully developed until adulthood.

Surges in the growth of white matter, the wirelike fibers that connect distant parts of the brain, happen between the ages of 6 and 13. As the brain develops, the part responsible for carrying out certain functions such as language skills and interpreting emotions by reading facial expressions, changes. There is a lot we still don't understand about brain development at this age, but we do know it is in a dynamic state, which may explain some of the ups and downs in an adolescent's emotions.

"As the growth of 'white matter' in the brain tails off, so does the ability to learn languages effortlessly."

How the bones develop

Healthy bone development in the preteen years prepares the bones for adult life. The stronger the bones are in young adulthood, the longer it will take for osteoporosis to set in. This is a bone disease that causes bones to become brittle and break easily. Bones continue to grow and get stronger until the age of 30—with the teenage years being the most important for development. Vitamin D, calcium, and phosphorus are vital for this process.

Calcium intake
Calcium requirements for the teenage years range from 800 to 1,000 mg a day, but studies suggest that many teenagers have calcium intakes that are below recommended levels.

Your child's health

As your child becomes more body-conscious, and possibly interested in others sexually, he may naturally begin to take better care of himself. However, many teenagers still need encouragement from their parents to brush their teeth correctly and bathe regularly.

Teeth and oral hygiene

By now your child should have a full set of secondary teeth, except for his wisdom teeth. He should brush carefully with a toothpaste containing fluoride at least twice a day to remove all plaque; every six months, go for a checkup with the dentist, who will recommend that he floss daily; and be aware of what affects his teeth, gums, and breath. These factors include:

Sugary foods—these interact with bacteria in plaque to produce acid, which causes erosion of enamel and cavities.

Smoking—this causes bad breath and tooth staining.

Alcohol—this contains sugar, which has the same effect as a sweet drink.

Mouth and tongue piercings—these should be avoided at all costs, as they can damage tooth enamel, and cause a hemorrhage or infection.

PERSONAL CARE *As children go through puberty, they have stronger body odor. Encourage them to shower regularly, and provide deodorant.*

Personal hygiene

Personal hygiene is never more important than in the teenage years, when the body is changing rapidly and producing sweat from underarms and feet, together with greasy skin and hair.

To look and smell clean, your child should:

▶ Bathe or shower daily, paying particular attention to feet and underarms.

▶ Use deodorant.

▶ Change underclothes and socks daily, and other clothes regularly, too.

▶ Wash his hair frequently.

▶ Take his shoes off when possible to allow his feet and shoes to dry. Feet have a huge number of sweat glands and need to "breathe."

▶ Stay away from cigarette smoke to keep hair and clothes fresh.

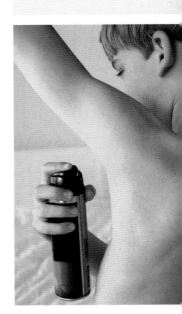

MONITORING HEADACHES
By keeping a record of headaches, you may be able to spot triggers, such as foods, and patterns, such as an occurrence on a certain day each week.

Dealing with headaches

Your child may get headaches, and the most common cause is stress, although they may also be due to migraines, sinusitis, and eye problems. Migraines are severe, usually one-sided headaches that often run in the family. They may temporarily affect vision and cause nausea and vomiting. Migraines are often debilitating and may respond to dietary changes, such as eliminating cheese, chocolate, and caffeine. Frequent migraines are sometimes treated with preventive medications.

If your child has regular headaches, increase his fluid intake, aiming for at least a quart (liter) of water per day. If he is drinking enough, he should need to urinate at least every 4 to 6 hours and should pass pale-colored urine. To ease the pain, use acetaminophen or ibuprofen early and regularly, without exceeding the recommended dose. If your child's headaches persist, take him for an eye test. If you think that stress is causing your child's headaches, try to get to the root of the problem and speak to his teacher if necessary.

Reasons to seek medical advice for a headache:

▶ No improvement after trying all the measures above.

▶ Headaches on waking up or at night.

▶ No response to regular doses of analgesics.

▶ The development of new symptoms such as a squint, poor coordination, weakness, or an abnormal gait.

▶ Vomiting in association with the headaches.

Vaccinations

In the US, all children between 11 and 18 years old should receive the meningococcal vaccine (MCV-4) to protect them from bacteria that can cause a blood infection and/or meningitis. It is recommended that girls receive a series of vaccines at age 11 or 12 to offer protection against human papilloma virus (HPV). This vaccine is given in three doses over the course of 6 months. The aim of this vaccine is to reduce cervical cancer in women. A single tetanus booster shot should be given between 11 and 12 years of age. If an adolescent has not received it previously, Tdap (tetanus, reduced diphtheria, acellular pertussis) should be given because it contains a vaccine against pertussis (whooping cough).

Understanding and skills

The age of 12 officially marks the beginning of adolescence, and your child will begin the stage of cognitive development that takes him through to adulthood. He may begin to make more personal decisions at school and at home, and begin to question authority and social norms.

Encouraging healthy debate

Your 12-year-old may by now be able to form and verbalize his own thoughts and views on a variety of topics, and this is something to be encouraged. There is nothing that will broaden your child's mind and enhance his cognitive skills more than healthy debate. Thrashing out a topic with you, or with another adult, will help him to think outside the box, defend his reasoning, listen to someone else's views, rebut what he doesn't believe in, and look for solutions.

To encourage your child:

▶ Show respect for your 12-year-old's beliefs. Always support "free speech," but demand the same respect in return. In other words, you will listen to what your child says, but you don't have to agree; you put forward your argument calmly, and invite rebuttals.

▶ Talk about current issues—for example, gun crime. Consider any disagreements you have as food for thought and a means by which you can both broaden your horizons. Open your mind to the belief that you can learn something from your child, and he will feel confident expressing himself and examining his own viewpoints.

   If your child is faced with a personal dilemma, an emotional issue may interfere with his ability to think in more complex ways and he may need your help to get a matter clear in his mind.

Computers and learning

The use of computers as an educational tool is controversial, and there are many who claim it diminishes creativity, encourages unhealthy habits, and promotes social isolation. One study found that sustained use of

BEING HEARD *If you can listen calmly to what she has to say, she will learn to listen to what you have to say in the same way—a valuable life skill.*

SURFING THE NET *The Internet is great for gathering information and checking facts, but be sure your child is using it responsibly.*

computers had no positive impact on academic achievement. However, used appropriately, a computer can be a useful tool. Educational computer programs can help to improve skills in subjects such as math, where interactive elements provide instant answers. Using the Internet can encourage your child to seek out answers on his own, pursue interests, broaden learning, and use a vast array of resources. However, your child needs to be made aware that he must not plagiarize other people's work by copying and pasting reference material and passing it off as his own.

Remember:

▶ Your child should spend no more than an hour or two a day on the computer; use other, additional resources, such as books, for schoolwork and projects; and have plenty of face-to-face interaction with peers.

Language and literacy

Your 12-year-old is likely to be able to read competently—even adult newspapers and magazines with topics of specific interest. By now he is able to categorize information and summarize it into his own words, indicating a leap in comprehension. He can also proofread his own work and may sometimes be his own harshest critic. A young adolescent may seem to lose words from his vocabulary, or be gaining words you would prefer he didn't. Language reflects emotional life, and the desire to be accepted by his peer group will result in his speaking more like his

Your teen's speech patterns

Through our interactions, we pick up new words and sayings and integrate them into our speech. Some expressions spread through the population and slowly change the language. Teens often use different words and phrases from their parents. It is important, therefore, not to dismiss new

speech patterns and the vocabulary used by your 12-year-old. If it's not rude, it's not necessarily wrong.

What is most important is that your child understands the word he is using, and can use a substitute to make himself understood in a world outside his peer group. So ask him to explain what a word or

phrase means; if it has a derogatory meaning, ask him to use something else.

Try to encourage a fascination with the way language changes across the generations; if your child enjoys words and can use them in different social situations, he will be one step ahead.

classmates and less like you at home. Speech patterns undoubtedly shift to conform to current trends, and "cool" expressions and slang will replace what once may have been a healthy vocabulary (see left).

The adolescent mute button

A strange thing occurs when a child enters adolescence: he develops a "mute button," which may be pressed when parental interaction is suggested. It is normal for children to clam up with their parents, to become reluctant to talk about certain (or any) subjects, and to reject parental interest. Part of this is a desire for privacy and a way of testing limits; another part is that your child really does have his mind elsewhere.

Many young adolescents simply don't feel like talking because they fear disapproval, but at the same time don't value parental opinions. To help overcome your teenager's silence:

Find some common ground Talk to your child about whatever interests him or her—music, cars, fashion, makeup, sports, TV, and video games— and keep up to date. If you can get a conversation flowing, you may be able to turn it in another direction.

Show respect for his ideas and opinions No child who is constantly rebuked or criticized will ever open up. If your child feels he can say anything without fear of reprisal, he will be more communicative.

Learning firsthand

One of the best ways to encourage learning is to allow your child to experience it firsthand. Children can learn about physics, biology, art, chemistry, geography, design— virtually anything—from exploring the world around them, seeing animals in natural habits, cooking, traveling, and even shopping. You will learn new things, too, if you partake of these activities.

Helping your child to learn:

★ He may find a classic science lecture boring, but get him out in the garden planting seeds and nurturing plants and he will learn in a manner he is likely to remember.

★ Learning to budget spending money and price things as you shop will teach your child invaluable financial skills.

★ Travel is ideal for broadening horizons, so be creative about your vacation destinations if you can.

★ Take your child to museums, galleries, and exhibitions.

Emotions and personality

Your preteen will have plenty to worry about, and every concern will seem huge to him. He is likely to agonize over being accepted or rejected by friends and be torn between striving for quirky individuality and trying to be popular with friends who demand conformity.

All these internal debates are going on for your child at those times when you think he's "spaced out." His tension often comes from trying to juggle so many issues at once. He will certainly get caught between loving you, yet not wanting his friends to witness parental assistance or affection; this could be seen as a sign that he is still dependent on you. He might be appreciative and affectionate in private but reject you fiercely in public. All this angst is an essential part of your 12-year-old's development, helping to form his values and individuality.

DISTANCING HERSELF
Your 12-year-old is striving to become independent, and this may feel to you like rejection. Try hard not to take it personally.

Conflict with parents

Clashes between parents and children can escalate in the preteen years as children no longer see their parents as their main role model. Your 12-year-old could now be copying the styles and attitudes of same-sex friends and celebrities rather than you. Without realizing it, you might be a little irked at this and inclined to be critical of his ideas. To your dismay, he may be making the same mistakes you did at his age, perhaps scaring off friends by being too needy, giving in to peer pressure, or not trying hard enough at school. Your natural inclination will be to try to stop this from happening, rather than accepting that few children learn from their parents' mistakes.
Remember:
▶ Your child has to try things out for himself and make mistakes to truly learn.

If you find conversations with your 12-year-old starting to go along the lines of "When I was your age…" you will find he tunes out immediately. To reduce these clashes, help him think through the pros and cons of new ideas rather than trying to tell him what to do. For example, if he is playing truant from school, ask him, "What do you like about disobeying the school rules and what will you gain or lose by doing this?" When you do this, you open up a debate and improve his decision-making skills.

"Remember, you remain in authority, both as your child's legal guardian, but also because you care about his welfare and, even though he'd deny this, you are wiser and more experienced than he is."

Your 12-year-old has an instinct to push the boundaries and challenge your decisions. It is essential to his developing sense of self. It can, however, be time-consuming and uncomfortable as every tiny thing may end in heated debate. Whether your preteen is nagging for a body piercing or a later curfew, it is worth considering whether you have adapted the limits you place on him enough to meet his increasing maturity and independence.

Emotional health

Developing emotional literacy is the ideal goal for your 12-year-old. This means being able to recognize, express, and manage his own emotions as well as tune in to and understand the feelings of others.

Your emotionally healthy preteen will be able to regulate his feelings most of the time but may need your help. For example, if he is concerned about a friend's not showing up on time, help him to work out some possible reasons and to keep his anger in check. He can use self-talk to soothe himself by thinking, "Maybe my friend is late because he's been kept after school, and he's not snubbing me." He might find ways to keep busy, rather than dwelling on the problem. Then, when the friend arrives, he will be more able to calmly ask about the delay rather than have an angry outburst.

How well children handle emotional upsets will to some extent depend on their personality. They also learn from their parents, so try to manage your own emotions in front of your child.

Remember:

❯ In some instances, your 12-year-old wants you to stand your ground firmly. This allows him to press for something outrageous without actually experiencing the fear of having to go through with it. Don't feel you need to give up your right to say "no."

Friends and friendships

Your preteen child is now intensely aware of the possibility of boy- or girlfriend relationships. Most 12-year-olds are still spending their time with friends of the same gender, but there is increasing contact with the opposite sex and romance is definitely in the air. At this age, showing an interest in romance can still lead to teasing and there will be considerable anxiety about being rejected, so contact between interested boys and girls often appears accidental—for example, bumping against each other in the hall or standing behind someone in the lunch line.

Boys may try to get a girl's attention in ways that could be interpreted as aggressive—for example, pushing or nudging. If this sort of approach is rejected, your 12-year-old can keep up the pretense of not caring, thus avoiding embarrassment. Both sexes show bravado about romantic relationships—for example, talking up the interest that has been shown in them and how they have rejected it. This is a way of expressing their basic ambivalence about moving from the relative safety of friendships into the world of dating.

Being accepted is a powerful motivator for your 12-year-old, and a prime way to get that sense of belonging is to join a clique or group of friends who identify with each other. They may have their own in-jokes, slogans, and dress code, which signals membership. The formation of a "gang" depends on having a number of young people who are in it and some who aren't allowed to join. Build your child's self-esteem at home so he feel goods about himself, whether he is "in" or "out" of the group.

BONDING WITH FRIENDS
Your child wants to belong, and will form cliques with her friends. She will be motivated to please them more than you, so expect disagreements.

Common concerns

▶ **My 12-year-old daughter seems to be developing physically far more quickly than her friends and is embarrassed by her figure. How can I help her?**

Being self-conscious is typical of a 12-year-old girl, but can be made considerably worse if she's reached puberty earlier than her peers, particularly if breast development and height have taken off.

Accept that this is a difficult time for your daughter and bear in mind that she may be being taunted about her appearance. If she is being bullied, act quickly to address it—for example, by ensuring that school staff take action. Practice with her some replies to the taunts along the lines of "I'm fine with how I look, thanks." Work on her pride in her developing appearance by encouraging her to stand tall, and make sure she has underwear and clothing that support and fit her curvaceous shape.

▶ **There always seems to be a new gadget my daughter demands. How can I stop this excess consumption?**

Possessions, whether they're the latest jeans or a phone, are the outward signs of status, and your 12-year-old, exposed to years of advertising, is likely to be materialistic. There are a multitude of influences outside the home that encourage this consumerism, over which you have no control. You do, however, control the purse strings and can ration purchases. Don't give in to every demand, and do reason with her about the value of possessions. For example, talk over what qualities she likes in others: is it their new phone or their sense of humor? Help her learn that self-worth is based on who we are, not what we own.

▶ **My 12-year-old loses things all the time. How can I help him keep tabs on his stuff?**

Increase the chances of your son's finding lost items by teaching him assertive search skills. For example, prompt him to take a mental journey forward from the last time

TAKING CARE OF POSSESSIONS *Teach him to care for his belongings, and resist replacing lost items until you are sure he has made every effort to find them.*

he saw the item; this gives him a route to search. Practice how to approach staff and ask about the lost item, or locate the lost and found. This way he will be more confident about searching actively and asking for help. Get him into the habit of using a mental checklist, going through everyday items one by one, asking himself, "Do I have my...." At first you may need to help with the list, perhaps going through key items together. Label everything so that you have a better chance that any misplaced items will be returned.

▶ **My son has recently become very opinionated. Why is this, and is it to be encouraged?**

Your son is in a dilemma; he no longer wants to be just like you, but he's not too sure about his separate identity. In trying to work out his sense of self, he'll try some different ways to express it. It is normal for children to take up new viewpoints, often the opposite of their parents', perhaps becoming vegetarian, questioning their faith, or taking an interest in politics. Much of the point of their opposition is to highlight their individuality, and your child will be disappointed if you don't notice or oppose some of these changes. But do be aware that you'll need to work hard to keep your cool if your son goads you with views very different from your own.

Your child's life

Being busy is the norm for your 12-year-old as he balances social life, school work, leisure activities, and family time. There is great variation in how much activity children of this age can cope with, so you need to monitor your child and ensure that he is getting the balance right.

"It will benefit your child to have periods of time where he can just relax and do nothing."

Your child may be happy to be busy every moment of the day, with no indication that he is overdoing things. If, however, you notice signs that he is overtired—for instance, if he finds it hard to wake up for school— you will need to negotiate some limits to his social life. Remember, he is with friends all day at school, so perhaps socializing can be cut back on school nights. Review his leisure-time commitments, too. If some of these are continuing out of habit, it may be time to cut out one or two.

Monitoring academic progress

When you stay interested in your child's homework, note the teacher's written comments, and talk topics over with him, you will become aware of his strong and weak points. Don't wait for parents' nights to speak with his teachers if you are concerned about your child's progress.

Helping with homework

Homework may be significant for your 12-year-old, and he will need your help to complete it on time.
★ A study area should have a flat, stable surface and be quiet, warm, well-lit, and free of distractions.
★ Ask what he is doing and find out how confident he feels about the assignment. Some homework requires finding information from books or the Internet, so help him with ideas for search strategies and teach him how to assess if material is of good quality.
★ Help him maintain concentration by reminding him to take a break every 30 minutes.
★ Keep him focused by making it clear that other, more pleasurable activities can only take place once homework is finished.
★ If your 12-year-old is really struggling with a subject, try not to cover this up by helping too much. It is better to get in touch with his teacher to figure out how to help your child improve.

If he seems to be falling behind in a subject, make an appointment with the relevant teacher to explore how the problem can be addressed. Perhaps he has been placed in a class above his skill level, or in one that isn't challenging enough and he is bored. He may have missed lessons or have a personality clash with the teacher. If he has fallen behind, then tutoring or homework clubs could make all the difference.

Losing interest in school

It is usual for some 12-year-olds to lose interest in schoolwork. For one thing, your child's peer group becomes infinitely more important at this age, and social interaction usually takes precedence. In addition, most 12-year-olds no longer crave the approval of their parents and teachers as much (a major motivation to do well in earlier years) and don't recognize the long-term benefits of slaving away for rewards that seem very distant. Given all these factors, it is not surprising that some children become disillusioned with school.

To help your child:

▶ Make it clear why an education is important and explain why it is desirable to do well at school.

▶ Consider whether your child is at the right school; sometimes a different approach to teaching and learning can motivate an apathetic child.

▶ Talk about what your child is doing in school and try to pinpoint the areas of the curriculum that do interest him.

▶ To encourage him, be positive rather than always criticizing. Talk excitedly about his future and what he might like to do; it may seem early, but if he knows that he wants to be a vet or a sports broadcaster, for example, it is helpful for him to know now what he needs to achieve.

▶ Set strict guidelines about homework and school responsibilities. Make sure he knows that he is allowed to have a social life, but only after homework and other school commitments are taken care of.

▶ Look out for signs of bullying (see page 199).

You may find your child dreams of being a rock star or sports star, but isn't prepared to put in the work to achieve these goals. While this sort of apathy is normal, if your child has lost interest in school and enthusiasm for most of the pursuits that once kept him busy, he may be depressed (see

DAYDREAMER *With such a full life, he may become preoccupied. Make sure he understands the consequences of lackluster grades.*

Dealing with truancy

For some children, school holds dangers of bullying, fear of failure, and feeling left out. Others are encouraged by friends to rebel by hanging out away from school. Once you know your child is truant, get him back to school as soon as possible, then monitor him closely between home and school each day, to be sure he arrives—and stays. Speak to his teachers to try to pinpoint reasons for his truancy and find ways of making school more appealing. Make sure your child is well prepared for school—some children skip school to avoid detention if they forget their gym bag, for example. For a very few children, going to school can cause so much anxiety that professional help is needed.

PRIORITIZING *Spending time with friends is important, but your child must get the balance right so that her social life doesn't prevent her from completing homework and getting to bed at a suitable time.*

page 283) or perhaps—although unlikely—even experimenting with drugs or drinking alcohol. Changes in behavior, and in particular, unusual apathy and loss of interest in friends, hobbies, and extracurricular activities, are all warning signs that should be investigated properly.

Going out on school nights

Your 12-year-old needs around nine hours of sleep each night to wake up ready to learn every weekday morning. Work out a bedtime that allows him to get the nine hours he needs, then work back one hour to give him time to wind down, and that gives you the latest time he can stay out on a school night. For example, if he usually gets up at 7 am, then he needs to be asleep by 10 pm, which means being home by 9 pm to prepare for bed. On top of the desire to socialize, your 12-year-old needs to allow time for homework, sports, practicing hobbies, such as musical instruments, and spending time with the family. These commitments must be fitted in before your 12-year-old goes out to socialize. You should always know where your child is, who he is with, and when he will return.

Don't sweat the small stuff

It is easy to get caught in a pattern of conflict with your 12-year-old if he is constantly challenging your authority and values. At this age, he will just tune you out if you are nagging or confronting him too often. If you and your preteen have fallen into this trap, review the situation. Work out which are the issues you need to take a stand over. Perhaps coming in late

and dumping stuff where it trips you irritate you intensely, but with other annoyances, just make your point and leave it at that. Leave your child alone if his behaviors affect only him. For example, he will soon learn to pick up his towel if it is still wet the next time he needs to use it.

"Everyday irritations, such as leaving clothes on the bedroom floor or eating too many cookies, can easily begin to dominate your relationship with your child."

Encouraging family values

Your 12-year-old may start to question specific family values, but he is unlikely to reject all the underlying standards you have taught. For example, he will still want to be kind, honest, and respect the property and privacy of others if these values have been instilled from an early age. His moral understanding has probably progressed and he will be able to see that rules are helpful to society because they protect people and promote fairness. He will, however, recognize that these rules are complex, sometimes contradictory, and that some can be negotiated.

Having debates with your 12-year-old on hot topics can help him explore values. The more you encourage discussion on subjects that question values and judgments, the more your child has a chance to work out where he stands, develop a sense of right and wrong, and form his own well-thought-out views on different topics.

Communicating with your child

To communicate effectively with your 12-year-old, try using "I" rather than "you" statements. "I" statements mean you express how you feel and try to understand the other person, whereas "you" statements can lead to guilt and conflict. For example, saying, "I felt hurt when you asked me to pick you up out of sight of your friends" describes the feeling without accusing your child.

Conversely, by saying to your child, "You were rude to ask me to pick you up out of sight of your friends," you are blaming him and are more likely to get a negative reaction. This difference may seem subtle, but try it to see if it improves communication between you.

Common lifestyle concerns

▶ **I'm concerned that when my 12-year-old hangs around with his friends, he is drinking alcohol. What can I do?**

It is so tempting for children to experiment with anything forbidden. In a recent survey, 48 percent of children age 10–15 admitted they'd tried an alcoholic drink.

How you react will affect whether your son hides his drinking from you. If you express concern but remain calm, you'll encourage him to confide in you. It helps to be knowledgeable about the health risks and consequences of drinking alcohol and the sanctions he could expect if the police got involved. You don't have to condone his behavior, but help keep him safe by offering suggestions about reducing risks. By being up to date, you can provide him with all the facts, without wrecking your credibility by exaggerating the risks. When the topic of risky behavior is out in the open with your child, it becomes less illicit, making it less exciting and desirable to him.

▶ **My son constantly texts friends, or chats on the Internet. Should I put a stop to this?**

This could be detrimental to your son's development if it is affecting his ability to socialize with friends in person and spend time with the family. Remote socializing means communication comes with much less information. For example, in person, tone of voice, gestures, and posture help to get a message across and can make the difference between a comment being interpreted as a joke, a back-handed compliment, or a massive insult. The limited information provided by messaging means misunderstandings are more common and your child has less opportunity to practice the full range of social skills.

Consider whether your son is socializing remotely because he lacks confidence in face-to-face friendships. Encourage him to see his friends after school and on weekends, and cut down the number

PHONE ADDICTION *If your son finds his phone irresistible and constantly checks it, set guidelines to help him minimize its use, such as turning it off at mealtimes.*

and duration of remote contacts. Put a limit on the time he can spend online and have one evening a week where the computer is out of bounds and the family spends time together. Do check the content of his Internet searches and online chats to be sure he is safe and only accessing appropriate sites.

▶ **My 12-year-old wants to have a party at home for her next birthday, but she wants to organize it and doesn't want us to be there. Should I allow this?**

Allow her to organize and host the party, but remain at home. You can keep a low profile, perhaps staying upstairs most of the time, but by being there you will be able to step in if problems arise.

Make it clear that she must set a limit to the number of guests and have a specific start and end time. Discuss how she will tackle any problems—for example, if alcohol is brought to the party, fights break out, or equipment failure messes up the music. It won't look cool if she rushes to get your help, but that may be the best solution. To avoid party crashers, make sure your teen uses paper invitations, rather than a posting on the Internet, which could attract strangers. Let the neighbors know the party is happening and reassure them you will be at home. This consideration should pay dividends in extra tolerance on the night.

14

13

12

11

10

9

8

7

6

5

4

3

YEARS

STARTING A RELATIONSHIP Girls at age 13 may feel they are ready for a "real" relationship, but the objects of their affections may be more reticent.

Your 13-year-old

"Academic pressure increases at this age, but your teen is likely to be preoccupied with outside interests."

FIT FOR LIFE Encourage her in sports and healthy pursuits to offset the many sedentary activities that are often favored by teens.

BOOKWORM If your teenager likes to read, make sure he has access to the books he likes and a quiet environment in which to enjoy them.

Growth and development

The mood swings associated with adolescence can start happening at an earlier age than 13, but they are usually associated with the teenage years. Knowing all about the hormone changes that affect your child can make you more understanding and tolerant at this challenging stage.

Hormonal changes

The whole point of puberty is to change the body of a child into a body capable of reproduction. This process is controlled by hormones, which is why people talk about "raging hormones" in teenagers. Boys and girls both release a hormone from the brain called gonadotrophin-releasing hormone, which stimulates the production of two further hormones, also produced in the brain. These hormones act on the testes in boys, to release testosterone and produce sperm, and on the ovaries in girls, to produce estrogen and release eggs.

In boys, once this process happens, it is continuous and not cyclical. In girls, however, once menstruation starts, and until menopause, the body is constantly preparing itself for reproduction. A cyclical pattern of hormones allows the lining of the womb (endometrium) to thicken and prepare for implantation of a fertilized egg. The hormones then cause release of an egg, and if it is not fertilized by a sperm, the level of hormones drops and the thickened endometrium, no longer needed for the implantation of an embryo, is shed. This is called a "period."

The role of each hormone:

▶ The specific roles of estrogen are to promote the development of the lining of the womb (see above), prepare the ovaries for release of an egg, and assist with salt and water balance in the body.

▶ Progesterone is more concerned with the procreation and survival of a fetus. It is secreted at ovulation, helping to prepare the womb for pregnancy and the breast tissue for milk production. Levels fall off in the second half of the menstrual cycle unless a pregnancy has started. Adjusting to these swinging hormone levels is difficult for some girls.

LOOKING OLDER *At 13, some girls begin to look like young women, while boys tend to still look like boys rather than young men.*

Physical changes in boys

If your 13-year-old boy is in early puberty, he will be growing slowly but steadily, increasing his muscle mass (see page 293) while becoming leaner. The body density of boys increases more than that of girls because muscle is denser than fat. The growth of boys' genitalia (see page 252) continues, and pubic hair is present in most, but only in an adult distribution in the minority. Your son may have the early signs of facial hair, although many do not, but his voice is unlikely to have changed yet.

Starting to shave

Most 13-year-old boys won't need to shave, but if they do want to, they should be shown how to do so safely. Girls of this age are likely to want to shave their legs and under their arms. Make your daughter aware that once she starts shaving, new growth will seem more conspicuous and she will be committed to shaving from then on. Children should be given their own razors (due to the potential risk of passing on bloodborne diseases such as hepatitis) and use shaving cream or soap to protect their skin.

Being active

Physically active children are at reduced risk for developing cardiovascular disease and are likely to have enhanced mental and emotional well-being. Exercise should be fun, varied, and part of everyday life. Many teenagers enjoy sedentary activities and need encouragement to exercise. Make sure they are getting out and about, especially on weekends.

FACIAL HAIR *In their early teens, some boys may have a light growth of facial hair. The first hair to grow is usually a mustache.*

Too much exercise?

As your teenager becomes more body-conscious, comparing herself to peers and role models, she may want to join a gym. This interest in exercise should be applauded as long as it is supervised by a trained adult who understands what is appropriate for the age and stage of the child. Some children do too much exercise—the two situations to be wary of are:

★ Excessive exercise in a child who you suspect may have an eating disorder (see page 297).

★ Overdeveloped muscles in a boy. This may be a sign that he has been given anabolic steroids. If steroids aren't involved, huge muscle development means he may be overstressing his joints and bones.

Your child's health

It may be alarming to think that your young teenager is possibly considering sexual activity. While sex at this age should not be encouraged, it is essential to inform teenagers about sexual health so that they can protect themselves from pregnancy and sexually transmitted diseases.

Many teenagers feel pressured into having sex for spurious reasons, such as keeping up with and impressing peers, wanting to get the first time "over and done with," and, for girls, often because they fear losing a boyfriend if they refuse sex. Although this can be a difficult and embarrassing subject to discuss, it is extremely important to be open and honest with your child about sex. Whatever our views, we must make sure that our teens can protect themselves from the first time they have sex.

What your teenager should know:

▶ It is never safe to have unprotected sex.

▶ The rate of teenage pregnancies and STDs is rising, and both are easily preventable by using condoms. Even if a girl is on the pill, the boy should always wear a condom.

▶ Condoms protect against all STDs including HIV, chlamydia, herpes, and gonorrhea.

▶ Girls should not rely on boys to carry or use a condom and should feel empowered to always insist they use one.

▶ Chlamydia is a particularly insidious disease as it often infects without producing symptoms. It is a major cause of infertility.

In the United States, the "age of consent" for sexual activity ranges from 16 years to 18 years, dependent upon the individual state laws. Age of consent means that one can have sex with another if the partner is consenting and of the same age or older. If coercion is suspected by a physician, this must be reported to law enforcement. Most adolescents require total confidentiality to discuss their sexuality with a health-care provider. However, the provider should encourage teens to be open with parents as much as possible.

GETTING PHYSICAL *Sexual attraction is a normal part of development. Some teens will begin to be more exploratory and seek sexual pleasure, even at this young age.*

Diet

Your 13-year-old may have a huge requirement for calories during a growth spurt and then eat much less when growth slows. She is more likely to snack and eat away from home, often junk food, so try to make sure the food you provide at home is healthy and includes carbohydrates (pasta, rice, bread, potatoes), vegetables and legumes, fruit, and dairy products. Encourage your child to drink plenty of water, and don't panic if she develops odd food cravings (see page 201).

Teenagers who become vegetarian often eat a very healthy diet as long as a wide selection of vegetables, starch, and dairy products are on hand. Beware the "vegetarian" teenager who only eats nonnutritious foods such as fries and doughnuts; she is not a true vegetarian, and will become iron-deficient if she is allowed to continue with such a nutrient-poor diet.

Acne

It is normal for teenagers to get acne. These unsightly and often painful pimples can occur on the face and body. Acne is caused by an abnormal response in the skin to the hormone testosterone. The pores in the skin become blocked by oil, and this causes pimples. Severe acne can be genetic. Acne usually starts in the early teens, peaks in the late teens, and clears by the mid-twenties. Acne can be helped in a number of ways

★ Although acne is not due to poor hygiene as such, it makes sense to keep hair washed and away from the face and to wash the face with soap and water twice a day to help unclog the pores. Antiseptic face washes can be particularly helpful.

Note that too-frequent washing can sometimes trigger acne because it encourages the skin to produce more oil.

★ Your child should avoid using oily hair and face products.

★ There is no data to support the idea that getting a suntan helps to clear up acne.

★ Despite popular myths about potato chips and chocolate, acne is not in any way caused by diet. However, a healthy diet, especially plenty of fruit and vegetables, can help keep skin clear.

Treating acne

★ Try an over-the-counter treatment, such as a lotion containing benzoyl peroxide,

applied to the whole affected area. This can cause redness or dryness, which can be overcome by applying it less frequently and using a moisturizer.

★ Antibiotics may be prescribed by your doctor or a dermatologist.

If all other options have failed in girls, the use of the oral contraceptive pill may be recommended to regulate hormones and help control acne.

Emotional impact

Acne undermines self-esteem and may make your teenager very unhappy, not least because she is at a self-conscious age. Be understanding and never allow teasing about her pimples.

Understanding and skills

For the first time, your 13-year-old may begin to focus on the future, so the messages you have been trying to get across about healthy living or education might start to filter through. Most importantly, you can help her to understand how her actions now will have an impact on her life.

Moral development

Setting a strong moral code in your family is important, as it serves as a foundation for your child's value system in years to come. It is important, therefore, to make your beliefs on certain subjects, such as honesty, materialism, sex, drugs, and family values, clear from early childhood onward, and to stick to your message even when challenged.

By the age of 13, your child wants to be liked and wants approval, and therefore her motivation for acting the way she does boils down to what others think of her. She will have worked out that people will like her if she is nice, and that by living up to other people's expectations, she can feel good about herself. This kind of thinking can be the source of cooperative, caring behavior. However, your child might feel confused about what is right and what others want her to do. It is fine if she is being influenced by people who are presenting positive moral values, such as kindness, honesty, and respect, but it will prove difficult if she is trying to please or impress someone who is lacking in morals.

Peer pressure

The challenge for you is to keep your child tuned in to positive values and make her strong enough to resist peer-group seduction into things like having sex, taking drugs, and drinking alcohol. She may be tempted to join in because "everybody's doing it." You have to remember that your young teen is only human and therefore she will value peer approval as much as you do, and at this age the pressure to conform can be very strong. This is why it is important to keep reiterating what you believe in, and why. Use examples to make your point and model them, and be honest and true to

"You may find that your child is more moral than you are, and anything perceived to be hypocrisy on your part will be swiftly picked up on."

your beliefs at all times. Not surprisingly, the ability to argue and reason develops in leaps and bounds during the 13th year, so be prepared for some disagreements but also, hopefully, some healthy debates.

Again, influenced by her peers, your teen is likely to have clear-cut beliefs and ideals and will probably challenge your morals and values, such as your political allegiances, or, if she is vegetarian, for example, the fact that you choose to eat meat. Even if you don't agree with her, try to respect her point of view and her choices. By using this approach, you are more likely to be able to have rational arguments with her. If you tell her she's wrong or too young to know about such things, she may just stop communicating with you altogether.

Language and literacy

Your 13-year-old will probably feel confident reading almost anything, and is likely to show an interest in more adult subject matter. At this age, many children outgrow children's stories and head into the older teens' section of the bookstore or library. Your child will be able to grasp more difficult

A healthy view of the world

Unfortunately, we live in a society where materialism, racism, and intolerance are rife; where there is a lackluster approach to caring for the planet, and little sense of personal responsibility.

We all want our children to see the good around them, and to feel part of the drive to make the world a better place, so influences are important. If your child learns about the world from soap operas, she will get a negative, compressed view of humanity; if she lives in a home where there is constant arguing, she will believe that this is a normal way to behave. If she witnesses violence and intolerance, she will absorb it: children learn what they live.

How to help your child:
★ Teach her about parts of the world that need assistance, and encourage her to get involved.
★ Teach her to recycle and to save resources.
★ Teach her about other cultures and races, and help her accept and appreciate their differences.
★ Show her tolerance and understanding so that she treats others in the same way.
★ Teach her values such as caring for others, kindness and courtesy, personal awareness, and promoting peace.
★ Get her involved in community initiatives and, if possible, travel off the beaten track a little so that she gets a taste of how other people live. This is the part of learning that creates a strong ethical core, and it will help to make your child a great citizen, both now and later.

plots and vocabulary, but you may find that she isn't as proficient at using the words that she can read and understand. While many 13-year-olds understand quite sophisticated topics and specialized words in writing, they can struggle to get their own ideas across on paper. Your young teen will be learning to relate words to actions and abstract thoughts. Talk about the words that are used, and what the author is trying to say.

Poetry may not be a family favorite, but it can be used effectively to talk about emotion and the use of words. Try also listening to popular music that your child likes; lyrics are a form of the written word, and can be used to improve literacy on all levels.

Creative writing

Many young teens struggle to communicate and find it difficult to identify and express themselves. Creative writing encourages children to use words in different ways, and to play with them, by exploring emotions and scenarios and problem-solving through the imagination. All of this enhances literacy and understanding.

To help your child:

▶ Suggest that she keep a regular journal and encourage her to cut out pieces of stories, names, words, or even pictures she likes, and paste them in. A creative journal becomes a useful resource for later writing.

▶ If your child doesn't feel it is too babyish, read to her, stopping at key points to ask what she thinks should happen next.

▶ Talk about endings and whether your child thinks they work. Suggest that she write an alternative ending, or adds another character.

Learning other languages

There are three main methods for teaching a second language for school-aged children who are not exposed to a second language at home. The first is "immersion training," which involves the child's spending part or even

Literacy and technology

If your child is more interested in being on her computer or cell phone than reading and can't be persuaded to cut down on screen time, don't panic. There are some great computer programs that can spark creativity and help with spelling and grammar. You may be concerned about your child sending lots of messages on her phone or computer, but there may be a positive side—she is still communicating through writing.

A 2006 study found that far from being detrimental to literacy, texting and chatroom-speak is beneficial for grammar. Researchers said they were "blown away" by the command of English, and the creativity and fluidity of language used. The study concluded that messaging and chatroom-speak are "an expansive new linguistic renaissance." Let your teen express herself through new media as well as through traditional reading and writing.

all of their school day exposed to the second language only. In partial immersion, several hours a day are dedicated to a particular language; in full immersion, all subjects are taught in it. The second and most common method of teaching a second language is when the language is taken as a distinct subject. This method works well, especially for younger children. Some studies support the idea that the best time to begin a second language is before adolescence, but others contend that older children with a mastery of the English language find it easier. In reality, it is never too late. Some schools include foreign language education in their study of varying countries and cultures. This method is not intended to produce fluency, but some students take away valuable terms and phrases.

Finally, a new way of learning languages is emerging. Based on the "mind-mapping" skills developed for studying and memory work, it teaches language in a vibrant and visual way that apparently lends itself to long-term memory.

To help your child:

▶ Locate books, DVDs, and music in the language your child is learning and take time to make them part of your child's day.

▶ Try to take your child to cultural events and movies in the second language. Just as she learned her first language by hearing it from a variety of sources, she will pick up the second language in much the same manner. The more exposure she has, the better.

EXTRA TUTORING
Additional tutoring can make all the difference if your child needs help with—or is interested in learning—a particular language.

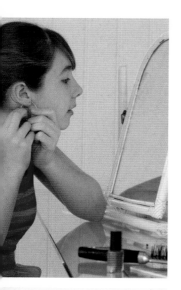

Emotions and personality

At age 13 your child is likely to become very self-conscious, and, with a heightened awareness about appearance, it will be common for her to agonize over pimples, clothes, and what people think of her. She will be very sensitive to any criticism, and need careful handling.

LOOKING GOOD *She will spend a lot of time scrutinizing her appearance and experimenting with clothes, hairstyles, and makeup. Give her space to do this.*

Your child will be so self-conscious that she feels everyone is looking at and judging her on her appearance. She will interpret the smallest glance as a critical stare, and you may be surprised by her strong reaction to what you intended as benign eye contact. If you do have to tackle a sensitive issue, such as personal hygiene (see page 253), do so with great care.

Often the simplest question about schoolwork or friendships will spark a seemingly exaggerated reaction of wanting to be left alone, alongside accusations that you are being nosy. Your daughter may seem to enjoy making a dramatic exit and follow it up with complaints about how unreasonable you are. Nevertheless, the time she spends alone will be productive and she may use it to think through and interpret the events of the day, perhaps by writing down her reflections in a diary or on a blog or social networking site, although you should make sure she knows how to use the latter in a safe and responsible way.

Constructive criticism

No one likes to be criticized, least of all your sensitive 13-year-old. However, sometimes feedback on her behavior is a must. For example, perhaps she has snubbed a relative by texting during a family visit. Start your conversation by stirring your child's empathy, perhaps asking how the relative might have felt when she kept texting, or how she might feel if someone texted when she was visiting.

Once you have gotten your point across that her behavior could be seen as impolite, ask your young teen to come up with a good course of action—for example, calling to apologize or sending a note. Once you have thought up with a few solutions, help her to choose one that offers a

"Provide your teenager with role models whose prowess is their humor, intellect, or spirit of adventure rather than their good looks."

way to repair the situation without losing face. Always address problems sensitively, and in private, since criticism in front of others can be very shaming, no matter how sensitively it is handled.

Striving for perfection

It takes time to go through puberty, and the halfway stage, between an immature and mature body shape, seems to take forever to your 13-year-old. The pressure to look perfect comes from within, but is fueled by role models such as celebrities, who are seemingly without a bump, bulge, or

Sorting out confusing feelings

Adolescence is a confusing time emotionally. When your 13-year-old is struggling to understand her feelings, give her a chance to talk it over. She probably won't want you to solve her problems, but she would like you to understand what's going on for her.

To help your child:
★ Choose a time when neither of you has anything urgent to do and find a private place to chat, where people can't interrupt.
★ Tell your teenager what you have noticed, perhaps that she seems to swing from tearful to frustrated, then excited.
★ Ask her to tell you about what is

happening for her, and reassure her that you want to listen and not to give advice or interfere.
★ Make sure you understand what she is saying by repeating some points back to her and asking how she felt at different times.
★ Finally, once she has described her situation, ask if there is anything you can do to help. Try to avoid offering direct suggestions, and don't take it personally if she rejects your help and advice.
　She may sometimes get angry and say "Just leave me alone" when you try to help. If this happens, give her space and time— that way, she is more likely to come and talk to you later.

EMOTIONAL SUPPORT *Create the right environment to talk. Let her share her concerns at her own pace, and listen carefully.*

blemish. To keep things in perspective, make sure your 13-year-old is realistic about her appearance. Draw attention to her good points to balance her focus on what she doesn't like.

Remember:

◗ You will never argue her out of self criticism, but you even the balance when you ensure that she identifies what is good about herself as well as what she would prefer to be different.

Friends and friendship

Friends are becoming increasingly important to your 13-year-old. They are there to offer reassurance, acceptance, and act as a sounding board for your teen. Don't be surprised to find your opinion rejected in favor of their views. Hanging out with friends will be a favored activity, yet there are few places young people can just meet to be together. Making your home a welcoming place means they have a safe space. You may not always agree with your teen's choice of friends, but keep an open mind and avoid being judgmental, especially about appearance. Telling your teenager not to hang out with someone is likely to lead to defiance and strengthen your teen's determination to spend time with that person, so it is better not to make an issue of it, unless you have very strong reasons.

RIVALRY *Interest in dating may lead to competition over partners. Even if there's an unspoken rule that friendship comes first, this may not happen in reality.*

Common behavioral concerns

▶ **I caught my son looking at a pornographic Internet site. Should I be worried?**
Interest in sex and the human body is at a height in your hormone-driven 13-year-old. For boys, a common channel for their curiosity and the relief of sexual tensions is found in viewing adult-content magazines or Internet sites.

It can come as a shock to find a men's magazine hidden under your son's mattress or risqué content in his Web search history, but this exploration is a normal part of his sexual development, and it's best, for example, to simply return the magazine to its place and let it pass. However, if your son is spending long periods viewing sexual content on the Internet, looking at highly pornographic material or inappropriate or underage sexual acts, express your concerns, no matter how embarrassed both of you feel, and limit what he can read or access.

▶ **My teenage son seems to have lost interest in just about everything. He no longer wants to see his friends, keep up his sports, and looks pretty sad. What can I do?**
If your son is sad and withdrawn for a short time—for example, for a few days—and then bounces back, there is little to worry about. However, if his mood has persisted or recurs frequently, he may be depressed and will need your help, and probably that of a health-care professional.

Support him by showing an interest in what has happened to him, by using gentle, open questions and listening carefully. Encourage him to keep going to school; having something to get up for every morning and keeping in touch with his friends helps keep him from falling into a declining mood. He may find it difficult to imagine that he'll ever feel better, and this is a red flag for you to seek professional help for him. It is crucial to intervene before he considers suicide.

STRUGGLING TO COPE *It's tough for parents to see their child in despair. Keep the lines of communication open and seek professional help if necessary.*

▶ **My son has started making homophobic jokes. We pride ourselves on being open to all lifestyle choices and are shocked. How should we handle this?**
It is your son's job to rebel. Putting aside and rejecting your views and values allows him a clean sheet to form his own opinions and work out who he is. However, this display of rebellion is highly offensive, and you need to step in to address it.

You could start by expressing your disapproval and pointing out that hiding his views in jokes is not acceptable. Explain why you hold your beliefs—for example, speak of the value of every human being and the importance of respecting each person's life choices just as you expect others to respect you. Praise your son for speaking well of others and interrupt quickly if he starts an unpleasant anecdote.

▶ **I'm concerned that my daughter is easily led, and I'm worried about her going to parties.**
If you are worried, talk to your daughter about how to avoid taking risks and, for example, coach her to have the confidence to say "No" to a lift if she thinks alcohol is affecting the driver. There is a risk that teenagers will experiment with alcohol and drugs at parties, meaning an increased risk of having casual sex. Highlight this issue with your child and talk about safe sex (see page 273).

Your child's life

As academic pressure increases, your teenager will need help and guidance to complete her studies well and on time, and the results of exams will begin to be more important. With puberty well underway, she will have lots to deal with and will be easily distracted, not least by the opposite sex.

Encouraging independent study

By the age of 13, children are expected to study independently, and this should be encouraged. Studies show that far too many teenagers are ill-prepared for further education, having never managed their own time, planned their own projects and essays, or worked independently. This process takes years to hone, so it is worth starting now. Ask your child what assignments she has for homework, when they are due, and find out if she should be studying for any exams. By all means, help with the planning. Many 13-year-olds are disorganized and will balk at the amount of work needed to complete a project or study for an exam.

How to help your child:

▶ Make her study space free of distractions, and insist that her phone and computer are switched off (unless the latter is required for research).

▶ Offer to quiz or check work, but don't be upset if she resists, and don't push it, either. You will know from her report card if she is falling behind in any subjects, and parents' nights will reveal areas of weakness.

▶ Remind her the week before a big project is due, or offer your help. It is always a good idea to suggest she get something down on paper, which you can check and make suggestions about, rather than helping with research or writing, which takes away her autonomy.

USING THE LIBRARY *If it's difficult to remove all distractions at home, encourage your child to use the library. She'll be more focused in this quiet learning environment.*

Study skills

The "30-minute daily study period" is an efficient way of learning. This is a period during which most people can concentrate well. If your child studies without a break for an hour, the last 20–30 minutes are likely to be less efficient, as concentration diminishes.

It will be much easier to encourage your child to sit down to study knowing that it is for a 30-minute stretch. If she has a lot of information to learn, break it into 30-minute segments, with breaks in between. Keep her supplied with healthy snacks and drinks while she is studying.

To help your teenager study:

★ Encourage her to plan. While most children resist studying, your child will be more inclined to study if she has clear and achievable targets. If she crosses off each item as she completes it, she will feel a sense of achievement.

★ Encourage "periodic retrieval." Instead of reading and rereading material, ask her to test herself periodically. Breaking the work into chunks, and quizzing her at the end of each, will help.

★ Don't stop at 100 percent accuracy. One researcher found he could improve retention by repeating it once or twice more after he had learned it. Once your child is at that point, a quick review might be all that is needed.

Your child's school

You may question the quality of your child's school, particularly if she doesn't seem to be motivated, or isn't learning enough or working to the best of her ability. Unfortunately, some schools do have poor teachers on their staff, and some schools fall below acceptable standards.

If you have the luxury of being able to move your child, then do so, but be aware that a 13-year-old plucked from her peer group and thrust into an unfamiliar setting may be distressed and find it difficult to cope. Even academically inclined children who want more stimulation will find the transition hard, so make sure the disruption is actually worth it.

Signs of a successful school:

▶ A charismatic leader, who sets the tone, and enthusiastic teachers.

▶ A strong ethos and a united approach to learning.

▶ Happy students.

▶ Minimal bullying, which is dealt with promptly.

▶ Plenty of extracurricular activities and a well-stocked library.

▶ Trips to enhance learning, and a good, supportive parent body.

▶ Good communication between parents and teachers, and between teachers and students. You should be able to contact the school and be assured of prompt attention. You should understand the grading system and be in touch with what is required for your child. If this isn't the case, then changes should probably be made.

Cheating issues

Some children cheat because of peer pressure, as a dare, or in desperation. All these reasons suggest that they need help. Make sure that your teenager knows that cheating on exams or plagiarizing is always unacceptable.

The problem is, of course, that the definition of cheating is somewhat blurred because of easy access to Internet resources, where information can be amalgamated into essays and projects and passed off as a child's own work. But this is still cheating. Help your child to understand that even if she fails to do well, at least it will be her own work that is being judged. By cheating, she will never learn or have a true gauge of what she is achieving and whether she is succeeding in a subject. Once your teen has gotten into the habit of cheating, she will come to rely on this to succeed academically. Explain that you would rather she failed and learned something than cheated and potentially damaged her academic success.

TEACHERS AND STUDENTS
Your child may not want to admit he doesn't understand something, but he should feel confident about approaching teachers with problems.

Encourage your child to understand that her greatest judge is herself, and she must be happy with and proud of everything she does. If your child cheats, ascertain why—for example, she may not have had enough time to study or she may just be struggling in a certain subject—and then work on resolving the cause.

Remember:

▶ By cheating, your child will never get that great sense of pride and joy from getting a good result and won't learn from her mistakes.

Keeping tabs

Many schools stop spoon-feeding parents with information when children are around this age, so if you are concerned about your child's work, get in touch with the school. Some schools have a parent–teacher contact book that is sent home every week, into which parents write comments, or pick up on those made by teachers. If information from the school is not forthcoming, don't hesitate to talk to other parents. The more knowledge you have, the better. Many 13-year-olds become defensive of their work and their privacy, and this is to be respected. However, your child does need to be confident that if there is a problem, you aren't going to become angry, and that you will support her. Ask pertinent questions, and flip through her books regularly to keep tabs. If you are worried about your child's progress, arrange to see the teacher of that subject or the head teacher.

Extracurricular activities

Many 13-year-olds are not eager to get involved in extracurricular activities. Their social lives revolve around peer group encounters, and the ubiquitous computer and cell phone. However, part of a child's education is learning other skills, such as sports, music, and drama, and getting involved in their school, perhaps by joining a debate club or working on the school newspaper. As much as your teenager resists, encourage her to do at least one activity per term, whether it is to take part in the school play, try out for a team, or join a club. If your child's school has nothing interesting to offer, perhaps she and her friends could approach the principal with some ideas of their own.

Socializing with the opposite sex

When your 13-year-old gets together with friends, it is likely to be much less visible to you than formerly. Often she will be out of your sight in her bedroom or at a friend's house, and her increasing interest in spending time with the opposite sex may cause you to worry. However, find out more before you become too concerned. For example, a close platonic relationship shouldn't be a problem, unless your teenager is restricting other social contacts. If, on the other hand, it is the possibility of sexual intimacy that is worrying you, then you need to talk this over right away (see page 273). Neither you or your child are likely to relish the conversation, but press on. Ask your teenager to be open and in turn be understanding about her feelings. If things are getting intimate, don't

ENCOURAGING HOBBIES
A hobby that combines learning skills with a social life is the one that will last longest, provide enjoyment, and mean the most to your child.

"Although she is still a child to you, accept that your teenager will begin to have an interest in the opposite sex."

try to stop the relationship (this will lead to resentment and rebellion), but be clear about how you expect her to behave. For example, you could agree that she keeps her bedroom door open and that you look in every so often. This way your teen's romance can flourish, while you can be sure that the level of intimacy is suitable for her age.

Types of parenting

It can be hard to adapt your parenting style to the demands of an increasingly independent young teenager and it is easy to fall into the trap of over- or underparenting.

Overparenting This entails being in charge, laying down rules, and dispensing material rewards and immediate consequences just as you did when your child was younger. This can cause your teen to feel resentful.

Underparenting This is when you loosen control too much, allowing your child to make too many choices herself when she actually still needs your guidance. This parenting style can result in your young teen's making poor choices and disregarding the rights of others.

Balanced parenting This walks a fine line between the two and involves collaborating to make decisions and respecting each other's rights and wishes. This is based on the understanding that you trust your young teen, and in turn she lives up to that trust.

Addictions

There are many reasons why teenagers drink, smoke, and take drugs: curiosity, boredom, to rebel against their parents' standards, or simply to enhance their enjoyment of music, parties, and relationships.

Teenagers have very little regard for the addictive nature of these substances, often holding the view that becoming dependent "won't happen to me," or, by minimizing their use, believing that the addiction is under control and can be stopped at any time.

Signs of addiction:
★ Mood swings.
★ Becoming secretive.
★ Needing more money than you would expect.
★ Deterioration of schoolwork.
★ Lying and being secretive.

★ Being giggly and too talkative.
★ Dizziness, headaches, and tiredness.
★ Long-lasting flu symptoms.
     It can be difficult to be sure there is a drug problem, since some of these signs are normal in adolescence, but find out about the effects of drugs and talk with your child if you are concerned. Seek professional help, if necessary.

Common concerns

▶ **My 13-year-old son is less than enthusiastic about going on vacation with us this year. What can I do to encourage him?**

First, don't take it personally. This reluctance is normal at this age. Unfortunately, your idea of bliss no longer suits your sociable, easily bored young teen. It is definitely time to compromise so that everyone gets as much as possible out of your family vacation. Start by making a wish list of each person's ideal location, accommodations, and cultural, sporting, and social activities. Get together and check the list against possible destinations to find a place that provides as much as possible to please each person. One way of making your son more interested is to allow him to bring a friend, if that's possible.

▶ **My partner and I are divorcing. How can I help my 13-year-old daughter get through this difficult time?**

Splitting up with a partner, whether it's mutual or not, is a highly distressing time. It is made more complex by the practicalities of moving out and arranging shared care of the children. In the midst of all this upheaval, your daughter needs to be kept informed of what is happening. She will be worried about what this means for her— perhaps a change of home location and/or school and almost certainly

less time with one parent. She'll want to voice what will work for her. When you respect at least some of her choices, you'll create a better transition for her.

Avoid getting her involved in conflict between you and your ex-partner—for example, don't ask her to join in with a critique of her other parent or pass messages between the two of you. Be temperate about how you speak about each other in front of her; you may no longer care for each other, but she still loves you both, and being torn between you is not good for her emotional health now or in the long term.

LIFE SKILLS *By being involved in household chores, your teenager will learn, for example, that clothes and bed linens do not magically wash themselves.*

▶ **My daughter hardly eats at all, and constantly weighs herself. What should I do?**

You're right to be concerned; these signs indicate your daughter may have an eating disorder (see page 297). Once eating problems take hold, they're hard to shake because weight loss is giving your child strong feelings of satisfaction and control, which increase her motivation to diet even further. To help your daughter, seek professional help now, as early treatment is usually more successful.

On a day-to-day basis, be open about what's worrying you. Statements like "I'm worried about you, I know you don't feel like eating, but is there anything I can do to help?" are caring without putting pressure on her.

▶ **I think our 13-year-old should start taking more responsibility by washing and ironing his own clothes. Is he too young?**

No, it is good to ensure that your teenager has gained useful life skills such as keeping his clothes clean and cooking basic meals.

Don't assume he knows how to carry out normal household tasks; explain how the washing machine works and show him how to iron, and then supervise him while he practices. If nothing else, helping out with chores will ensure that he appreciates what you do and doesn't take you for granted.

14

13

12

11

10

9

8

7

6

5

4

3

YEARS

NURTURING TALENTS By now
your teen will know where
her strengths lie. Respect her
interests and encourage her in
subjects she's good at, even if
they aren't academic.

Your 14-year-old

"Your teen's independence will be well established and she will have her own life."

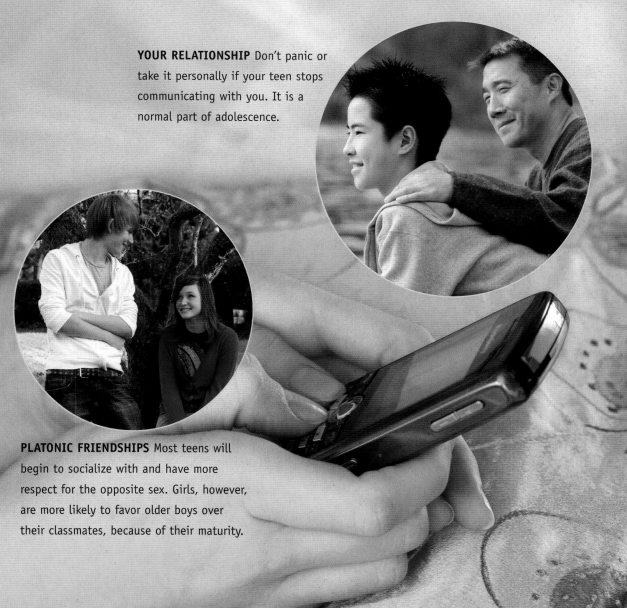

YOUR RELATIONSHIP Don't panic or take it personally if your teen stops communicating with you. It is a normal part of adolescence.

PLATONIC FRIENDSHIPS Most teens will begin to socialize with and have more respect for the opposite sex. Girls, however, are more likely to favor older boys over their classmates, because of their maturity.

Growth and development

By the time your child is 14, you will have a full-fledged adolescent on your hands. Your child may in fact have grown to be taller than you by now, which can be difficult to come to terms with! If your teenage daughter still hasn't reached puberty, you should seek medical advice.

Boys and muscular development

As puberty develops in boys, their muscle mass increases and their fat decreases. Although they are likely to put on weight, most of this will be due to the muscle they have gained, rather than fat. A boy's change in body shape is a long process and continues well into his late teens and often into his twenties. How much the muscles develop depends on how much they are used; athletic boys will become far more muscular than sedentary boys. Body shape and size also have a strong genetic component, so physically a boy will often start to look increasingly like his father.

Delayed puberty

If your daughter is showing no signs of puberty (see page 186) by the age of 14, and you haven't already seen her doctor, take her for a checkup now. Late puberty in girls is much less common than late puberty in boys and is more likely to have an underlying medical cause. Girls of 14 who are not developing at the expected rate should be referred to a specialist.

Around age 14 is the time when the fastest growth rate occurs in the average boy. If your son has not yet started puberty, don't panic; it is normal for many boys to go into puberty late. Some boys of 14 are happy to be reassured that they will catch up eventually, but others may feel left behind and be adversely affected by their late development, especially if they are singled out by others for being small and looking young. Many boys and their parents appreciate the opportunity to talk to a specialist and discuss whether any treatment may be helpful. Testosterone injections to speed up the process are an option if a boy is still showing no signs of puberty by the age of 15 or 16.

FILLING OUT *As well as growing taller, a boy going through puberty will become broader and his body will change shape.*

LATE RISER *Although it can be frustrating for you, it is a normal part of your teenager's sleep pattern to sleep in. Allow this on weekends to let her catch up on sleep.*

Sleep and growth

Throughout childhood, levels of growth hormone that are detectable in the blood are higher during the night than during the day. Levels of other hormones, such at cortisol, are lower at night. This is known as the circadian rhythm, and it is vital for the body to function normally.

Because of the way these growth hormones work, growth occurs primarily during sleep, and teenagers who miss out on sleep will have to catch up at some stage. It is common for teens to have great difficulty getting up in the morning, and this is often due to a very late bedtime or the inability to fall asleep quickly. Good sleep hygiene (see page 227) is therefore essential.

Teenagers who have a serious sleep problem that is impinging on their health and education are sometimes helped by taking melatonin. This is a hormone, secreted by the brain at night, which can be bought in supplement form, but discuss this with your child's physician first.

Food and mood

If your teenager lives on junk food, this may explain some of his moods. It is quite common for children of all ages to become irritable when they are hungry and, as we know, this may continue into adult life. We all need to have a decent blood-sugar level in order to be able to concentrate, and some people, particularly those without surplus fat, become hypoglycemic when they are hungry. This can be a problem at school and cause behavioral problems as well as poor concentration. This is one reason why a teenager's diet is so important.

Breakfast is a very important meal and should ideally contain complex carbohydrates, such as those found in whole-grain cereal or oatmeal. These carbohydrates take a long time for the body to break down and release sugar gradually until lunchtime. Children who skip breakfast often have a high-glucose snack such as a bar of chocolate instead, which gives them a quick sugar "rush" followed by a rebound "slump" in sugar levels. Healthy snacks that will keep your teen fuller for longer are nuts, seeds, fruit, slices of raw vegetables, and nutrition bars, as long as they are not high in sugar. There is also no doubt that good-quality school food improves behavior and concentration and can even decrease illness rates.

Your child's health

While dealing with minor irritations such as pimples will consume your teenager, it is his lifestyle that will begin to be the biggest threat to his health. He is likely to be tempted to try alcohol now and in the coming years—this is becoming an increasing problem for young people.

Skin problems

By age 14, many teenagers will have experienced acne (see page 274), and many will have oily skin and greasy hair. These are due to production of sebum, a greasy substance from the glands next to each hair follicle. This is a result of hormone production and is a normal part of puberty.

Eczema (see page 115) is another common skin problem in children. It tends to flare up at times of stress and, especially in teenagers, may also be triggered by cosmetics, perfume, and hair dye. Treatment is aimed at removing the cause if possible, using emollients to prevent the skin from drying out, and using intermittent steroid creams sparingly for troublesome patches. Antibiotics may be prescribed for infected eczema.

Alcohol and your child's health

Alcohol is a powerful drug, but unlike many other drugs, in small quantities it is relatively harmless. Advice about how much is too much, and at what age it is appropriate to offer a glass of wine in the home, is conflicting. There are widely differing cultural and religious views, with some families banning any alcohol until age 21, and others allowing a glass of wine with a meal from as early as 14.

In countries such as France, where alcohol is often offered to teenagers with the family meal, binge drinking is less common than elsewhere. In contrast, as alcohol is now relatively cheap and easy to obtain in the UK, there has been a sharp increase in dangerous binge drinking in teenagers, with serious medical consequences. As a parent, you need to accept that your teenager might be tempted to experiment with alcohol, and so it is a good idea to discourage him from doing so. He needs to know all of the

PREVENTING PIMPLES
Once your teenager gets pimples, you will find she takes better care of her skin. Tying hair back can help to reduce outbreaks.

"Alcohol is the major contributing factor in hospital admission in an ever-increasing number of young people."

risks associated with drinking alcohol. Children who are admitted drunk to a hospital are then usually referred to social workers for an in-depth assessment and professional advice.

Caffeine intake

Since caffeine is found in carbonated beverages as well as tea and coffee, most teens will consume some caffeine often. Caffeine in reasonable quantities (two or three caffeine-containing drinks daily) does not cause problems for children, but if your child is having trouble sleeping, he should avoid drinks containing caffeine in the evening.

High doses of caffeine in certain drinks and tablets are aimed at giving an extra "lift" and keeping a person awake. Teenagers commonly take them during exam time, but this is not recommended as they cause the heart to beat faster, possibly resulting in heart-rhythm abnormalities. A teenager who is resorting to high doses of caffeine to stay awake needs to look at why he is not getting enough sleep and address that problem first. Your child should plan his time effectively around exam time so that he doesn't have to stay up late studying.

Urinary tract infections (UTIs)

These are infections, usually bacterial, of the urine in the bladder and sometimes in the kidneys. Symptoms include pain on urination, passing urine frequently, stomachaches, smelly urine, and fever. Girls are more likely to get UTIs than boys as the urethra (the tube leading out of the bladder) is shorter in girls than boys and bacteria can get into the bladder more easily. Sexually active girls are also susceptible to UTIs, which is why such infections are sometimes known as the "honeymoon disease."

What to do:

▶ Take your child to the doctor to have her urine tested if she has symptoms of a urinary tract infection.

▶ Give her acetaminophen or ibuprofen for pain and fever as needed.

▶ Encourage her to drink plenty of fluids.

See your doctor right away if:

▶ Your child appears very ill to you, or if she develops vomiting along with the urinary symptoms.

Eating disorders

Weight is often a concern to teenagers, in particular to girls, and this is not helped by a celebration of the super-thin in the media.

Anorexia nervosa is a condition in which a person's body weight falls 15 percent (or more) below the norm for her height. This is achieved by self-starvation, with many sufferers reducing food intake to an absolute minimum, and doing excessive exercise. It is also characterized by obsessive behavior.

Bulimia is a condition in which a person eats excessively and then exercises, vomits, or uses laxatives and diuretics to offset the effects of overeating. Around 0.5–1 percent of adolescent girls suffer from anorexia, and 2–3 times more are bulimic. While eating disorders are most common in girls, 10 percent of sufferers are boys.

The majority of people with eating disorders deny any problem. The cause is not known, but is considered to be psychiatric, and more common in children with perfectionist tendencies, a strong desire for social approval, and a need for control. A poor self-image is almost always at the root of an eating disorder.

The physical effects

Both anorexia and bulimia lead to significant, often life-threatening, weight loss. In particular, anorexics risk decreased immunity, cessation of menstruation (potentially causing fertility problems later), anemia, and delayed puberty. More seriously, heart, kidney, and gastrointestinal problems are common, as well as thinning of the bones (osteoporosis).

In bulimia, damage to the gut, caused by taking laxatives, and damage to the teeth from excessive vomiting can sometimes be lifelong. There may also be serious dehydration and vitamin and mineral deficiencies, bringing other symptoms.

Warning signs

★ An obsession with weight, calorie counting, and going on strict diets.
★ Exercising obsessively.
★ Frequently being "not hungry" or "too busy" at mealtimes, and often choosing to eat alone.

ATTITUDE TO FOOD *Anorexics invent their own rules about how much they should eat. They might fear that more than two mouthfuls of something will make them fat.*

★ Disappearances to the bathroom after meals (to induce vomiting).
★ Mood changes, including angry outbursts, isolation from friends, and depression.
★ Rashes, dry skin, hair loss, and itching.
★ Cessation of periods.

What you can do

Watch your child carefully and seek medical advice if she appears too thin. Early intervention is more successful than trying to cope yourself. Forcing your child to eat may simply frighten her and strengthen her resolve.

Make family meals regular so that you can see what your child is eating. It is not realistic to weigh a teenager, but it is good to encourage children to understand that weight charts (see page 52) are important, and that they can use them into adulthood.

As a parent, model healthy eating habits and positive attitudes to food. Furthermore, be aware that you have a powerful influence on your child's self-esteem and body image. In one study, self-esteem scores of children ages 9–11 were lower when they thought their parents were dissatisfied with their own bodies. However, even secure children can suffer from self-esteem and emotional problems after an upset, so don't blame yourself. Seek help from professional organizations (see page 310–311).

Understanding and skills

You will be delighted with your 14-year-old's maturity and new sense of responsibility one moment, and then despair when he does something childish the next. This is normal. During adolescence, development goes slightly awry, so you will see progression in some areas and regression in others.

Although your 14-year-old will be better able to express his feelings through an improved vocabulary, he may often be uncommunicative and even silent at times, and have an ever-changing range of different emotions. This can be a confusing time for you and for him; he might have the physical development of a 16-year-old, typical cognitive development for his age, and the social skills of a 10-year-old.

CHAOTIC LIFE *Your teen is likely to be badly organized. The part of his brain that is responsible for planning and prioritizing is not fully wired yet.*

Supporting risk-taking

At this age sense is often overridden by a "leap before you look" mentality, because the part of your teen's brain that deals with gut reactions and emotions is working at top speed. If your child seems foolhardy and gets a thrill from risk-taking, let him make mistakes, as long as what he is doing

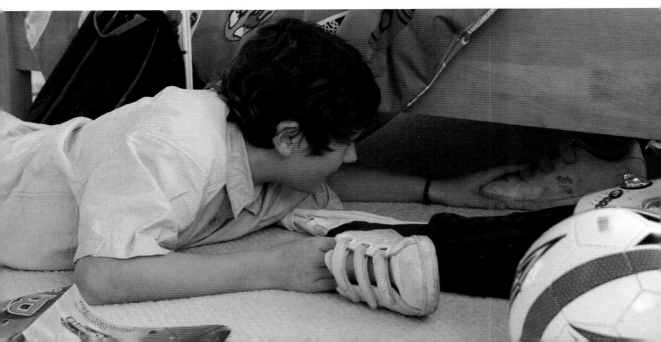

Teaching empathy

Teenagers are able to feel empathy for others. Sadly, however, many don't—simply because they have never been taught how to be empathetic and rarely see it modeled. We live in a society that is often self-oriented and geared toward personal gain.

To help your teen be empathetic:

★ Don't be afraid to show your child that you are upset when he is rude or violent. A cold, angry parent responding to a cold, angry child will lead to a power struggle, whereas a warm parent who shows the occasional weakness, and the ability to be "human," can teach a child compassion for others and that it is okay to be upset rather than angry.

★ Teach your child to notice kindness. If someone does you a favor, say, "That was so helpful."

★ Show empathy yourself. If your child is caught being nasty to a sibling, for example, show him that you identify with what he must have been feeling. It teaches him that others can see his point of view. However, say that the behavior was unacceptable, and you want to know how he can make up for his actions. Also explain how his sibling will be feeling.

★ Reinforce the message that there is usually something good about everyone. Encourage him to step into someone else's shoes and see their viewpoint.

isn't dangerous or unhealthy. It is important to put faith in his occasional maturity, but remember that you will need to offer a helping hand. Young teens do stupid things, so be as patient as you can.

Guide your teen in the direction of healthy risks, and away from daring and dangerous activities such as drinking alcohol and taking drugs. Healthy risk-taking means pushing your teen past his comfort zone—for example, he might want to go a bit wild on the art front and write something risqué and unconventional, or maybe do something that he would never normally consider, such as trying out for the basketball team or taking up a new and challenging outdoor pursuit.

Remember:

▶ Unhealthy adolescent risk-taking may appear to be rebellion, but it is actually a part of your child's struggle to test out his identity by providing self-definition and separation from others.

▶ Most cases of addiction (taking drugs, drinking alcohol, gambling, and overusing the Internet or video games) mask a need for excitement. Studies show that children who are regularly stimulated, with full, active lives, are not only less likely to engage in unhealthy risk-taking, but are better able to manage their time, deal with stress, and develop healthy

"If teens have nothing in their lives but the mundane, they are likely to look for stimulation elsewhere."

habits that will continue into the adult years and are in place for life.

▶ Because adolescents are wired to seek excitement and take risks, we need to help them find plenty of healthy opportunities to do so.

Language and literacy

By the age of 14, your teenager will be thinking in broader terms, and be able to see how things are connected to each other, refining abstract thought and even difficult abstract ideas. You will find that the way he learns changes during this period, as comprehension develops and he is expected to take greater responsibility for his own studies.

Fun projects will be replaced by work that encourages him to think for himself, and to link concepts to provide an argument. He will be capable of differentiating right from wrong, and distinguishing fact from opinion, as well as evaluating the credibility of various sources of information. He will therefore read not just for pleasure but to gain knowledge and to apply critical thinking.

During this year, your child will be capable of making advances in all aspects of his thinking, and this will be reflected in more adult reading skills and levels, and a much more varied and vibrant vocabulary. He is

Improving comprehension

To help your teen get the most from books and other reading material, bear in mind the following;

★ Good readers need environments that help them focus. Make sure your child has a quiet space in which to curl up and concentrate.

★ Encourage your child to stop reading after every paragraph and ask himself to summarize the information. If he hasn't grasped the main idea, he should go back and read it again.

★ It helps to visualize what is being read. Ask your child to pretend he is a director, turning a book into a movie: What does he see? What is the setting? What do the characters look like? What should or will happen next?

★ It is also useful for your teen to relate the text to a personal experience, or compare it to another book he has read or a movie he has seen. This helps to cement understanding.

★ Ask your teen to pay attention to structure. Get him to read subheadings and titles, and anything and everything, including captions. These all work as parts of a puzzle and provide valuable clues.

★ Your teen should pace himself. Reading too quickly means he may not pick up key elements; too slowly and he may lose interest. The pace can be accelerated when the reading is easier, and slowed down in trickier parts.

capable of speaking in adult terms, although not always consistently, and confidently using adjectives and adverbs, as well as metaphors and other linguistic tools, although more often in writing than orally. You can help this process by encouraging your child to read anything and everything, and to describe his world accurately and in detail.

Learning to spell

Many children struggle with spelling, particularly if they aren't avid readers, and a lot of teens much prefer using abbreviated text talk to the real thing. There has been some confusion recently about how best to teach children to spell, which has meant that in many countries a large number of children have "fallen through the cracks," and do not have the spelling skills they need.

You can help your child by:

▶ Doing crosswords and playing games such as Scrabble together. If your child wants to win, he has to spell words correctly, and the competitive instinct of the average 14-year-old should kick into gear.

▶ Get him used to letter-writing—or even typing emails—for thank-you notes and invitations. Encourage him to read back what he has written. Most children will see their mistakes, and this is a good way to learn.

▶ Make use of your computer's spell-checker, but make sure your child stops and looks at the word that is wrong before choosing the correct one. Encourage him to look up words in a dictionary sometimes.

▶ Be light-hearted about mistakes, and make them fun. Pit family members against each other and put a list of misspelled words on the refrigerator. "If everyone makes mistakes, your child won't feel singled out.

▶ If your child is embarrassed about his inability to spell, download some spelling lessons from the Internet and encourage him to try them out; there are also some good interactive spelling tests that will give instant results.

▶ Encourage your child to read, even if he will only read the sports page of the newspaper. Good readers are good spellers.

Remember:

▶ Poor spelling is not a sign of poor intelligence. Some children are sloppy or merely uninterested, whereas for others there may be learning difficulties at the root. Don't make your child feel inadequate for being a poor speller.

WORD GAMES *Scrabble is a great way to learn new words and practice spelling. It also encourages use of a dictionary to check words.*

Emotions and personality

Your 14-year-old is a "work in progress." He is busy figuring out who he is, what his values are, and where he fits into his family, peer group, and community. So it is no wonder that he seems inward-looking and unsure how to react as he tries out new opinions and types of behaviors.

"He can switch between the petulance of a toddler and the angst of a teen within minutes, and will be as tired of being at the mercy of his moods as you are."

To an observer your teenager's behavior may appear rather self-indulgent, but it is developmentally very important. He is reflecting on what kind of person he wants to be and is trying ideas on for size. He may have a period of being cool and aloof to see if that attracts new friends, or experiment with being studious and helpful, or edgy and risk-taking. By his late teens, all this trial and error will have given him the information he needs to be sure of his identity.

Handling moodiness

The hormonal changes of puberty and the new emotional challenges of romance can render your 14-year-old unbearably moody. You can't change his hormones and have little control over the ups and downs of his friendships, but you can be a steady, calming influence. Whether he is uptight or upset, avoid becoming emotional yourself, give him space to be alone if he needs it, then offer to listen to the problem when he is ready. Take him seriously, but don't jump to solve problems for him or you may find you are being drawn into things even though he has let the issue go.

Becoming less affectionate

Showing you care about your teenager gets a little more complicated as he matures because it is not cool for him to approach you for a kiss or hug, especially in public. Be reassured, though, that your 14-year-old still wants to be close and may be affectionate in private, sitting up close to watch TV or wanting a goodnight kiss. You will also be developing more subtle ways to show you care about each other. For example, a pat on the back, squeeze of the arm, wave, or touch of the hand communicates your warmth. Your teenager may be ambivalent about approaching you for affection; he needs your acknowledgment, but will not want to appear babyish. So do make the first move yourself when you are in private, but in public let him guide how you express your love for him.

Challenging behavior

Your teen will be driven to try risky behavior (see page 298) to show that he is no longer a child, and you will be equally motivated to keep him safe. The tension between these perspectives means your authority will be challenged as he strives for looser boundaries and less supervision.

Resolution through compromise and negotiation is a dull but effective solution. For example, you may want to set a curfew of 11 pm on weekends, and he may see no reason to be back before 2 am. He is probably working on an inflated idea of his own ability to protect himself, so you will need to build in some limits for his behavior. For example, you might loosen the curfew a little for a party but pick him up yourself to make sure he gets home safely. Teenagers respond better to boundaries than to a laissez-faire attitude of allowing them to make their own decisions. Of course, not all rebellion ends well. If your 14-year-old is getting involved with crime or substance abuse, or being exploited sexually, then seek help from a certified counselor immediately.

GOOD TIMING *The key to communicating effectively with your teenager is to read his mood and pick your moment carefully.*

Self-harm issues

Self-harm involves deliberately inflicting injury or mutilation on your own body to gain relief from strong emotions. Girls are four times more likely to self-harm than boys. It may involve cutting, biting, or burning, among other methods, and is usually carried out alone and hidden from the family. The feeling of relief from anger, frustration, or anxiety is often followed by negative feelings of guilt and a loss of self-esteem.

What to do:

★ If you think your teenager is self-harming, speak with him calmly about your concerns.

★ Even if you are shocked or alarmed, try not to show it, as this may reinforce his guilty feelings. It is your care and attention he will value most.

★ Gently ask what is bothering him, but avoid interrogation. His feelings and explanations may come out later, when he is ready to share them.

★ Find out if medical attention is needed and make sure your child knows how to seek emergency assistance when you are not around.

★ Seek help from a health-care professional if self-harm persists.

Avoiding the nagging trap

Nagging a teenager doesn't work. Repeating an instruction over and over again is frustrating, and your 14-year-old will simply tune you out.

How to get your message across:

▶ To get your teen's attention and cooperation, select a good time to make your request—for example, wait until he has finished playing a level on his computer game or hung up the phone.

▶ Then stop what you are doing, go up close to him, and clearly state what you want. Stick around, so he knows you are serious, and thank him when he has been cooperative.

▶ If he doesn't want to do as you ask right away, then agree on a time scale—for example, to bring all his laundry down within the next hour. This way, you don't need to keep asking. But if he doesn't follow through, do give him a consequence; perhaps he has missed the chance to have his favorite clothes washed until the next day.

GETTING SERIOUS If your teen has found someone she connects with, a relationship is likely to develop, but be prepared for many ups and downs.

Friends and friendship

Friendships are changing for your 14-year-old. Where before he had mostly same-sex friendships, you will notice now that a larger mixed-sex group is forming. This is usually the result of two groups, one of boys and one of girls, overlapping or merging through dating.

If your child is dating, this will often be a group event, too, with several pairs hanging out together rather than couples spending time alone. Your 14-year-old will be increasingly reliant on friends to analyze relationships, find support to break up with a partner, or be comforted if he has been dropped by his girlfriend. The intensity of friendships means highs and lows as things go well or badly, and your support will be needed to pick up the pieces if relationships break down.

Common behavioral concerns

▶ **I am constantly battling my 14-year-old daughter, who seems to think that no one else matters except for her. If things don't go her way, she makes a huge fuss and pesters us until we give up our plans to make way for hers. What's going on?**
Your 14-year-old is trying to assert herself, but is coming across as selfish and demanding. You may need to answer her pestering with the "broken record" approach, firmly giving the same reply whenever she nags. For example, simply repeat, "I can't take you shopping now because your brother has baseball practice. I'll take you to the mall tomorrow." If nothing else, this will bore her into accepting the decision.

Involve her in making family decisions as much as you can; this way she will be more likely to go along with them.

▶ **I am at the end of my tether with my 14-year-old son's argumentative nature. How can I best handle this?**
Remain calm and don't argue back. For example, if he states, "What would you know?" simply say "Please don't be rude" rather than, "I know plenty, thanks. Who do you think runs the house and pays the bills?" This response sounds defensive and will lead to a full-blown argument. Walking away and trying to communicate with your son once he has calmed down will be most effective.

▶ **My young teen has dramatically changed her appearance. Is this normal?**
Trying dramatic new styles, looking different from your generation, and declaring membership of a group through appearance is entirely normal behavior for 14-year-olds.

Even if you hate your daughter's look, be reassured that it shouldn't last long, since fashions change quickly. However, if your teen is breaking school rules with her appearance, then you need to take action. For example, if her clothes are very revealing or too casual for school, try to agree on when your teen should wear "normal" clothes and when her more extreme fashion statements are appropriate.

Supporting from the sidelines

The way you support your 14-year-old in his schoolwork, sports, and hobbies means a lot to him and will be important to his self-confidence and continued success. When you watch your teen perform in drama, music, or sports, for example, or you attend parents' nights, you show that you are interested and concerned with his life. He will notice this support, even though he might not say anything.

However, while you want to back your teen up in every aspect of his life, and will undoubtedly be very proud of his achievements, be careful not to smother or embarrass him with overblown praise and attention. Just be sincere—he will value a few quiet words of praise over long speeches that exaggerate his many talents.

HOMEWORK *Take an interest in your child's homework, but be realistic and accept that at this age he is unlikely to be enthusiastic about doing it.*

Your child's life

Keeping your busy teen motivated to do schoolwork can be a challenge, as he has plenty of competing demands on his time. Dating, hanging out with friends, listening to music, and just thinking can take up much of his free time, and studying will be far down on his list of priorities.

Your teen will work most effectively when there are clear rules about homework—for example, that assignments must be completed each night before he can see, text, or email friends. Motivate him by taking an interest in his studies, being supportive, and trying to engage him in what he is learning. At times of intense study, offering rewards for completing work and preparing for tests may help him focus.

Remember:

❯ It is all too easy to pay a lot of attention when you think your teenager is slacking and ignore him when he is working hard. Turn this around by giving him lots of praise for putting in effort.

❯ It is solid hard work that creates long-term achievement, so focus your praise on his effort rather than whether he comes in first or wins prizes.

Anxiety about schoolwork

The pressure to do well at school can be overwhelming for your 14-year-old, and it may make him anxious. He might make excuses, such as inventing minor illnesses, to avoid going to school. There could also be physical signs such as being shaky and tearful, and emotional signs, such as speaking about himself as useless or stupid.

This shows your child is in a cycle of self-doubt, which will be exacerbated if he misses classes and falls behind. Help him cope with anxiety using positive self-talk—for example, exchanging the thought "I'm dumb" with "I can do this." Practice muscle relaxation with him to reduce physical anxiety; get him to let his shoulders drop, shake out the tension from his hands, and take a deep breath. Let school staff know how he is feeling and work with them to offer support and reassurance.

Teaching responsibility

Your child may want to do more for himself but not feel confident, so break each task down step by step. For example, he may want to go to an amusement park with friends for the day. To do this, he needs to find the cheapest tickets for the park, make travel arrangements, and agree on a time to be home. All this means using his Internet search ability, phone skills, budgeting, and negotiation skills. Most of all, he needs to be able to make decisions, weigh up his options, and make sensible choices.

If he has a weekly allowance, or earns money from a paper route, for example, he needs to spend the money responsibly. Don't tell him what he can and can't buy, but do advise him if you think he is wasting it. He should know that he has to save up for items he really wants.

Sibling bullying

Squabbling, then negotiating and compromising, is a normal aspect of sibling behavior that teaches your child skills to resolve everyday disputes. However, sometimes arguments turn into damaging sibling bullying. If this is happening at home, your first priority, naturally, will be to protect the child who is being bullied. Work on a safety plan with your child so he knows what to do if he is threatened or hurt—for example, shout "Stop!" and call for you right away, or escape to a neighbor's house if he fears assault. Increased supervision of siblings is

> "The best way to teach responsibility is to give your 14-year-old a chance to take on new challenges."

When your teen is a bully

Hearing that your teenager is bullying others can be shocking and shaming. There are many possible reasons: perhaps he too is being bullied, feels sad or bad about himself, or has problems understanding how his actions hurt others. Bullying can make your teen feel powerful, and give an instant sense of importance at the expense of the other person. Step in to stop your child by expressing your disapproval and giving consequences, such as less freedom. The next step is to resolve the problems that started the bullying—for example, ensuring that he himself is safe from bullying, is well supervised at times when he's been bullying, and has help addressing any difficulties. Work on building up his empathy; get him to imagine how others feel when he threatens or hurts them. When you work with the school to support your teen in being kind to others, his behavior is likely to change.

essential until the problem is resolved—for example, do not leave them at home together without adult supervision. The bullying sibling needs help to change. You may consider writing a formal agreement with him about how he should behave, including being kind to others, not taking things without permission, and resolving disputes using words. Don't be afraid to call the police if serious assaults are happening that you cannot control.

Balancing work and play

Being an adolescent is exciting, fun, and very, very tiring. Your 14-year-old is using up lots of energy just managing the physical needs of his rapidly developing body, the demands of school, and the effort of maintaining peer group, romantic, and family relationships. If you think he is wearing himself out, step in to limit some of his after-school activities. He is likely to be relieved if you suggest he cuts some practice sessions for a few weeks. Get him to turn off his phone and close his email program by 10 pm so that he doesn't get dragged into late-night communications.

Common concerns

▶ **I am offended by the violent and sexist lyrics of my son's favorite songs. Should I stop him from listening to them?** Disapproving of, or banning, certain music is a surefire way to make it more interesting to your son. Try to avoid criticizing; generations of parents have reacted by putting down their teenager's choice in music and simply reinforced the myth that parents just don't understand!

Instead, listen to your child and find out why he likes each musician and explain what bothers you about the lyrics.

This is a rare chance to discuss difficult subjects like racial and sexual prejudices and get your son to question his own views. It is not possible to protect him from all negative attitudes, but encouraging him to think about what he listens to is your best defense against unwanted influences.

▶ **My daughter leaves a trail of belongings behind her. How can I address this?** Instead of just complaining to her, motivate your daughter to be neat with some new storage boxes, and files and folders for her schoolwork. If she chooses the colors and designs, then using them will be more appealing. Work with her to develop a plan to be neat; this could include putting her things away as soon as she comes in and keeping all schoolwork in her study space.

If she achieves this degree of tidiness, perhaps you can tolerate a mess in her bedroom, for example. Do, of course, make sure she's not copying any untidy habits you have by cleaning up your act, too.

Useful organizations

Action on Smoking and Health (ASH)
2013 H Street, NW
Washington, DC 20006
Web: www.ash.org
Excellent source of information and advice on giving up smoking.

American Academy of Child & Adolescent Psychiatry (AACAP)
Tel: (202) 966–7300
Web: www.aacap.org
Non-profit organization; offers family resources, as well as a directory of accredited child psychiatrists.

American Academy of Pediatrics
141 Northwest Point Boulevard
Elk Grove Village, IL 60007
Tel: (847) 434–4000
Web: www.aap.org
Provides general information related to child health.

American Counseling Association
Tel: (800) 347–6647
Web: www.aacap.org
A professional and educational counseling association.

American Diabetes Association
ATTN: National Call Center
1701 North Beauregard Street
Alexandria, VA 22311
Tel: (800) 342–2383
Web: www.diabetes.org
Increases understanding and offers help for those with diabetes.

American Dietetic Association
Tel: (800) 877–1600
Web: www.eatright.org
News, information, and tips on nutrition; offers a directory of nutritionists.

American Homeschool Association
PO Box 3142
Palmer, Alaska 99645
Tel: (800) 236–3278
Web: www.americanhomeschoolassociation.org
Covers all aspects of home education.

American Psychological Association (APA)
750 First Street, NE
Washington, DC 20002
Tel: (800) 374-2721
Web: www.apa.org
News, information, and resources pertaining to mental health.

American Red Cross
National Headquarters
2025 E Street, NW
Washington, DC 20006
Tel: (703) 206–6000
Website: www.redcross.org
Runs first-aid courses and offers first-aid help and information.

American Speech-Language-Hearing Association
2200 Research Boulevard
Rockville, MD 20850
Tel: (800) 638–8255
Web: www.asha.org
Supporting those with all aspects of communication disabilities.

Art Junction
Email: contact@artjunction.org
Web: www.artjunction.org
Website offering activities, projects, and resources designed to educate and foster artistic expression in young people.

Association for Library Service to Children
50 East Huron
Chicago, IL 60611
Tel: (800) 545–2433, x2163
Web: www.ala.org/ala/alsc/alscresources/resources.cfm
Email: alsc@ala.org
Offers a list of links for parents about safe internet surfing as well as information about finding books.

BAM! Body and Mind
Web: www.bam.gov
CDC website that addresses kids' health, nutrition, fitness, and stress.

Canadian Health Network
Web: www.canadian-health-network.ca
Aims to help Canadians live active lives and stay healthy.

Canadian Pediatric Society
2305 St. Laurent Blvd
Ottawa, ON K1G 4J8
Tel: (613) 526-9397
Web: www.cps.ca
Great resource for parents seeking information on various child and adolescent health, behavior and development issues.

Canadian Parents Online
101 Auburn Way
Quispamis, NB E3E 3C5
Tel: (506) 847-9057
Web: www.canadianparents.com
Advice on topics from healthy eating to surviving the high school years. Includes message boards, blogs, podcasts as well as an Ask an Expert section.

Child Care Aware
3101 Wilson Boulevard, Suite 350
Arlington, VA 22201
Tel: (800) 424–2246
Web: www.childcareaware.org
Information and support for working parents.

Children and Adults with Attention Deficit/Hyperactivity Disorder (CHADD)
8181 Professional Place, Suite 150
Landover, MD 20785
Tel: (301) 306–7070
Web: www.chadd.org
Provides support and information for parents and sufferers.

Compassionate Friends
PO Box 3696
Oak Brook, IL 60522
Tel: (877) 969–0010
Web: www.compassionatefriends.org
Grief support for parents who have suffered bereavement.

Family Education Network (FEN)
501 Boylston Street, Suite 900
Boston, MA 02116
Tel: (617) 671–2000
Web: www.familyeducation.com
Parenting resources and information for kids of all ages.

Food Allergy and Anaphylaxis Network (FAAN)
11781 Lee Jackson Highway
Suite 160
Fairfax, VA 22033
Tel: (800) 929–4040
Web: www.foodallergy.org
Email: faan@foodallergy.org
Helpful information and resources about food allergies.

Healthy Mothers, Healthy Babies Coalition
2000 North Beauregard Street
6th Floor
Alexandria, VA 22311
Tel: (703) 837–4792
Web: www.hmhb.org
Email: info@hmhb.org
Information on the health and safety of mothers, babies, and families.

International Dyslexia Association
40 York Road, 4th Floor
Baltimore, MD 21204
Tel: (410) 296–0232
Web: www.interdys.org
A wide range of help and advice for those living with dyslexia.

KidsHealth
Web: www.kidshealth.org
Excellent site for children and teenagers about food and fitness.

Kids Sports Network USA
8206 Roughrider, Suite 104
San Antonio, TX 78239
Tel: (210) 654-4707
Web: www.ksnusa.org
Promotes quality nonschool sports and fitness for children aged 3–19.

National Aphasia Association
350 Seventh Avenue, Suite 902
New York, NY 10001
Tel: (800) 922–4622
Web: www.aphasia.org
Organization for those with speech and language impairment.

National Association for the Education of Young Children
1313 L Street NW, Suite 500
Washington, DC 20005
Tel: (202) 232–8777
Web: www.naeyc.org
Information on high-quality early education for parents and educators.

National Association of Anorexia Nervosa and Associated Disorders
ANAD Box 7
Highland Park, IL 60035
Tel: (847) 831–3438
Web: www.anad.org
Offers information and hotline counseling for those suffering from eating disorders, and for their families.

National Eating Disorders Association (NEDA)
603 Stewart Street, Suite 803
Seattle, WA 98101
Helpline: (800) 931–2237
Web: www.nationaleatingdisorders.org
Information and help on all aspects of eating disorders.

National PTA
541 North Fairbanks Court
Suite 1300
Chicago, IL 60611
Tel: (800) 307-4PTA
Web: www.pta.org
Information for parental involvement in public schools.

National Sleep Foundation (NSF)
1522 K Street, NW, Suite 500
Washington, DC 20005
Tel: (202) 347–3471
Web: www.sleepfoundation.org
Help with sleep problems.

Parents Without Partners
1650 South Dixie Highway,
Suite 510
Boca Raton, FL 33432
Information Line: (800) 637–7974
Web: www.parentswithoutpartners.org
Support for single parents.

Planned Parenthood Federation of America
434 West 33rd Street
New York, NY 10001
Tel: (212) 541–7800
Web: www.plannedparenthood.org
Information on talking to your kids about puberty, birth control, and sexually transmitted diseases.

Reading is Fundamental (RIF)
1825 Connecticut Avenue, NW
Suite 400
Washington, DC 20009
Tel: 1 (877) RIF-READ
Web: www.rif.org
Children's and family non-profit literacy organization.

The Stuttering Foundation
3100 Walnut Grove Road, Suite 603
PO Box 11749
Memphis, TN 38111
Tel: (800) 992-9392
Web: www.stutteringhelp.org
Offers free online resources and support to those who stutter and their families.

US Department of Education
400 Maryland Avenue, SW
Washington, DC 20202
Tel: 1-800-USA-LEARN
Web: www.ed.gov
Provides information and assessment of schools, allowing parents to make informed choices.

US Food and Drug Administration (FDA)
5600 Fishers Lane
Rockville, MD 20857
Tel: 1-888-INFO-FDA
Web: www.fda.gov
US government agency offering information on food safety and nutrition.

Vegetarian Resource Group
PO Box 1463
Baltimore, MD 21203
Tel: (410) 366–8343
Web: www.vrg.org
Great source of nutritional information and advice, with healthy recipes for kids.

Index

A

acne 274, 295
addictions 288, 299
ADHD (attention deficit
hyperactivity disorder)
54, 60, 128
adolescence
definition 255
see also all topics relevant
to 12–14-year-olds
affection, 145, 258, 302-3
after-school activities 79,
128, 165, 180, 199, 217, 287
aggressive behavior 90-1
alcohol 221, 253, 267, 273,
283, 288, 295-6, 299
"all my friends are doing
it," 235, 260, 275
allergies 115, 163, 209, 295
allowance money 130,
174-5, 193, 238, 257, 307
anabolic steroids 272
anaphylaxis 209
anemia 78, 228
anger
children 35, 122, 127, 214,
217, 237, 240
parents 47, 217
see also tantrums
anorexia nervosa 251, 297
see also eating disorders
anti-HPV (human papilloma
virus) vaccination 254
anxiety & stress
clinginess 84, 127
fear of failure 165, 169-70,
171, 196, 237
fears 91, 172
headaches 254
night terrors 67
physical symptoms 161-2
puberty-related 226, 227,
234, 246, 261
school-related 81, 84, 173-4,
175, 238-9, 306
separation anxiety 33-4,
39, 69
teenage transitions 247
approval, parental see
positive attention

arguing 87, 122, 146, 149,
212, 229, 237, 276, 305
assertiveness 34, 66, 90, 305
asthma 163
attention deficit hyperactivity
disorder (ADHD) 54, 60, 128
attention-seeking behavior
39, 93-4
attention span see
concentration
attention to children, parents'
see positive attention

B

B vitamins 15, 137, 179
baby fat 157, 206
bacterial infections 26, 27,
81, 115, 163, 296
balanced parenting 288
bargaining see negotiating
bathing see personal hygiene
bedrooms & bedroom
sharing 46, 98, 218-19, 308
bedwetting 54, 138, 139
nocturnal emissions 208
behavior
3-year-olds 34-6, 39, 43-4, 45
4-year-olds 64-7, 73
5-year-olds 90-4, 96-9
6-year-olds 122-4, 127
7-year-olds 145, 146, 147-9,
151-3
8-year-olds 166, 168-9, 172
9-year-olds 189, 191, 197,
201
10-year-olds 211, 212, 213,
214, 216, 217, 221
11-year-olds 226, 229, 234,
235, 236, 237
12-year-olds 257, 258-61,
263-7
13-year-olds 273, 275-6,
280-1, 283, 286-9
14-year-olds 298-300,
302-3, 304, 305, 306-8
ground rules 64, 97, 124,
151-2, 193, 235, 280
knowing right from wrong
see moral reasoning skills

behavior cont.
positive reinforcement
35-6, 39, 43-4, 65, 67,
73, 93-4, 123, 235, 238
school 96, 97, 197, 201
siblings 43-4, 98-9, 123,
151-2, 239-41, 307-8
twins 39, 54
see also specific aspects
(e.g., tantrums)
bikes 55, 79, 111
biting 39
bladder control & problems
54, 81, 138, 139
BMI (body mass index)
charts 52
board games 72, 86, 159,
164, 172
boasting 93
body fat levels 157, 206
body hair 135, 186, 205, 225,
251, 272
body image & awareness
4-year-olds 54
6-year-olds 131
7-year-olds 145
8-year-olds 157, 172
9-year-olds 201
10-year-olds 207, 210, 219,
220
11-year-olds 234
12-year-olds 253, 261
13-year-olds 272, 274, 280,
281-2
14-year-olds 293, 305
body mass index (BMI)
charts 52
body odor 253
body proportions 21, 206, 293
bones
bone age 22
development 22, 82, 102,
206, 244, 252
fractures 22, 136, 188
books, stories, & reading
3-year-olds 29, 30
4-year-olds 57, 60-1
5-year-olds 87-9, 95, 96-7
6-year-olds 119, 120
7-year-olds 133, 136, 137,
143-4, 153

books, stories, & reading cont.
8-year-olds 162, 166-7
9-year-olds 192-3
10-year-olds 212
11-year-olds 231-2
12-year-olds 256
13-year-olds 269, 276-8
14-year-olds 300-1
learning to read 60-1, 88-9
libraries 61
bossiness 66-7, 127, 195
boys
anabolic steroids 272
bedwetting 139
development milestones &
problems 60, 61, 86
dyspraxia 53, 110
erections 208
facial hair 205, 251, 272
friendships 126, 170, 182,
185, 213
getting girls' attention 260
growth spurts 205, 225,
251, 274, 293
imaginary friends 63-4
nocturnal emissions 208
pornography 283
puberty 135-6, 205-6, 208,
225, 251-2, 271, 272, 293
strength & muscle mass
205, 272, 293
brain development 21-2, 51,
56, 159, 252, 298
breakfast 114, 294
breast development 135, 157,
186, 205, 207, 225, 261
"broken record" technique
92, 305
bulimia 297
see also eating disorders
bullying 96, 153, 172, 173,
199, 220, 307-8

C

caffeinated drinks & soda 16,
23, 84, 139, 208, 247, 296
calcification, bones 22
calcium 15, 22, 84, 102, 178,
206, 244-6, 252
caloric requirements 78-9

candy 25, 102, 122-3
car seats 54
carbohydrates 17, 103, 114, 137, 161, 274, 294
card games 58, 80, 86, 164
caregivers *see* child care; parents
cause & effect 118
cell phones 218, 220-1, 267, 279, 280
cereals & grains 17, 78, 84, 114, 161, 294
challenging behavior
  3-year-olds 34-5, 39
  4-year-olds 66-7, 73
  5-year-olds 90-4, 96
  6-year-olds 122-4, 127
  7-year-olds 145, 146, 149
  8-year-olds 168, 169, 172
  9-year-olds 189, 191, 197, 201
  10-year-olds 214, 216, 217, 221
  11-year-olds 226, 229, 234, 235, 236, 237
  12-year-olds 257, 258-60, 261, 263-7
  13-year-olds 273, 280-1, 283, 286, 287-8, 289
  14-year-olds 298-300, 302-3, 305, 307-8
  twins 39, 54
  see also specific problems (e.g., bullying)
chapped lips 115
chatrooms 174, 267, 279, 280
cheating 172, 286
chicken pox 84
child care 33-4, 40-2, 72, 95
chlamydia 273
choices & control, 4–8 years 67, 102, 103, 106, 127, 146, 147-8, 149
chores *see* household tasks
circadian rhythms 246
clay & dough 29, 96, 117
clinginess 84, 127
cliques & gangs 173, 260
clothes, shoes, & getting dressed
  3-year-olds 18, 36
  4-year-olds 51
  5-year-olds 79, 97
  7-year-olds 149
  11-year-olds 225, 234
  12-year-olds 253, 261
  14-year-olds 305

clumsiness 118
coordination *see* fine motor skills; gross motor skills
cognitive development *see* understanding & cognitive development
cold sores 115
colds 26, 55
collections 141
communication *see* listening skills; speech & language
community involvement 211, 276
competitiveness 92-3, 110, 148, 198
  cheating 172, 286
  competitive parenting 79
  fear of failure 165, 169-70, 171, 196, 237
comprehension 212, 231-2, 256, 300
computers & computer games
  educational uses & benefits 89, 121, 140, 255-6, 279, 301
  modern manners 212
  safety 174, 202, 222
  time limits 104-5, 159, 171, 195, 256, 267, 308
concentration
  3-year-olds 24, 28
  4-year-olds 48, 58, 60, 70-2
  5-year-olds 74, 88, 96
  6-year-olds 116, 118, 128-9
  10-year-olds 212
  12-year-olds 262
  14-year-olds 294
condoms 273
confidence & self-esteem
  3-year-olds 35, 36, 37
  5-year-olds 85, 98-9
  6-year-olds 110, 125-6
  7-year-olds 145, 148, 149
  8-year-olds 166, 168, 171, 172
  9-year-olds 192, 196
  10-year-olds 210-11
  11-year-olds 236, 237
  12-year-olds 260, 261, 267
  13-year-olds 274
  14-year-olds 297, 305, 306
conflict *see* disagreements & conflict
conjunctivitis 83
consistency
  parental 34, 65-6, 175, 185, 200, 235, 260

consistency cont.
  routines 40, 45, 69, 72, 104, 150, 162, 175, 198-9
constipation 25, 54
constructive criticism 280-1
consumerism & excess consumption 234, 261, 276
contraception 273
copying & mimicry 44, 45, 86
cosmetics 185, 234
counting *see* math; numbers & counting
crafts
  3-year-olds 29
  4-year-olds 53, 71
  5-year-olds 79, 85-6, 96
  6-year-olds 117
  8-year-olds 159
  clay & dough 29, 96, 117
  painting & drawing 24, 29, 52, 71, 79, 85-6, 96, 110, 117, 125
creative writing 166-7, 278, 279, 280, 301
criticism
  constructive criticism 280-1
  self-criticism 148, 237, 282
crushes *see* dating & crushes

D

dairy products 15, 102, 178, 206, 274
  milk 25, 81, 84, 178, 206
dating & crushes
  10-year-olds 213, 214
  11-year-olds 222, 234, 236
  12-year-olds 260, 268
  13-year-olds 273, 282, 287-8
  14-year-olds 304
death 153
debating skills 190, 231, 255, 259, 268, 276, 308
decision-making 146, 147-8, 305
dehydration 21, 26, 82, 254
delayed puberty 251, 293
depression 216, 246, 263-4, 283
development *see* specific types (e.g., physical development)
developmental milestones & checks 86, 112
diabetes 82, 161

diapers 25
diarrhea & vomiting 83
diet & nutrition
  3-year-olds 15-17, 22, 23, 25
  4-year-olds 15-17, 51, 53, 71, 72-3
  5-year-olds 15-17, 78-9, 81, 84
  6-year-olds 102-4, 114, 122
  7-year-olds 102-4, 137, 138-9
  8-year-olds 102-4, 157, 161
  9-year-olds 178-9, 201
  10-year-olds 178-9, 206, 209
  11-year-olds 178-9, 226, 228
  12-year-olds 244-6, 248, 253
  13-year-olds 244-6, 274
  14-year-olds 244-6, 294
  acne 274
  breakfast 114, 294
  caloric requirements 78-9
  cooking together 102, 142, 159
  encouraging healthy eating 102-4, 138, 157, 178-9, 209, 219, 244-6, 274
  family mealtimes 72-3, 97, 297
  food allergies 209
  food familiarity 16
  food hygiene 26, 27, 56
  junk food 102, 103, 244, 274, 294
  meal planning & preparation 103, 131
  migraines 254
  overweight children *see* obesity
  packed lunches 71, 219
  picky eaters 15, 16, 25, 73, 103-4, 178, 201, 274
  snacks 16, 25, 51, 127, 139, 157, 161, 178, 248, 294
  vegetarians 137, 274, 276
  see also specific foods (e.g., vegetables); specific nutrients (e.g., vitamins)
disagreements & conflict
  between playmates 90-1, 98
  between siblings 43-4, 98-9, 123, 151-2, 239-41, 307-8
  parent–child *see* challenging behavior
discipline
  6–8 years 124, 131, 145, 172, 175

discipline cont.
9–11 years 197, 216, 237
constructive criticism 280-1
parenting styles 199-200,
264-5, 280-1, 288, 304
divorcing or separating
parents 175, 289
"doctors & nurses" game 54
dogs 27, 38, 91
dominoes 29
double-jointedness 82
dough & clay 29, 96, 117
drawing & painting 24, 29, 52,
71, 79, 85-6, 96, 110, 117, 125
dressing *see* clothes, shoes,
& getting dressed
drinks
alcohol 221, 253, 267, 273,
283, 288, 295-6, 299
bedwetting 54, 138, 139
caffeinated/carbonated
drinks 16, 23, 84, 139,
208, 247, 296
juice 15, 16, 244
water intake 16, 21, 82,
138, 254, 274
drugs 275, 283, 288, 299
DTP vaccinations 27, 254
dyscalculia 192
dysgraphia 192
dyslexia 121, 136, 158, 192
dyspraxia 53, 110

E

ears
ear piercing 201
hearing problems 25, 83
infections 83
eating disorders 81, 138, 157,
209, 226, 251, 272, 289, 297
eczema 115, 295
electronic games 104-5, 121,
140, 159, 171, 195, 299
electronic reading devices 89
emotional development
3-year-olds 31, 33-9, 42, 45
4-year-olds 57-8, 62, 66,
67, 70
5-year-olds 86, 89, 90-4
6-year-olds 118, 122-7
7-year-olds 145-9, 153
8-year-olds 161-2, 168-72,
173, 175
9-year-olds 194-7

emotional development cont.
10-year-olds 213-17
11-year-olds 226, 227, 232-3,
234-7, 238-9, 240
12-year-olds 258-61
13-year-olds 271, 278,
280-3, 289
14-year-olds 294, 298, 299,
302-3, 304, 305
labeling feelings 62, 66,
89, 145, 197, 232-3, 298
parents' emotions 47, 70,
86, 217, 258, 266, 299
parents separating or
divorcing 175, 289
see also specific emotions
(e.g., love)
empathy 66, 118, 233, 259,
280, 299
emulation & mimicry 44,
45, 86
encopresis 54
endometrium 271
enuresis 54
erections 208
erotic (wet) dreams 208
estrogen 186, 226, 271
exercise & physical activity
3-year-olds 14-15, 23
4-year-olds 14-15, 55, 63
5-year-olds 77, 79, 80, 87, 94
6-year-olds 104, 109-10
7-year-olds 104, 133, 149
8-year-olds 104, 154, 157, 159
9-year-olds 178, 179-80, 187
10-year-olds 178, 179-80,
208-9
11-year-olds 178, 179-80
12-14 years 247, 269, 272
gyms 187, 272
over-exercising 136, 272
sports 63, 79, 109-10, 136,
178, 187, 247
swimming 80
eyes
headaches 254
infections 83-4
sight problems 56, 158

F

facial changes 77, 206
facial hair, boys 205, 251, 272
failure, fear of 165, 169-70,
171, 196, 237

family
attitudes to alcohol 295
behavior ground rules
64, 97, 124, 151-2, 193,
235, 280
child-care providers 41
chores *see* household tasks
& cleaning
cooperation & teamwork
129-30
decision-making 146,
147-8, 305
extended family 41, 99,
129, 241, 280
"family values" 241, 266,
275-6
grandparents 99, 129
leisure time 46-7, 72, 141,
208-9, 241, 247
mealtimes 72-3, 97, 297
outdoor activities 14-15,
55, 72, 208-9
siblings 43-6, 98-9, 123,
151-2, 239-41, 307-8
vacations 257, 276, 289
visiting relatives 129, 241,
280
see also parents
fantasy 67, 91, 166
imaginary friends 63-4
imaginative play 29, 31,
63-4, 85-6, 88, 166-7
tooth fairy 77
fats 17, 23
favoritism 123-4, 240
fears 91, 172
feelings *see* emotions
fever 26
fiber 17, 161
fine motor skills
3-year-olds 24
4-year-olds 52-3
5-year-olds 74, 79-80, 86
6-year-olds 110
7-year-olds 136
8-year-olds 159, 167
clumsiness 118
dyspraxia 53, 110
fish 15, 53, 84, 102, 206
flash cards 88-9
fluids *see* drinks
fluoride 111
folic acid/folate 15, 179
food *see* diet & nutrition
food allergies 209

fractures 22, 136, 188
freedom *see* independence
& self-sufficiency
friendships
3-year-olds 36-7
4-year-olds 62, 64, 69, 70
6-year-olds 102, 106, 126,
127, 128
7-year-olds 133, 149
8-year-olds 170, 173
9-year-olds 179-80, 182,
183, 185, 194, 197
10-year-olds 179-80, 213,
214, 217, 221
11-year-olds 179-80, 222,
235-6
12-year-olds 244, 249, 259,
260, 264, 267
13-year-olds 244, 282, 287-8
14-year-olds 244, 291, 304
cliques & gangs 173, 260
imaginary friends 63-4
socializing 179-80, 235,
264, 267, 282, 287-8
see also peer pressure;
social skills
fruit & juice 15-16, 17, 71,
78, 84, 161, 178, 244, 274
frustration 35, 90, 148, 149

G

games *see* play; specific
games (e.g., card games)
gangs & cliques 173, 260
genetic inheritance
acne 274
ADHD 60
asthma 163
bedwetting 54, 139
dyslexia 121
eczema 115
migraines 254
personality & temperament
44-5
physical development 21, 22
sports ability 109
gifted children 151
girls
breast development 135,
157, 186, 205, 207, 225,
261
developmental milestones
86

girls cont.
  eating disorders 138, 157, 209, 226, 251, 272, 289, 297
  friendships 126, 170, 185, 213
  growth spurts 186, 205, 206, 225-6, 274
  handwriting 136
  imaginary friends 63-4
  makeup 185, 234
  menstrual cycle 135, 186-7, 228, 271
  puberty 135-6, 157, 186-7, 205, 225-8, 251, 261, 271, 293
  self-harm 303
  vitamins & minerals 178, 179
glasses & eyesight 56, 158
goal-setting 210, 263, 285
going out alone 105, 169
gonadotrophin-releasing hormone 271
goodbyes 34, 39, 62, 69, 127
gossip 197
grains & cereals 17, 78, 84, 114, 161, 294
grammar 30, 119, 143, 166, 193
grandparents 99
gross motor skills
  3-year-olds 24
  4-year-olds 51-3
  5-year-olds 77, 79
  6-year-olds 107, 109-10
  dyspraxia 53, 110
growing pains 82
growing up too soon 234-5
growth *see* physical development
growth charts 22
growth hormones 14, 15, 21, 294
gyms 187, 272

H

hair, washing *see* personal hygiene
handwashing 26, 55, 56, 115
handwriting
  4-year-olds 52-3, 58
  6-year-olds 110, 120
  7-year-olds 136

handwriting cont.
  8-year-olds 158, 167
  dysgraphia 192
  left-handers 80, 167
hanging out 179-80, 267, 282
hay fever 209
head size & shape 21, 206
headaches 254
health
  3-year-olds 26-7
  4-year-olds 55-6
  5-year-olds 78, 81, 82-4
  6-year-olds 112-15
  7-year-olds 138-9
  8-year-olds 160-3
  9-year-olds 188-9
  10-year-olds 207-9
  11-year-olds 227-8
  12-year-olds 253-4
  13-year-olds 273-4
  14-year-olds 295-7
healthy eating *see* diet & nutrition
hearing problems 25, 83
height 22, 51, 77, 109, 135, 154, 172, 251
  growth spurts 157, 178, 186, 205-6, 225-6, 251, 274, 293
  posture 207
hobbies *see* leisure activities; talents & interests
home alone 217
homework
  5-year-olds 95
  6-8-year-olds 104, 125, 174
  9-year-olds 198-9
  10-year-olds 218, 221
  11-year-olds 237, 238-9
  12-year-olds 262
  13-year-olds 284-5
  14-year-olds 306
homophobia 283, 308
honesty 67, 216, 221
hormones
  estrogen 186, 226, 271
  gonadotrophin-releasing hormone 271
  growth hormones 14, 15, 21, 294
  melatonin 294
  progesterone 271
  stress hormones 161
  testosterone 205, 226, 271, 274, 293

house rules 64, 97, 124, 151-2, 193, 235, 280
household tasks & cleaning
  3-year-olds 29, 44, 46
  4-year-olds 73
  5-year-olds 86, 97
  6-year-olds 103, 129-31
  10-year-olds 211, 218-19
  11-year-olds 231, 237
  13-year-olds 289
  14-year-olds 308
HPV (human papilloma virus) vaccination 254
humor 37-8, 66, 87, 94, 211, 229
hygiene 26-7, 55-6, 115, 218-19
  see also personal hygiene
hyperactivity 23
hypermobility 82

I

illnesses
  3-8 years 26-7, 55, 78, 81, 82-4, 138-9, 161-3
  see also specific illnesses (e.g., colds)
imaginary friends 63-4
imaginative play 29, 31, 63-4, 85-6, 88, 166-7
immersion training, languages 279
immune system 26, 55
immunizations 27
impatience 168
impetigo 84, 115
independence
  3-5 years 33, 36, 42, 58, 70
  6-8 years 102, 105, 148, 150, 169
  9-11 years 196, 200, 203, 211, 213, 217, 220, 235, 238, 240
  12-14 years 247, 258, 264, 267, 283, 284, 303, 307
infections 26, 27, 55, 81, 82-4, 115, 139, 163, 296
injuries 22, 136, 188-9
interests & talents 144, 151, 164-5, 196, 230, 287, 290
Internet 174, 256, 267, 280, 283, 286

iron 15, 78, 102, 161, 178, 179, 228, 246
iron deficiency 78, 228

J

jigsaw puzzles 29, 57, 129, 159
joints 82, 136
jokes *see* humor
journal-writing 278
juice 15, 16, 244
junk food 102, 103, 244, 274, 294

K

kitchen hygiene 26, 27

L

language *see* speech & language
large muscle development 18, 24, 77, 79, 109-10, 205, 272, 293
  see also gross motor skills
learning difficulties 121, 136, 158, 173-4, 192
left-handedness 80, 110, 167
leisure activities
  3-year-olds 29
  5-year-olds 79-80
  7-year-olds 141-2, 148
  8-year-olds 159, 164-5, 169
  9-year-olds 179-80, 190-1, 195, 196, 199
  10- & 11-year-olds 179-80, 235
  12-year-olds 262, 264
  13-year-olds 287
  14-year-olds 306, 308
  after-school 79, 128, 165, 180, 199, 217, 287, 308
  as a family 46-7, 72, 141, 208-9
  outdoors 14-15, 55, 72, 104, 169, 208-9
  see also specific activities (e.g., play)
letter & word games 31, 119, 121, 166, 232, 301

"letting go" see independence & self-sufficiency
libraries 61, 284
lisping 31
listening skills 62, 96, 97, 123, 195, 197, 210, 255, 281
literacy see books, stories, & reading; comprehension
logic & problem-solving 116, 117-18, 149, 165, 229-31
look-and-say 60
love
  parents for children 19, 33, 62, 74, 122, 123, 172, 240, 247
  see also dating & crushes
lunch boxes 71
lying 67, 153, 166, 191

M

magnesium 161
make-believe play see imaginative play
makeup 185, 234
manners 67, 73, 96, 97, 122, 127, 152, 212, 233
masturbation 54, 228
materialism 261, 276
math
  3-year-olds 28-9
  4-year-olds 57
  6-year-olds 116-17
  7-year-olds 140
  8-year-olds 165-6
  10-year-olds 221
  dyscalculia 192
  parental inadequacies 221
  telling the time 29-30, 57, 65, 87, 117, 200
mealtimes, family 72-3, 97, 297
measles 27, 84
measuring & quantities 57
meat 17, 27, 78, 102, 137, 179
medical advice, when to seek see specific problems (e.g., precocious puberty)
melatonin 294
memory 29, 58, 86, 87
menorrhagia 228
menstruation & menstrual cycle 135, 186-7, 228, 271
migraine 254

milk 25, 81, 84, 178, 206
milk (primary) teeth 27, 77, 111
mimicry & copying 44, 45, 86
minerals & vitamins 15, 22, 78, 137, 161, 178, 179, 206
  see also calcium; iron
mixed-race children 153
MMR vaccination 27
mood swings 127, 226, 234, 271, 288, 294, 302
moral reasoning skills
  4-year-olds 67
  6-year-olds 118, 131
  7-year-olds 152-3
  8-year-olds 172
  9-year-olds 191, 194-5
  10-year-olds 216
  11-year-olds 235, 236
  12-year-olds 266
  13-year-olds 275-6, 286
  14-year-olds 300
  see also specific problems (e.g., lying)
motor skills see fine motor skills; gross motor skills
muscle development 18, 24, 77, 79-80, 109-10, 205, 272, 293
  see also fine motor skills; gross motor skills
music
  learning an instrument 144, 199
  teens' choices 308
"mute button" 257, 291

N

nagging 207, 264-5, 304
nature study 141
negative thinking 126, 165, 196, 237
negotiating skills
  5-year-olds 87, 92
  6-year-olds 122-3
  7-year-olds 141, 146, 149
  10-year-olds 212
  11-year-olds 231, 234, 235
  14-year-olds 303
neurons (nerve cells), pathways & networks 21-2, 51, 56, 159, 252
night terrors 67

nights away from home 129
nocturnal emissions 208
non-prejudice see respect & tolerance
nose blowing & wiping 26, 55
nudity 219
numbers & counting 28-9, 57, 116-17, 140
  see also math
nursery & preschool 25, 33-4, 39, 40-2
nursery rhymes 29, 31, 58, 121
nutrition see diet & nutrition

O

obesity
  3-5 years 23, 25, 51, 78-9, 81
  6-8 years 112-14, 157, 158
  12-14 years 246
  calorie requirements 78-9
omega-3 fatty acids 53
oral hygiene & tooth care 23, 27, 77, 102, 111, 160, 189, 253
orthodontics 189
outdoor activities 14-15, 55, 72, 104, 169, 208-9
ovaries & ovulation 271
overparenting 229-30, 288

P

pacifiers 39
packed lunches 71, 219
painting & drawing 24, 29, 52, 71, 79, 85-6, 96, 110, 117, 125
parents
  attention to children see positive attention
  "broken record" technique 92, 305
  children copying parents 44, 45
  competitive parenting 79
  computer skills 174
  conflicts with children see challenging behavior
  consistency 34, 65-6, 175, 185, 200, 235, 260
  constructive criticism 280-1
  embarrassing children 145, 258, 302-3

parents cont.
  emotions 47, 70, 86, 217, 258, 266, 299
  favoritism 123-4, 240
  feeling rejected 258
  "grow up" messages 234-5
  helping children learn 257
    see also specific topics (e.g., math)
  "I" & "you" statements 266
  keeping your cool 47, 217, 221, 237, 261, 305
  labeling & comparing children 45, 98-9, 117, 123-4, 164
  love for children 19, 33, 62, 74, 122, 123, 172, 240, 247
  lying 153
  manners 67, 73, 96, 127, 152, 233
  "mute button" 257, 291
  nagging 207, 264-5, 304
  nudity 219
  overparenting 229-30, 288
  parenting styles 199-200, 264-5, 280-1, 288, 304
  parent-teacher evenings & contacts 123, 125, 201, 287, 305
  questions 30, 59, 69, 144, 159, 165, 185, 190
  reinforcing good behavior 35-6, 39, 43-4, 65, 67, 73, 93-4, 123, 235
  risky behavior 221
  role models 147, 191, 197, 233, 258
  separating or divorcing 175, 289
  spoiling children 146
  stress 47, 86
  underparenting 288
  see also discipline; family
parties 148, 267, 283, 303
peanut allergy 209
peer pressure
  "all my friends are doing it" 235, 260, 275
  clothes & appearance 149, 213, 234
  diet & junk foods 102, 244
  language 167
  rejecting public displays of affection 145, 258

peer pressure cont.
risky behavior 216, 236, 275, 286
  toys 127
  values & beliefs 213, 229, 236, 275-6
pencil grip 24, 52-3, 58, 80, 110
penis 135, 205, 251-2, 272
periodic retrieval 285
permanent (secondary) teeth 77, 111, 160, 189, 253
personal hygiene
  4-year-olds 56
  9-year-olds 188
  12-year-olds 253
  13-year-olds 272, 274
  acne 274, 295
  handwashing 26, 55, 56
  shaving 272
  teeth & tooth care 23, 27, 77, 102, 111, 160, 189, 253
personality & temperament 44-5, 69, 92-3, 168, 258-60, 261
pester power 91-2, 146, 149, 261, 305
pets 27, 38
phonics 60, 88
physical activity *see* exercise & physical activity
physical development
  3-year-olds 18, 21-5
  4-year-olds 51
  5-year-olds 77-81, 82
  6-year-olds 109-11
  7-year-olds 135-6
  8-year-olds 154, 157-9
  9-year-olds 178, 185-7
  10-year-olds 178, 205-6
  11-year-olds 178, 225-6
  12-year-olds 244, 251-2
  13-year-olds 244, 271-2
  14-year-olds 244, 293-4
  growth spurts 157, 178, 186, 205-6, 225-6, 251, 274, 293
  see also specific aspects (e.g., height)
picky eaters 15, 16, 25, 73, 103-4, 178, 201, 274
piercings 201, 253
plagiarism 256, 286
planning skills 168, 284, 285, 298, 307

play
  3-year-olds 28, 29, 31, 33, 36-7, 42, 43
  4-year-olds 48, 54, 57, 58, 59, 61, 62-5, 72
  5-year-olds 85-7, 88, 90-1, 92-3
  6-year-olds 119, 120, 126, 128-9
  8-year-olds 159, 164, 166, 170, 172
  9-year-olds 182, 195, 196
  children with dyslexia 121
  cooperative 36-7, 42, 43, 62-3, 64-5, 90-1, 159
  games *see* specific types (e.g., card games)
  solitary 196
  see also specific types (e.g., imaginative play)
poetry 278
pornography 283
portions & portion sizes, 3-5 years 15, 17
positive attention
  to 3-year-olds 33, 35-6, 39, 43-4, 46
  to 5-year-olds 93-4
  to 6-year-olds 123, 125-6, 131
  to 9-year-olds 195, 197
  to 10-year-olds 211
  to 11-year-olds 238
  to 12-year-olds 257
  to 14-year-olds 305
positive thinking 196, 237, 306
possessions
  consumerism 234, 261, 276
  losing 261
  possessiveness 64-5, 97
posture 207
potty humor 37, 66, 94
potty training 25, 54, 81
praise 35-6, 44, 73, 88, 90, 125, 168, 211, 240, 305
preschool & nursery school 25, 33-4, 39, 40-2
precocious puberty 135-6, 206
pregnancy 45-6, 271, 273
pretend play *see* imaginative play
primary teeth 27, 77, 111
privacy 58, 145, 151, 218-19, 228, 240, 248, 251, 280

private tutoring 192, 279
problem-solving & logic 116, 117-18, 149, 165, 229-31
progesterone 271
projects 190-1, 218, 230, 284, 300
pronunciation 31, 59, 193, 232, 233
protein 17, 103, 137, 179
puberty
  7-8 years 135-6, 157
  9-11 years 185, 186-7, 205-6, 208, 225-8, 234
  12-14 years 246, 251-2, 261, 271-2, 293
  see also specific aspects (e.g., breast development)
pubic hair 135, 186, 205, 225, 251, 272
punishment *see* discipline
puppets 31

quality time *see* positive attention
questions 30, 59, 69, 144, 159, 165, 185, 190

racism 153
  see also respect
rashes 84, 209
reading *see* books, stories, & reading
refrigerator temperature 27
regression 45
relaxation techniques 239, 306
research 256, 262
resilience 125-6, 148, 196, 210
respect & tolerance
  4-5 years 71, 97
  6-8 years 130, 131, 153
  7-year-olds 153
  9-11 years 185, 233, 237
  12-14 years 276, 283, 308
responsibilities *see* household tasks & cleaning; independence & self-sufficiency
retention control 54

rickets 206
right & wrong, understanding *see* moral reasoning skills
risky behavior 221, 236, 267, 273, 275, 283, 288, 303
  healthy risk-taking 298-300
road safety 54, 81, 105, 111, 169
role models 147, 172, 191, 197, 210, 220, 233, 258, 281
rooms & room sharing 46, 98, 218-19, 308
routines & continuity 40, 45, 69, 72, 104, 150, 162, 175, 198-9
rubella 27, 84
rules 131, 172
  family 64, 97, 124, 151-2, 193, 235, 280
  money 175, 193

S
safe sex 273, 283
safety 38, 80, 169, 217, 303
  allergen avoidance 209
  Internet & chatrooms 174, 202, 267, 280, 283
  road safety 54, 81, 105, 111, 169
sandboxes 27
sanitary protection 187, 228
sarcasm 229
school
  4-year-olds 48, 69-71
  5-year-olds 95, 96, 97
  6-year-olds 104, 105, 123, 124, 128
  7-year-olds 104, 105, 140, 150
  8-year-olds 104, 105, 154, 173-4
  9-year-olds 180, 186, 191, 193, 197, 198-9, 201
  10-year-olds 180, 203, 207
  11-year-olds 180, 222, 226, 231
  12-year-olds 262-4
  13-year-olds 284-7
  academic difficulties 173-4, 192, 198, 231, 262-3
  after-school activities 79, 128, 165, 180, 199, 217, 287, 308

school cont.
after-school care 72, 95
    allergy & asthma
        management 163, 209
    anxiety factors 81, 84, 173-4,
        175, 238-9, 306
    bullying 96, 153, 172, 173,
        199, 220, 307
    clothing & appearance
        rules 201, 234, 305
    field trips 129
    gifted children 151
    gossip 197
    illnesses affecting
        attendance 81, 83-4, 228
    language teaching 278-9
    losing interest in 263-4
    math lessons 140, 166
        middle school 180,
        235-6, 238-9
    packed lunches 71, 219
    parent-teacher contacts
        201, 287
    parents' nights 123,
        125, 305
    projects 218, 284, 300
    quality & standards 285-6
    school bags 207
    school refusal & phobias
        175
    sex education 186
    starting school 48, 69-71,
        105
    study skills 238-9,
        284-5
    tests 150, 170, 192, 238-9
    tiredness 104, 208
    toilet problems 81
    traveling to 105
    truancy 259, 264
    unwelcome friendships
        217
    see also homework
science 117-18, 141-2
scissors 29, 53, 80, 110
scoliosis 207
scrotum 205, 251-2, 272
search skills 261
second languages 278-9
secondary (permanent)
    teeth 77, 111, 160, 189, 253
secondary schools 180, 235-6,
    238-9
secrets 58, 182, 194-5, 217,
    219, 249, 280, 288, 303

selenium 161
self-awareness 210-11
self-consciousness
    7-year-olds 145
    8-year-olds 157, 172
    10-year-olds 207, 210,
        219, 220
    12-year-olds 261
    13-year-olds 274, 280, 281-2
    14-year-olds 293
self-criticism 148, 237, 282
self-esteem *see* confidence
    & self-esteem
self-harm 303
self-sufficiency *see*
    independence & self-
    sufficiency
separating or divorcing
    parents 175, 289
separation anxiety 33-4, 39,
    62, 69
    clinginess 84, 127
sets & groups 57
sexual development &
    sexuality
        kissing 214, 221
        masturbation 54, 228
        natural curiosity & sex
            education 54, 131, 169,
            185, 213, 221
        nocturnal emissions 208
        pornography 283
        same-sex preferences 214
        sexual health &
            contraception 273, 283
        sexualized behavior 169,
            214, 221, 273
        see also dating &
            crushes; puberty
shape discrimination 57
sharing 64-5, 97
shaving 272
shoes *see* clothes, shoes, &
    getting dressed
shoplifting 216, 236
showering *see* personal
    hygiene
shyness 37, 171
siblings 43-6, 98-9, 123,
    151-2, 239-41, 307-8
sight problems 56, 158
skills development
    3-5 years 36, 51-3, 70-1,
        79-80

see also specific skills
    (e.g., speech & language)
skin problems 84, 115, 209,
    274, 295
slang & speech patterns 167,
    233, 256, 257
sleep
    3-5 years 14, 46
    6-8 years 104, 137, 139, 162
    9-11 years 179, 207-8, 227
    12-14 years 248-9, 264, 294
    night terrors 67
    sleep disorders 162, 294
    wet dreams 208
slouching 207
small muscle development
    24, 79-80, 110, 205
    see also fine motor skills
smoking 253, 288
snacks 16, 25, 51, 127, 139,
    157, 161, 178, 248, 294
soda/caffeinated drinks 16,
    23, 84, 139, 208, 247, 296
social skills
    3-year-olds 37, 42, 43
    4-year-olds 62
    5-year-olds 90-1, 92, 96-7, 98
    6-year-olds 118, 122, 127
    7-year-olds 152
    8-year-olds 170, 171, 173
    9-year-olds 180, 194
    10-year-olds 180, 211
    11-year-olds 180
    community involvement
        211, 276
    see also friendship; respect
socializing, 10-14 years 179-80,
    235, 262, 264, 267, 282, 287-8
soiling 54
solitary play 196
spectacles & eyesight 56, 158
speech & language
    3-year-olds 25, 28-31
    4-year-olds 58-60, 61, 66
    5-year-olds 86, 87
    6-year-olds 118-19
    7-year-olds 142-3, 145, 146
    8-year-olds 166-7, 168
    9-year-olds 191-3, 197
    10-year-olds 210, 211
    11-year-olds 231-2
    12-year-olds 256-7
    13-year-olds 276-9
    14-year-olds 300-1
    gossip 197

"mute button" 257, 291
    problems 25, 61, 83, 121
    "public" speaking 191-2
    second languages 278-9
    slang & speech patterns
        167, 233, 256, 257
    swearing 193, 233
spelling 119, 301
spoiled children 146
sports 63, 79, 109-10, 136,
    178, 187, 247
    over-exercising 136, 272
    swimming 80
star charts 54, 139, 199
staying home alone 217
STDs 273
stealing 191, 216, 236
stomachaches 81, 175, 227
stories *see* books, stories, &
    reading
strength 205
stress
    children *see* anxiety &
        stress
    parents 47, 86
    stress hormones 161
stubbornness 122
study skills 238-9, 284-5
sunburn 115
supplements, vitamin &
    mineral 78, 178, 206
swearing 193, 233
swimming 80

T
table manners 73
talents & interests 144, 151,
    164-5, 196, 230, 287, 290
tampons 187
tantrums 35, 39, 67, 148,
    211, 214
teamwork, family 129-30
teasing 37-8, 126, 214, 260
teeth & tooth care 23, 27,
    77, 102, 111, 160, 189, 253
temperament & personality
    44-5, 69, 92-3, 168, 258-60,
    261
testes/testicles 135, 205,
    251-2, 271, 272
testosterone 205, 226, 271,
    274, 293
texting 220, 267, 279, 280
thinking skills

abstract thought 190, 300
cause & effect 118
comprehension 212, 231-2, 256
debating skills 190, 231, 255, 259, 268, 276, 308
logic & problem-solving 116, 117-18, 149, 165, 229-31
negative thinking 126, 165, 196, 237
planning ahead 168, 284, 285, 298, 307
positive thinking 196, 237, 306
research 256, 262
search skills 261
world view 276
time, concept of & telling time 29-30, 57, 65, 87, 117, 200
tiredness 104, 208
toilet hygiene 26, 56, 115
tolerance *see* respect & tolerance
tooth fairy 77
tooth care *see* teeth & tooth care
Toxocara 27
toxoplasmosis 27
toys
  3-year-olds 28, 29, 31, 39
  5-year-olds 85
  7-year-olds 146, 151-2
  peer pressure 127
  sharing 64-5, 97, 151-2
  transitional objects 39
transitional objects 39
travel
  going out alone 105, 169
  nights away from home 129
  school trips 129
  to school 105
  vacations 257, 276, 289
tremors 24
truancy 259, 264
tutoring, private 192
TV
  3-5 years 14, 15, 47, 55, 73, 83
  6-8 years 104-5, 128, 143, 153, 171

TV cont.
  9-11 years 189, 195, 208, 212, 240
  12-14 years 247, 276
twins 39, 45, 54, 61

U

underage sex 273
underarm hair 186, 205, 225, 251
underparenting 288
understanding & cognitive development
  3-year-olds 21-2, 28-30, 42
  4-year-olds 51, 57-61
  5-year-olds 85-9
  6-year-olds 116-21
  7-year-olds 140-4
  8-year-olds 159, 164-7, 168
  9-year-olds 190-3
  10-year-olds 210-12
  11-year-olds 229-33
  12-year-olds 252, 255-7
  13-year-olds 275-9
  14-year-olds 298-301
  academic difficulties 173-4, 192, 198, 231, 262-3
  dyslexia 121, 136, 158, 192
  see also specific aspects (e.g., speech & language)
urine & urinary tract infections (UTIs) 81, 139, 296

V

vacations 257, 276, 289
vaccinations 27, 254
vegetables 15-16, 17, 78, 84, 102, 103, 161, 178, 206, 274
vegetarians 137, 274, 276
virus infections 26-7, 55, 115, 254
vitamins & minerals 15, 22, 78, 137, 161, 178, 179, 206
  see also calcium; iron
vocabulary development *see* speech & language

volunteering 211
vomiting & diarrhea 83

W

walking to school 105
water intake 16, 21, 82, 138, 254, 274
weight
  3-year-olds 25
  4-year-olds 51
  6-year-olds 109, 112-14
  8-year-olds 157
  10-year-olds 208-9
  11-year-olds 226
  12-14 years 246, 293
  baby fat 157, 206
  BMI charts 52
  problems *see* eating disorders; obesity
wet dreams 208
wetting 54, 81, 139
  nocturnal emissions 208
whole grains 161, 294
"why" questions 30, 59, 144
withdrawal & depression 216, 246, 263-4, 283
word & letter games 31, 119, 121, 166, 232, 301
world view 276
worriers 172
writing *see* creative writing; handwriting

"Parenting is as much about instinct as anything else, but we all need a little help sometimes to confirm that we are getting things right."

Acknowledgments

Text attributions
Page numbers below refer to pages, or parts of pages where indicated, written by that author:

Carol Cooper: 25–31, 39, 55–61, 81–4, 112–15, 116–118, 127, 137–142, 149, 152 (last paragraph), 160–3, 164–5, 166 (1st paragraph), 167 (2nd paragraph only), 172, 188–9, 207–9, 274 (box)

Claire Halsey: 33–8, 43–7, 62–7, 72–3, 90–9, 122–6, 128–31, 145–8, 151 (except box), 153 (except last paragraph), 153, 168–71, 172 (1st and 3rd questions), 173–5, 194–7, 199 (box only), 200, 213–17, 218–19, 220 (box only), 221 (except box), 234–7, 238–9, 258–61, 262 (box only), 264–7, 280–3, 287 (last para only), 288–9, 302–8

Su Laurent: 21–4, 51–4, 77–80, 109–11, 135–7, 157–9, 185–7, 205–6, 225–8, 251–4, 271–4, 293–7

Karen Sullivan: 14–17, 40–2, 67 (box), 69–71, 85–9, 102–5, 116–21, 140–4, 150, 151 (box), 166 (except 1st paragraph), 167 (except 2nd paragraph), 178–80, 190-3, 198–9 (except box), 210–12, 220 (except box), 229–33, 240–1, 244–7, 255–7, 262–3 (except box on 262), 275–9, 284–7 (except last para 287), 298–301

Authors' acknowledgments
Claire Halsey would like to thank Vicki McIvor.
Su Laurent would like to thank the entire DK team and Alex, Emily, and Eddie, her three children, for making being a mother such a wonderful experience, and her husband, Peter, for his support at all times.

Publisher's acknowledgments
Proofreader: Andi Sisodia
Indexer: Sue Bosanko
Editorial assistance: Nicola Parkin
Photographer's assistant: Jamie Bowler
Photoshoot assistant: Susanna Sanford
DK picture librarian: Romaine Werblow
Picture researcher: Harriet Mills and Sarah Hopper
Schools: Honeywell Infant & Junior schools, London, and King Alfred School, London, with particular thanks to Lorraine Deville.
Location agencies: Amazing space, 1st Option, and Oak Management
All the children and parents who took part in the photoshoots: Lawrence Bache, Arthur Bagnall, Millie Bagnall, Thomas Battson, Joe Bertram, Marta Blaiklock, Joe Brandon, Lewis Brown, Willow Bush, Ellen Cooley, Rachel Cooley, Jake Croton, Maja Da Costa, Amelia Ellenger, Henry Ellenger, Anna Fitzgerald, Jessica Forge, Toby Forge, Lottie Head, Phoebe Head, Benjamin Hewitt, Hannah Hewitt, Florence Hoffman, Henry Hoffman, Cameron Irving, Biba Kang, Jas Kang, Sky Kang, Alice Kenny, Fleur Kenny, Gus Lingwood, Kit Lingwood, Robyn Liu, Crispin Lord, Eleana Macauley-Rowe, James Macauley-Rowe, Rosie McMahon, Ellie Millard, Hamlett Millard, Ben Nossiter, Megan O'Connor, Jay Orriss, Atinuke Osuntokun, Benjamin Osuntokun, Kikelomo Osuntokun, Samuel Owen, Alex Paterson, Sam Powell, Edward Reader, Emily Reader, Abigail Richson, Weljah Richson, Daniel Smith, Talya Smith, Michael Sutcliffe, Ammi Takahashi, Kai Takahashi, Adam Vallack, Miles Wagner, Kayleigh Wennerland, Sean Wennerland, Oliver Wilson, Ben Woodard. Plus pupils from Honeywell Infant & Junior schools and King Alfred School.

Picture Credits
The publisher would like to thank the following for their kind permission to reproduce their photographs:
(Key: a-above; b-below/bottom; c-center; l-left; r-right; t-top)

Alamy Images: Bubbles Photolibrary 98, 281; f1 online 149; Jenny Matthews 283; Nordicphotos 201; Alex Segre 127; Steve Stanford 273; Rob Walls 178; **Bubbles:** 39; **Corbis:** Heide Benser 152, 190; Cameron 185, 222-223; Kevin Dodge 213, 248cl, 260; John Henley 278; A. Inden/zefa 103; Ronnie Kaufman 255; Tom & Dee Ann McCarthy 41; Roy Morsch 269cl; Gabe Palmer 289; LWA-Dann Tardif 225; Alfred Saerchinger/zefa 251; Anna Peisl/ zefa 264; Ausloeser/zefa 147; Emely/zefa 237; Mika/zefa 214; **Getty Images:** Ableimages 247; altrendo images 150, 258; B2M Productions 208; Jean Louis Batt 161; Victoria Blackie 115, 198; Guy Bubb 84; CAP 267; ColorBlind Images 184, 284, 293; John Cumming 268-269; DCA Productions 294; Nick Dolding 134; John Giustina 125; Gone Wild/Photographer's Choice 304; Colin Gray 241; Hill Street Studios/Stock This Way 291; ISU 188; Bruce Laurance 256; Clarissa Leahy/Stone 295; Jonnie Miles 169; Steve Murez 80; Nacivet 139; Thomas Northcut 235; Sami Sarkis 222cl; Stephen Stickler 301; Gala Narezo/ Taxi 227; Jerome Tisne 114; Stefan Wettainen 297; **PunchStock:** 156, 163, 254, 279.

All other images © Dorling Kindersley
For further information see: www.dkimages.com